HURACAN

DIANA McCAULAY

HURACAN

A Novel

PEEPAL TREE

First published in Great Britain in 2012
Peepal Tree Press Ltd
17 King's Avenue
Leeds LS6 1QS
England

ISBN13: 9781845231965

Supported by
ARTS COUNCIL
ENGLAND

For Jonathan; Jamaican born
And for everyone who stayed

"No tribe, however insignificant, and no nation, however mighty, occupies a foot of land that was not stolen."

Mark Twain, *Following the Equator*

"Now my disorder of ancestry proves as stable as the many rivers flowing around me. Undocumented I drown in the other's history."

Olive Senior, "Cockpit Country Dreams"

BOOK 1

REUNION

1986
Kingston

"White gal!" the barefoot man shouted, pointing at her with a half empty bottle of white rum. He wore a vest and torn shorts and his eyes glared. Leigh McCaulay turned her head away – it was a familiar, damning description, echoing from her childhood. She watched the traffic light, which remained on red. She knew where she was – the corner of Windward Road and Mountain View Avenue, coming in from Norman Manley International Airport. She was not a tourist. She wanted to explain this to the man. I was born here. I am coming home.

"Pay him no mind," Danny said. "Him don't know better." They had just met. He had been sent by her new employer to collect her from the airport.

The light changed and they drove on. The man remained where he was, leaning against an unrendered concrete wall covered with peeling, bleached-out posters advertising dances and plays. His anger seemed to have passed. He tipped the bottle of white rum to his head and Leigh could see his throat muscles working. How to describe him – poor man, sufferer, black man, rum head, *bhuto*, Jamaican man?

Her arrival had passed so quickly – the aeroplane descending through cloud, jerking and swaying, the passengers gasping in fear and surprise. Her seat mate had been wearing three hats, one on top of the other and he had prayed loudly, repetitively. "Fahda God, do mi beg you, tek wi down safe. Do, mi beg you. Do…" Then, the plane landing and the people clapping, the flight attendant welcoming returning Jamaicans, the good-humoured tussle to get hand-luggage, people standing too close in the aisles, and the moment when the aircraft door swung open and sunshine fell into the cabin, and then she was standing at the top of the boarding stairs, wanting to pause, to take it all in, the smell of the salty dense air of the Palisadoes spit, long grass waving, bleached at the ends, on the overgrown verges beside the runway, where, she imagined, animals might wander over to graze. Above it all, the Blue Mountains behind Kingston. But the people behind her pushed and murmured and kissed their teeth so she had to go down the stairs. Then she was inside the terminal building, in the long lines (the immigration officer stamped her Jamaican passport without comment), and the Customs Officer was bored by her duffle and backpack, then she was outside in the heat where noisy crowds pressed the barriers lining the walkway. This is a black country, she had thought, involuntarily, and was irritated at herself. But her eyes sought and found the only pale face in the crowd, a middle-aged man standing behind the rows of people, looking over their heads. She had walked towards him, but another man on the wrong side of the barriers reached for her bag and barred her way. "Taxi, miss?"

"No, thank you."

"Me carry your bag," he said, tugging at her duffle. He was a big man and his forced grin showed missing teeth.

"No, thank you," she said, more emphatically. She pushed past him, wondering if she still sounded Jamaican. Americans had always been confused by her fair skin and Jamaican accent. Perhaps her accent had been watered down by the years away, though Jamaican voices were still what sounded normal to her. "I don't have an accent," she was fond of telling those who commented on her manner of speech. "*You* have an accent."

She had stood a little apart from the crowds, catching her breath, hoping for a lull, a chance to process what had seemed enormous, but, as it unfolded, was really quite mundane. A woman returns to the island of her birth after her estranged mother's death. She has been away for fifteen years. She has taken a job in Kingston. A simple narrative. No one else approached her and she felt conspicuous, as if a circle had been drawn around her that no one would cross, as if she were a teenager at a party, waiting to be asked to dance. The letter had said she would be met. Other people were being met, greetings were shouted, luggage was piled on the sidewalk, taxis and minivans pulled up, loaded and drove away. She fumbled in her pocket for the address of the place she would be staying, "with the Libbey family" the letter had said – perhaps she would have to find her own way there. She could no longer see the white man. Then her eye caught a cardboard sign that seemed to have her name – it had been written in ballpoint pen and was barely legible. She went closer to make sure – yes, it was her name. A lithe young man wearing a worn white shirt tucked into khaki trousers held the sign. He was looking beyond her at the porters and passengers coming from Customs.

"Hello," she said. "I'm Leigh McCaulay."

"Miss?" the man said, still looking behind her.

"I'm the person you've come to meet. I'm Leigh."

He stared at her then. "You come to Kingston Refuge?"

"Yes."

"Miss McCall?"

"McCaulay. But Leigh is fine."

"For Kingston Refuge?"

"Yes. For Kingston Refuge. Leigh McCaulay." Why was he doubting who she was? "I was told I would be met," she said, and the words sounded wrong, imperious.

"Me did think you…" Then she understood – he had been told she was a returning Jamaican and he expected a black woman. "O-kay, Miss!" he said, suddenly energetic, reaching for her duffle. "Me is Danny." He pointed to a place on the sidewalk. "You wait there. Little further up, past the crossing. Police don't like if me stop on the crossing. Me get the car. Is a blue Toyota."

"Thank you." She walked away from the thrumming crowd. Why in the place where she had been born did her nationality require explanation? Yet the place was familiar, welcoming; the noise, the heat, the smell of things rotting. She thought of people walking their dogs in New York with plastic bags in hand, the twisting motion they made with their wrists as they cleaned up after their pets. Here no one picked up dog poop. She stood at the side of the road, her face turned to the sun.

They drove with the windows down, Danny's elbow resting on the window. The car had no seat belts. A strong wind blew from the sea and Leigh wanted to stop as they drove along the Palisadoes, remembering how her grandmother had taken her there in the late afternoons, whenever her parents came to town. "What's the point of that?" her father had asked. "We have much better beaches in Portland. Take her to the Institute for some culture." Leigh's grandmother ignored this. Generally a stickler for the proper attire for girls of her class – frilly dresses and patent leather shoes – Grammy had allowed her to wear pedal pushers and flip flops for their excursions to Palisadoes. She would drive her boxy grey car – an Austin? – onto the beach and Leigh would tumble out onto the grey sand of the spit that separated Kingston Harbour from the rollers of Big Sea. Palisadoes' muted shades of brown and grey *was* very different from Portland's jewel tones of emerald, turquoise and opal, but she had loved the arid strip of land with the occasional cactus; the clack of the stones as the waves surged over them. During those afternoons, she would search for the roundest stone with the most unusual colour, always disappointed when the stone dried out at home and lost its luminous glow. She used to think they were moon stones, fallen from the night sky and holding the light of the moon inside – until they were taken away from the beach. She wanted to ask Danny to stop, so she could walk on the grey stones of the beach, just long enough to collect a single one, to smell the sea as she readied herself for sleep that night, but she didn't want to seem strange. She remembered that Nanny Ros used to throw her stones away.

Big Sea was as rough and the harbour calm as she remembered them. Across the harbour there were many new high-rise buildings, and the scars of construction on the green hills. Purple clouds massed behind the Blue Mountains and she knew it would rain. She was surprised by the pile of gypsum at Harbour Head and the dust-drenched cement works, not because they were new, but her memory had left them out. They drove past Rockfort and the mineral baths, past the rum shops and market women on Windward Road and the battered zinc fences and the goats in the streets, and Leigh remembered the weekend when her grandmother had taken ill for the last time, the illness that had released her father. He had taken Leigh to Kingston with him, she could not remember why. Grammy had asked him for steamed fish and mashed potato and Leigh had gone with her father to buy fresh fish at Rae Town, surely somewhere near?

"Is Rae Town near here?"

"The fishing beach? Further up. You want go there?"

"Not now. Maybe another time." Fairlight. Fishing. Dad. Zoe. The air no longer smelled of the sea, but of diesel fumes and

14

old dust. When Leigh had left Jamaica, there had not been many traffic lights in Kingston and none in Portland. A boy approached the car on her side. "Miss, beg you a lunch money." He wore only a pair of grubby shorts. Being asked for money was another suppressed memory. She was flustered and unwilling to reach for her purse. She had no Jamaican money. "Miss, do. A hungry…"

"Here, yout'," Danny said. He reached across her and gave the boy a coin. "Why you not in school?" The boy tossed the coin into the air, caught it and ran to another car without answering. Seeing the boy took her back to going with her parents to see a ship docked in Port Antonio, one of the banana boats which took bananas to England and returned with pink-skinned tourists, the women in floral dresses and elaborate hats, the men in suits and bow ties. The visitors threw coins into the water and black boys dived for them. The coins spiralled down and the boys had to get to them quickly before they settled in the silt of the sea floor. She had wanted to join the boys, sure she could swim and dive just as well, perhaps better, but her father said it was not appropriate and her mother sighed and looked away, her eyes hidden behind her dark glasses.

By now her excitement had ebbed and she longed to be inside, out of the heat, with a drink in her hand. Lemonade. Passion fruit. June plum. Even mouth-puckering tamarind. "Do we have much farther to go?"

"No. Soon reach. You born in Kingston, Miss?"

"Portland."

They had left the main roads and Leigh was no longer sure where they were. Then she caught sight of the mountains and knew they would guide her as she began to learn her way around downtown Kingston. The mountains to the north, the sea to the south. "Are you taking me to the Libbeys?" she asked. They were in an older residential community, the houses built close to the streets, many in poor repair.

"Umm-hmm. They not there right now but Miss Beryl expecting you. Father Gabriel say you start work on Monday, give you tomorrow to do some business, right?"

"Yes, I have to see a lawyer."

"Me come for you Monday morning, show you where to go."

"I'm sure I can find my way," she said. "But thank you."

15

"No, me come. 'Round eight-thirty."

"Do you work at the shelter?"

"Eeh-hee."

"What you do there?"

"Little of this, little of that." He stopped the car on the street and Leigh saw a zinc-roofed house with a big mango tree in front. "Me bring you bag," he said. Leigh got out of the car and stood in front of a narrow iron gate. A short flight of stairs led to a verandah enclosed by metal grillwork – there were no signs of anyone home. The front door was shut behind the grill and there were two wooden rocking chairs on the verandah amid a profusion of potted plants, some in old paint tins. "Miss Beryl!" Danny shouted from behind her, making her jump. He banged on the gate with a stone. "Open up!" No one came. "You wait here, Miss Leigh," Danny said. "Me go find her."

Leigh stood beside Danny's car and the sun beat down. Another move to yet another place. Then the front door opened and Danny came onto the verandah with a key. He opened the grill gate and beckoned to her. She was up the stairs and out of the heat, just as the rain started.

The maid, Beryl, showed her to her bedroom and then to the kitchen where she pointed to a covered plate on the stove. "Supper," she said. "Fry chicken. Mek sure you lock up good before you go sleep. See di key-dem here – front door and grill. Mr. Conrad and Miss Phyllis back tomorrow." She spoke slowly, as if to a child, and then left quickly.

The room was simply furnished. A single bed pushed against one wall, covered with a white chenille bedspread and a mosquito net tied in a large knot above it. A bedside table with a lamp, sitting on a crocheted doily. A faded picture of the Last Supper, hung too high. A small wooden desk and chair. The chair was the type Leigh remembered from her school days, with a round seat and railed back – it would probably fetch a good price in an American antique shop. A worn armchair. A battered hanging press, with a spotty mirror on the front. There was a sash window without curtains; the bottom half was nailed shut and the glass had been painted white. She could see the rain through the open top half.

She unpacked her duffle. She had not brought much with her. When she had dismantled her New York life, she had seen just how rootless she was. She owned almost nothing – thrift store furniture, minimal kitchen equipment, a basic uniform of jeans and boots and sweaters. She did not buy books, preferring instead to join the local library in the cities she had intermittently occupied. She had once had a few photographs of her Jamaican childhood – her best friend Zoe, the Portland cove, the dinghy, her dog Rex, her mother, father and brother leaning on the verandah railing at Fairlight – but they had all been destroyed by a burst pipe in her first year of graduate school. At the time, she had been glad – she did not want to look at her father's face, or her mother's. And her much older brother, Andrew, was by then a stranger who sent Christmas cards from England signed "Best wishes". When the sopping photos had been pulled from a pulpy cardboard box on the floor of her bedroom, she had thrown them out without regret. Her unencumbered life had once seemed as full of possibilities as it was empty of attachments, but when she packed to go home to the island she had left when she was fifteen, she had felt transient, someone who barely existed. She had moved through the world but the world did not move through her. Two unremarkable degrees, a series of supposedly socially useful jobs at soup kitchens and homeless shelters and health clinics, superficial college and workplace friendships, smiling acquaintances with pharmacists and grocery store operators, lovers who aroused her body but failed to know her mind. She was a ghost, but not even capable of a decent haunting.

Her boss had shown her the advertisement for the job at a homeless shelter in Kingston a few days after news of her mother's death had reached her. He had shrugged when she told him she was leaving. "Going home, are you? Hope it works out. Keep in touch now." Her last lover, skinny Kevin, had helped her haul away the few pieces of furniture she owned; he did not pretend they would ever meet again. Her apartment was no doubt already occupied by someone else, dreaming New York dreams. Now she was in another house owned by strangers.

She wondered whether she should eat, but wasn't hungry. A sense of anticlimax had sapped her energy. She put the plate of food inside the noisy fridge, propped up with a slab of wood to compensate for the uneven floor. There was a pitcher of juice in the fridge but she wasn't sure she should drink it. She poured herself a glass of water remembering how she had been embarrassed the first time she visited an American home, when she asked where they kept their drinking water. "Umm, in the tap," they said, over-politely.

She wished she could go for a walk, but after Beryl's warning to lock up good decided to leave this for another day. She went to her room and lay on the bed. The rain was easing. She was *fine*. She had been alone in many such rooms, it was what she did – Gainesville, Washington DC, Atlanta, Chicago, New York. She undid the mosquito net and let it fall and liked the cocoon it made. The beds at Fairlight had mosquito nets. Fifteen years. Fifteen years grounded; fifteen years a nomad. The first fifteen years she had slept in the same bed, in the same house, saw the same view; her birthright a house on a hill. As soon as she could, she would return to Fairlight. It had been sold, of course, but it would still be there; that was the thing about land; it paid no attention to its owners. The hill would be there and so would the cove and the sweep of the coast and the pale grey squalls far out to sea. The journey that churned like surf on sand was over. She was home.

Next day she took a taxi to the lawyer's office. The Libbeys had not returned. A crowing rooster had woken her before it was light. She had found tea in the cupboards and a slice of hard dough bread in a chipped bread bin; she had eaten on the verandah, looking at the people on the street. Some nodded to her and she waved back.

The taxi driver smoked, dangling his right hand out the window. Traffic was heavy. She paid him with US dollars without calculating the conversion to Jamaican dollars and his thanks were effusive. He sped away in a shower of gravel before she could come to her senses and demand some of the money back. The morning was fair and she lingered for a moment in the street looking up at the lawyer's office. She had not known what to wear for this meeting. A car horn blasted and she jumped onto the sidewalk. As the car raced by, the driver flung his arm at her in a familiar gesture of disdain. Nobody messed with Jamaicans. She smelled sewage and saw greasy black water pooled in gutters and potholes.

Inside the office, a short, brown man told her Mr. Bucknor was not available. He had been called away by a family emergency.

"But I have an appointment."

"Indeed. But yours is a simple matter and Mr. Bucknor has authorized me to deal with it. I'm Turland Lambeth. Mr. Bucknor's associate."

Two surnames and a pompous manner to go with them. He invited her to sit in a neat office. The window behind him threw his face into shadow.

"We're happy to *finally* make contact with you, Miss McCaulay," he began, and she felt a flash of guilt. Her mother had died and she had not known. There had been no flicker of warning, no sense of foreboding, no dreams, waking or sleeping. She had not shed tears, had not felt sadness, regret or failure. Her mother, the mystery, would remain a mystery. When last had she thought of her, even in anger?

She wanted to explain to the lawyer, to say, I wasn't close to my mother, or rather, she wasn't close to me. She held her tongue.

"Your mother's will is in probate. The process could take up to three years and..."

"How did she die, Mr. Turland?"

"Mr. Lambeth. My name is Mr. Lambeth."

"I apologize. Mr. Lambeth. How did my mother die?"

"A car accident, I understand. You were not informed?"

"My brother wrote to me, but... here." She dug into her backpack and handed the lawyer the letter. "Dear Leigh," Andrew had written. "I am not sure this will find you, but I got a call from Jamaica yesterday. Mom died in a car crash. By the time you get this, the funeral will have been held. I was not able to go; big project at work. Isabella couldn't take leave either, what with the kids' schooling. I tried the last telephone number I had for you, but they said you no longer lived there. They had a forwarding address, but no phone number. I wish you would at least let me know where you are. Anyway, that's the news. Mom died. I suppose this might come as a shock, but I'm not going to pretend we were close. Phone me if you are able to. Andrew."

Turland Lambeth looked up. "Yes. Well. I don't know the precise details of the accident, if that's what you're asking." He folded the letter and returned it to her.

Leigh remembered her mother as a hesitant driver. "Where was it? Was another car involved?"

"Um. As I said, I don't know the precise details. The file… it seems to have been temporarily misplaced."

"The file is lost?"

"It is *not* lost. Were Mr. Bucknor here, the file would be available, but he had to leave so suddenly…"

"Then how do you know anything about my case?"

"Please, Miss McCaulay. Let me finish. This is a simple matter and I have been thoroughly briefed. Your mother's estate is in probate. It will take a while. Her will was simple; she left everything to you and your brother, divided equally. Mr. Bucknor has written to him. Once you can establish your identity – a birth certificate would be best – I can advise you as to the size of the estate. Your portion of the money will be released once probate is concluded."

"I don't have my birth certificate," she said. "I left Jamaica with a passport and it was renewed. My mother would have had my birth certificate."

"Well, there were some papers and personal effects. Your father has them, I believe. Have you seen him?"

"Not yet. I arrived yesterday."

"Failing that, you'll have to reapply to the Registrar at Spanish Town. It can be a frustrating and lengthy process."

"I'm not in a rush," she said. "I live here now."

He raised his eyebrows. "Excellent. I hope you're being careful – Kingston is a dangerous city. Especially for a young woman."

"So I've been told," she said. "How do you get paid?"

"Our fees will be deducted from the estate when probate is completed. Do you have a local mailing address?"

Leigh took the Libbeys' address from her pocket. Better memorize this, she thought, if I lose it, I'll have to go back to New York. The silliness of the thought made her smile.

"If that's all…" Mr. Lambeth stood and she was dismissed.

Outside, she saw a bank on the other side of the road and she went in to change her money. She separated the US and Jamaican dollars into different pockets. No more happy taxi drivers. The rest of the day and weekend stretched ahead. She would take a walk. In the summers spent with her mother in Kingston after her parents' divorce, she had not been allowed anywhere near downtown. Now she took in the modern office buildings beside the overgrown lots, the ruins of churches and warehouses, the piles of garbage overflowing from the sidewalks into the streets. She walked past a pile of red bricks at the side of the road. "Bricks, Miss?" the boy sitting next to them asked. A street sign said Duke Street. She wished she had a map. Then she saw the harbour ahead and was glad to have a destination.

She walked for hours, until the sun was directly overhead, realising the streets were laid out in a grid pattern with tiny, broken lanes in between. People sat on low walls or in the open doorways of rum shops; groups of men played dominos, slamming down the tiles; women selling goods – coolers, trays and baskets, fruit, sweets, cigarettes, drinks – sheltered under huge umbrellas or tarpaulins tied to the wrought iron fences. Ragged children peered from dark doorways. The lawyer had said Kingston was dangerous; Portlanders agreed: they were a cut above Kingstonians. Theirs was the most beautiful part of Jamaica, and the safest, and the most famous, gilded by its association with celebrities – Errol Flynn, Robin Moore of *Green Beret* fame, the Princess Nina Aga Khan. Leigh knew that in the first ever Tarzan film, Johnny Weissmuller had swung from thick lianas in the Portland bush. She was Kingston born – her mother had travelled to the Nuttall Hospital to give birth to her – but Portland grown. Could living and working downtown be as dangerous as they said?

There was nothing romantic about Kingston, but there was a noisy vibrancy that spoke of survival, of refusal to despair. Earthquakes had devastated the place more than once – when were the dates? There had been a fire too, and the city had been razed. Yet here it still stood, crumbling, smelly, teeming. A stray dog sniffed at her ankles and she held out her hand, but it flinched away.

People called to her – asking her to buy from them, begging, offering to walk with her. Her skin seemed to reflect light like a mirror, flashing into these people's eyes; they either turned their heads away or demanded something from her. It had been the same as a child; then she had burned her skin in the sun, hoping to pass for brown, wanting unremarked passage.

She bought a coconut from an old man with a handcart who wielded his machete with terrifying skill, but his smile was sweet. She drank the cold coconut water with a straw as she walked, and when it was finished wondered where to put the shell. A Jamaican would just throw it into the next open lot. She would be considered mad if she got into a taxi with it. She was a Jamaican. She put the nut down in a clump of guinea grass and immediately a goat appeared and began to lick at the shreds of flesh around the opening. It was October and she knew the afternoon rain would soon begin. She congratulated herself on this knowledge, but then the skin on her arms itched and she knew she had got her first sunburn. Aloe vera. Nanny Ros would have called it *sinkle bible*. Maybe there would be some in the garden at Waverly Street.

She thought of her brother, Andrew, eight years older, an impossible gap when they were young. He had studied architecture in England and stayed there, married an English woman, had English children. She had not seen him since she had been in college, when he had visited her in Gainesville and taken her to dinner at a Red Lobster. Who had called Andrew with the news? Had it been her father? She thought of the last address she had for him in Trelawny. She had no idea what he was doing there. She thought of him standing on the jetty at Fairlight, waiting to tell her he was leaving her. Leaving them. She heard the crash from her mother's bedroom and heard her own voice say, "Mummy?"

The Libbeys returned that night. "Leigh, right?" Phyllis Libbey said, walking up the front stairs with a basket full of produce. "How you spell that? Sorry we not here when you reach, mi dear, but we back now. This my husband, Conrad. Conrad! Which way him turn? Bet you him inspecting the pumpkin vine. Beryl give you everything you need? Come inside, nuh, lock the grill gate. You shouldn't sit out here with it open, too many mad people on the street."

"But isn't Mr. Libbey still outside?"

"He will bawl out when him ready. What Beryl cook?" Phyllis peered into the three covered plates on the stove. "Huh. Fricassee chicken again. That woman have not one bit of imagination. I better boil up some yam or Conrad going complain 'til the middle of next week."

Over supper, Leigh learned about the Libbeys. They had two grown children, neither of whom had stayed in Jamaica, so they rented out their spare room and bathroom to foreigners – Peace Corps or social workers in Jamaica on short-term contracts. Conrad Libbey seemed to be about seventy. "Retired civil servant, me dear," he said, "worked for forty years with the Ministry of Agriculture. They thought I would stay there until they had to sun me, but I left when the time was right." He winked at Leigh. Phyllis was perhaps ten years his junior, wearing a tight, flowery dress cut low over an ample bosom. "Had enough, Leigh?" she said, passing the bowl of yellow yam again.

"More than enough, thank you."

"You have plans for the weekend? I got some shopping and errands and you could come with me, see something of Kingston," Phyllis said. "Church on Sunday; of course I know sometimes Americans don't go to church, but you're welcome to come. Six-thirty sharp."

"Thank you – but I probably don't have the right clothes for church," Leigh said. "I'd love to drive with you, though, get my bearings a little."

That night, the house was full of human sounds, muffled coughs, the scrape of a chair, low voices. Leigh smiled into the darkness. She made a list in her head. One, find out how my mother died. Two, find my father. Three, go to work. Four, find my way around Kingston. Five, go to Portland, see Fairlight. Six, find my friends. Seven, put down roots. Right down to bedrock.

There was no eighth item on the list.

On Monday morning, Danny rattled the padlock on the grill gate just after eight. The Libbeys were not yet up but Leigh was ready. She was glad of the lift. It marked a difference – no one in America had come to show her the way, ever, unless you counted college orientations. Danny was dressed as he had been at the airport, but his face looked scrubbed and there were a few drops of water in his hair. He smiled as she got into the car. "You have a good weekend, Miss?"

"Leigh, Danny. My name is Leigh. No need for the Miss." He turned down the radio. "No, leave it," she said. "It's fine." He smiled at her again but left the radio down low.

They crawled through traffic. Vendors sold newspapers on street corners and Leigh thought she would subscribe to a Jamaican newspaper. "I went to Duke Street on Friday," she said. "Is Kingston Refuge near there?"

"One street over. How you did get to Duke Street?"

"Taxi. Then I walked around until the rain started. Went down by the harbour. Got sunburned."

"Sometime you have to careful where you walk downtown," Danny said. "Aii Jelly!" he shouted as they went past a coconut seller. Leigh looked around to see if he was the same seller she had bought from, but the man's face was lowered and she couldn't tell. She was going to tell Danny about her dilemma over the shell, but she decided not to.

"Where you from, Mi… Leigh?"

"Told you already." She wondered if he was testing her. "From here. Born in Kingston, grow in Porty."

"Never been to Porty."

"Is beautiful. I want to go and see my old house."

"Where you mother and father come from?"

"Here too. Born here." This was a tedious and familiar line of questioning.

"Four generations," she would say, though she was sure only about three. "My great grandfather was a Scottish missionary." *Not* some estate owner, was what she meant. A missionary. Someone who left his comfortable home and travelled to the Indies to preach to the people. A good man. She knew almost nothing about the man. Missionaries were controversial, but they were definitely better than slave masters.

"For true?" Danny said. "A missionary?"

"Yes."

"Where him live?"

"I don't know," Leigh said, and the admission seemed slightly shameful.

"Where him grave is?"

"Don't know." She knew Danny was waiting for an explanation. "I left Jamaica when I was fifteen, my parents split, my mother took me away. Maybe I'll look for the missionary's grave."

"So where you parents?"

"My mother died couple months ago. Car accident. My father – he's somewhere in Trelawny. I have to find him."

"Never been to Trelawny neither."

"Tell me about the refuge."

"What you want know? Is a place for homeless people, give them food, place to stay, if them want. Most of them don't want to stay. Run by some priests."

"How is it funded?"

"How you mean, funded?"

"How it get money?"

Danny shrugged. "Dunno. Sometime they have barbecue, that kinda thing." He seemed uncomfortable with her questions and she became silent. A man suddenly stepped in front of the car and Danny braked sharply. The man wore only tattered material wrapped around his waist, almost a loincloth. He was barefoot and filthy and thin, his hair long and matted.

"Danny!" he yelled. He appeared delighted rather than alarmed. "Wha' gw'aan? Who dis?" He peered through the windshield.

"Guinep! After me did nearly kill you! You think you can beat out and duco?"

The man threw his head back and cackled. "You a good driver, Danny-boy. You nah kill me." Danny shook his head and drove on.

"Guinep, you called him?" Leigh said.

"Eeh-hee. 'Cause that's all him eat. Him nearly dead when guinep season done. Every year him nearly dead."

"Does he come to the shelter?"

"Sometime. But not when guinep bearing."

"How are you settling in, Leigh?" Father Gabriel asked, a month later.

"Fine, Father," she said. "It's good to be home." This last statement was expected. Jamaicans who had never left the island expected deference from the prodigals. They, the faithful, had stuck it out – the politics, the crime, the poverty, the flirtation with socialism, the austerity programmes, the empty supermarket shelves. They had not run. They had not had the benefit of a foreign education. They were born yahs, grow yahs, never left yahs. They were the tough ones, the ones who deserved Jamaica.

"How's your accommodation?"

"Fine."

"You get along with the Libbeys?"

"Absolutely. Everything's fine, Father."

"What about your family here? Have you connected with them?"

She sighed. She preferred American workplace boundaries. Father Gabriel was an old-school Jesuit priest; if she let him, he would have patted her head. "About to, Father," she said and left him. She had telephoned her father once, but the phone had not been answered.

Kingston Refuge was run by the Roman Catholic Church – one of a variety of programmes they ran for the poor – visits to shut-ins, a homework programme for children, a Sunday school. Their offices and the shelter were located in a shabby old building on East Street, partly brick and partly concrete. It was in poor repair, but from its high ceilings, trimmed with crown moldings, and the sweep of its sash windows it had obviously been important, but no one working at the shelter knew its history. The Institute of Jamaica was further down the street and she decided that sometime she would go to see if there were any documents on the old buildings of downtown Kingston, or maybe records about missionaries who had come to Jamaica.

There was not all that much to do at the shelter, and she quickly understood that her position was a condition of their funding, even though the priests thought it unnecessary. The shelter had a few bunk beds, bright new bathrooms, lockers for people to store their possessions, and a games room where their users could play dominoes and, occasionally, table tennis. Two meals were provided – a proper cooked lunch at noon, served in

Styrofoam containers, which Leigh often encountered littering the streets – and soup with a hunk of hard dough bread at six.

Although her title was Director of Programmes, she found she was merely in charge of registering those who used the centre – this was another requirement of their grant – and those who used the centre were profoundly suspicious of this step. Leigh suspected they would double their clientele if no one had to register. The form required an address and even a signature – for homeless people! Many of those who staggered through the doors could not read and were ashamed of their illiteracy. Leigh soon found herself offering to sign for them, using her left hand. She sat at a desk in a corner, facing the entrance, in charge of the buzzer that would release the glass door so that those deemed sufficiently unthreatening could enter. A drop-in centre, she thought, where there were far too many obstacles to dropping in.

"How do I tell if someone is threatening?" she had asked Father Gabriel, when he first explained her role.

"Well, their eyes."

"What about their eyes?"

"And whether or not they have a weapon." He pointed at a big sign on one wall – "Absolutely no weapons of any kind."

"Suppose the weapon is hidden?"

"You'll soon get the hang of it," he said, waving his hand at the top of her head, remembering just in time the newfangled ideas about the role of women. By the end of her second day at work, Leigh knew that most of the people who came in could not read the sign about weapons. So she pressed the buzzer for anyone who could stand – it was irrelevant for those who lay like rubbish on the sidewalk outside. Guinep walked by at least once a day, waved at her, grinning wildly, but never came in.

Danny worked at the shelter doing odd jobs – cleaning, driving, even helping with the cooking on occasion. He had walked with her through the nearby streets each lunchtime during her first week, introducing her to the vendors. Seya who sold bananas, oranges and ground provisions from country; Alberta, for warm bottled drinks and cheese crunchies; Carmella for sky juice; and old Jelly, the coconut seller, *her* coconut seller. Danny told them Leigh was his friend, and they should not

27

overcharge her. After that, the vendors often gave her a *brawta*, a tangerine or an extra squeeze of syrup on her sky juice. When Danny walked with her, the bold stares of the men and the comments on her colour lessened.

From one of her co workers, Delilah Mendez, Leigh learnt that Danny came from Jordan, a so-called garrison community. She had read about these communities in the USA, and now in the *Gleaner* she followed the stories about near universal unemployment, vandalized schools, reprisal killings and fights over turf. Kingston Refuge gave opportunities to poor youths – Danny was a beneficiary. He had made it through his all-age school, was functionally literate but that was about all that could be said about his education. He had never known a father and had seen his two older half-brothers murdered in the street in the crossfire of warring gangs before he was twelve. He slept in a small room at the back of the house on East Street and was anxious to please. Good material, Delilah said. He was twenty-two, slim and long-limbed, the bones of his skull visible under his skin. Leigh noted the slight flattening at his temples, the curve of his cheekbones, the cleft of his chin. His eyes were light brown and slanted upwards at the corners. He smiled easily; the inside of his lips were pink. An American volunteer at the shelter had left him her Walkman and he was never seen without it. Leigh thought she should feel motherly towards him, but she also thought about slipping his shirt off his shoulders and running her fingers over the tight skin of his arms, right the way down to his fingers. She pushed those thoughts away – she had no intention of making any of her old mistakes.

She was determined to like her slow job and her slow life with the Libbeys. Her rent included breakfast and dinner; mealtimes were strictly observed and began with prayer and hands held. She regressed to being a schoolgirl. Once Phyllis even asked if she had remembered to wash her hands before coming to table. She tried to tune out Phyllis's incessant chatter about church gossip, and Conrad's rants about politics. He hated Prime Minister Edward Seaga, and inveighed against his policies, the rising debt, the ever-devaluing dollar. Everything in Jamaica was in terminal decline.

But after her solitary years in America, she found the close attention of the Libbeys comforting. It would chafe in time, and then she would move on, but for now she liked the zinc-roofed house, which was no better or worse than its neighbours. She liked the rooms crammed with furniture and knick-knacks, the uneven green-flecked floor tiles, the muttering fridge, the riotous garden where Conrad waged a constant war against the fowls from next door. She liked the verandah where the Libbeys sat every afternoon, drinking lemonade or coconut water, listening to the radio, exchanging greetings with their neighbours, picking dead leaves off the potted plants. Conrad had bought home a rocking chair for her within her first week – so the verandah now had three chairs.

But there was nothing to do at night. The Libbeys wanted her home by dark. Too dangerous to be downtown then. They hated it when she walked anywhere. Leigh had found a convenient lift with Delilah, who drove right past her street to and from work. Delilah left at five p.m. precisely, so she was home by five-thirty and the evenings lay ahead. She would help herself to a drink from the fridge and sit on the front step, enjoying the soft light of late afternoon. After supper, the Libbeys retired to their front room, in front of a small colour TV and watched old American sitcoms. Leigh said her good nights and went to her room. She showered, then lay on her bed, staring at the square of the night sky through the top of the window, listening to the sounds of traffic and the croaking lizards, rasping in call and response like competing preachers at their pulpits. Dogs barked and sirens sounded. Her mind was empty. She never really knew what time she fell asleep. Often she woke, imagining she heard the sounds of her childhood, the clank of oarlocks, the bubbling of the hull of her dinghy skimming over the water, and the crash of shattering perfume bottles, jewellery, compacts, lipstick, hairbrushes on the day her father left her mother.

She had been in bed that day, reading *Black Beauty*. It was a Saturday, and normally she would have been out – on her bicycle to the Port Antonio market to buy food for a cookout in the bush, or in the dinghy trying to row around Alligator Head, which would take her into the calm waters of San San Bay, and up to the

Little Island, where she could beach the dinghy and climb to the top and look out over the reef to the indigo sea, shading her eyes, hoping to see Cuba, just ninety miles to the north. Rowing around Alligator Head needed the calmest day possible – she had only made it around the headland a few times. But she was recovering from an upset stomach and her mother had decreed that she should stay in bed one more day, on a diet of ginger ale and dry toast. She was bored and restless. She was usually alone on Saturdays – Zoe, had work to do at home. When Leigh had been younger, she had read storybooks about English children, and they'd had to do "chores" like Zoe. Leigh never had to do chores. She had demanded a chore from her mother, but when she discovered this involved sweeping and dusting and ironing and folding clothes and cooking, she became less enthusiastic. It had sounded better in the Famous Five books. Zoe had to do those things for her mother and her five brothers and sisters, but Zoe did not seem to mind.

Leigh heard a crash from her mother's dressing room – she called it her *boudoir*. "Mummy?" she called. There was no answer. She was breathless. There was something about the crash that suggested that this was not an accident, not the careless knocking over of a bottle of perfume. "Mummy?" she said again, and walked to the door of her parents' bedroom suite. She knocked gently and there was still no answer. She walked in. She was wearing her new cotton pyjamas, a little large, taken out from the storage cupboard as a treat for her illness, and the top slipped off her thin, sunburned shoulders. She adjusted it and ran her fingers through her hair, to avoid a lecture on her appearance. Her mother had taken her for a haircut that year and her hair was very short. When longer, it was untidy, verging on not being "good hair".

"Mummy?" she said for the third time.

Her mother turned her blotched face towards her and Leigh took a step back, because she had never seen her mother look anything but composed and painted. When she swam on calm summer days, she did not get her hair wet; she held her hand high, with a cigarette between her fingers, using an awkward one-armed dog paddle. This woman with swollen eyes and quivering mouth and uncombed hair was not her mother.

"What happened?"

Her mother held up a piece of notepaper. "He's left us. Your father. He's left us. He's run off with some bimbo." Leigh saw her mother's cosmetics on the ground – that was the crash she had heard. Her string of pearls had broken. She must have swept them to the floor. "Shh, Mummy," she said. "Don't cry." She hovered, confused. "Shall I get you a hankie?"

"Go and play, Leigh," her mother said. "I can't deal with you now."

Leigh backed out of the room. It could not be true. Her father would not have left, not without telling her good-bye. Her stomach clenched and she thought she needed the bathroom, but she swallowed and her gorge settled. In her room, she tore off her pyjamas and pulled on her bathing suit, now too small and stretched out, the cloth faded. Her mother had given her permission to leave the house. It was going to be a Saturday like any other.

She ran down to the cove and straight into the water. She swam out to sea, thinking of islands, perhaps an uninhabited one. Her favourite story was Robinson Crusoe, because it reminded her of herself and Zoe. She could see them alone on an island, she the captain; Zoe, Man Friday. They would eat coconuts and lobster and have adventures.

The salt water stung her eyes and she rolled on her back and floated. She could hear underwater sounds, strange clicking noises that her father had not been able to explain. She knew they were the voices of fish. She floated into a cold fresh-water bubble welling from the sea floor and shivered. She churned her arms and legs to mix the icy fresh water with the warm salty sea. She looked to the shore and saw her father standing on the jetty. He was dressed in a suit and tie and she knew then it was true. He was leaving them. He was leaving *her*. She put her face in the water and settled into a steady crawl, away from him, heading for the open sea. Maybe she could swim all the way to Cuba.

Leigh remembered this as the day her mother cried, and how, later, she used to sing those words in her mind to the tune of "American Pie". Her father left just after the summer holidays had begun, the summer of 1970, and by that September, Leigh was no longer at school in Portland, but was boarding at the Hampton

School for Girls in St. Elizabeth. Her dog, Rex, had been given away to a family with a farm where, she was told, he would be able to run free. She knew this was a lie. Fairlight had been sold and her mother was in one of Kingston's first apartment buildings, defiantly entertaining a twenty-five-year-old lover.

"You find your father yet?" Phyllis Libbey asked. They sat on the verandah, drinking lemonade. The afternoon sun poured through the burglar bars and made patterns on the floor.

"Not yet. Been busy at work. Called a few times; no answer." Leigh hoped this was brief enough to discourage further questions.

"You been here more than a month. Family important," said Conrad Libbey. "You have a famous name."

"I do?" Leigh knew Conrad fancied himself a historian.

"Are you related to the abolitionist or the Lord?"

"Neither, as far as I know. My great grandfather was a missionary."

"Wasn't there a McCaulay who died a few months back? A car crash in Montego Bay?"

"Montego Bay? My mother was killed in a car crash, but I don't know where."

"Wasn't just a car crash… Didn't they…?"

"Shh, Conrad. Some things not good to talk," Phyllis said.

"What do you mean, some things not good to talk?"

"Pay him no mind. Him read death notice 'til him fool. Don't know McCaulay from McIntosh. It was a lady name McIntyre him was thinking of."

"McIntyre, yes," Conrad agreed. "Somebody else."

"My church sister," Phyllis said. "Carla McIntyre. Moved to Mo Bay and *bam*, dead. You never know the hour or the day. Bad things happen in Mo Bay. Godless place."

"Where's Beryl?" said Conrad. "Me thirsty. That woman always missing in action."

Beryl, their helper, was a stout woman with a vacant manner. Leigh had learned the word "maid" was now considered demeaning. Beryl came to work every day before seven, changed in a small, outside bathroom into a blue uniform with a white apron, set the table, prepared breakfast, cleared the dishes, washed and dried them, cleaned the house, did laundry by hand on Mondays and Thursdays, sitting on a stool in front of a large tin pan, hung out the clothes on the line in the back, prepared lunch, served it to Conrad who was nearly always home, and cleared it away. Only then would she sit and drink a heavily sweetened cup of tea. Then she made the day's fruit drink and began supper. She left the supper dishes on the top of the stove, the food portioned on each plate, each covered with a thin white towel. At six, Phyllis covered each plate with another plate and put them all into a slow oven. Leigh often found the food only barely warm and cooked with too much oil. Once a week, on a Friday night, Beryl made dessert – home-made ice cream, which she churned in a green bucket, or sweet potato pone, banana bread or coconut jelly, sprinkled with brown sugar. On Sundays, the Libbeys had a big, late lunch; supper was buttered white bread with a cup of cocoa. Leigh had gained weight since being in Jamaica.

Beryl unlocked her childhood memories – so much of her growing up had been supervised by maids and gardeners. Her Nanny Ros wore a white cap and starched apron, and smelled of thyme. She had only bottom teeth and Leigh used to sit on her lap and count them. When she wanted to be rude, she called her Seven-tooth Nanny. It was Nanny Ros who woke her, got her ready for school, packed her lunch, and walked with her to the gate. She was collected by a neighbour, but it was Nanny Ros who was waiting at home for her. She allowed outdoor play until four o'clock, then it was time for "tea and tidy". It was Nanny Ros who walked with her to the cove and stood waiting while she paddled or threw stones into the sea, who told her tales of the fearsome galliwasp – should Leigh ever catch sight of this awful reptile, race for the nearest water! – who told her of River Mumma lurking under bridges, particularly the Flat Bridge on the Rio Cobre, waiting to suck you down so you drown, and of the Rolling Calf with eyes like headlights, signalling all manner of calamity. Leigh never repeated these stories to her parents; even when very young she knew they were somehow unacceptable, stories from a people not her own. She never developed a phobia of lizards, she approached Flat Bridge without a twinge of fear, and never, ever dreamed of the Rolling Calf.

She remembered their laundress, Laverne, who sang hymns as she bent over the wash pan; and the gardener Ken, who showed her how to catch peenie wallies in a bottle to light the corners of her room at night, where to feel for janga under the big rocks in Portland's many streams, how to climb trees and stalk the lizards she did not fear, using a noose constructed from the fibres of coconut trees. It was Ken who cut and stripped the branches of June rose bushes and made her bows and arrows; Ken who, when she approached puberty, pulled her onto his lap and slid his fingers under her shorts. He had kissed her with an open mouth too, she not yet twelve; the taste of his tongue made her feel sick, and she ate an entire box of imported marshmallows to replace Ken's taste with something else. She had not thought of that moment behind the garage in years. Watching Beryl at work in the kitchen brought it back, the black people moving like shadows in and out of Fairlight, the dinghy, the cove with its crescent of white sand and the tickle of seaweed on her feet, her skinny body buoyant in the water, her bicycle, her slingshot, the grass quits that fell to her increasingly well aimed stones, and Zoe, her fishing buddy, and the bread man who brought hard dough bread and bullas in a mule cart. He had one day offered her a ride in his cart, his black hand grasping hers to help her up, his palm dry and hard as stone. This had caused trouble when Nanny Ros found out. "Him touch you?" she demanded, holding Leigh's shoulders too tightly.

"Ow!" she said. "You're hurting me! He just helped me into his cart."

"Him touch you anywhere?" Leigh shook her head, understanding suddenly that the kind of touches Nanny Ros worried about were the kind Ken had administered under her shorts, right in her own garden. Bad things could happen even though the fences ran around the base of a hill and your house was right on top.

Growing up, she had accepted the household staff as normal, as if the house somehow came equipped with such people. Everyone had maids; at any social gathering a fair amount of conversation was devoted to the subject – how laundresses could no longer iron, not in the way they used to, how it was best to give them the old kind of iron, the ones that had to be heated in a coal pot and used with thin pieces of cloth to protect the clothes, because maids simply could not handle electric irons; who had been fired because she was found entertaining a man while on duty; who had walked off the job without notice; who had come to work with her children – well-mannered and neatly dressed children, but still… And who had committed the cardinal sin of stealing – leaving for the once-a-month weekend off with a bag of sugar or even a leftover chicken leg just beginning to grow mould. Such transgressions had to be met with the harshest discipline, or where would it lead.

Leigh listened to these conversations more uncomfortably as she edged into her teens; Zoe was the daughter of a maid. She did not want to have to supervise a maid, but this seemed to be her destiny. She did not want her white skin that attracted envy and dislike and the possibility of violence. She loved her home on the hill, but knew it was in some way bound up with the colour of her skin. She loved to sit on a rocking chair on the verandah to watch the weather sweep across the sea, loved the fair light that fell through louvre windows making stripes on her bed, loved the tangle of trees around the house, and the cove, her cove. But she did not want the girls at school to know where and how she lived.

Leigh carried the laundry tub into the back garden at Waverley Street. It was nearly dark and Phyllis had warned her that clothes might be stolen. She was not a good washer. Her hands were weak and she couldn't make the right squishy noise, nor wring out the large items, especially her sheets. Somehow she always managed to drop or trail something in the dust. But what was she trying to prove by doing her own laundry by hand? In America, she had either taken her clothes to laundromats, or the buildings she had lived in had washers and dryers in the basement. Washing her own clothes made her forsake her jeans – they were too hard to wash, scraped her knuckles and took too long to dry. She was slowly replacing them with light cotton trousers, bought from sidewalk vendors on Princess Street – a place Phyllis had told her was strictly off limits to decent people.

Her mother would not have approved. She would never have sunk her manicured hands into a tub of laundry. She would have made a sound of great irritation and told her she was depriving someone of a job. Warned her about ruining her hands.

She had been reminded of her mother's friends when Father Gabriel invited her to a cocktail party shortly after her arrival. She had bought a cheap dress and evening shoes on Princess Street – she had not worn a dress since childhood. She went with Delilah to the party at an uptown hotel, an old coffee plantation, Delilah had told her, and feeling awkward, she had stood amongst the groups of glittering women and distracted men. The men had no interest in her at all; they were making business deals. The shiny women ignored Delilah, standing at her side, but they spoke to Leigh.

"What brought you home?" they asked and Leigh mumbled a response. They did not ask why she had left.

"You're working at the shelter on East Street!" Leigh agreed that she was. Eyebrows went up, heads were shaken, and advice given about never walking the streets alone, about being home by dark, and getting a car as soon as possible. "It's dangerous down there," the women said, fingering their necklaces.

"Many good people live there," Leigh said. Delilah pinched her arm, which she understood to mean, be quiet. No, she would rather have cocoa tea and patties than this gin and tonic world.

She dropped the clothes in the wash pan, watching them balloon as they trapped air. She needed to contact her father – why was she procrastinating? The slowness of her days filled her with lassitude. There was no hurry. He did not know she was here.

She had learned the address she had for him was for some kind of farm in Trelawny and she wondered how he had come to be there and why he was in possession of his ex-wife's personal effects. Her parents' break up had been acrimonious. Had he attended her mother's funeral?

For a while Leigh had known about her father's various business ventures – he had owned a fleet of taxis, sold real estate, imported goods banned by the socialist government in the late 1970s, started a fabric wholesale business, traded in used cars, grown and exported pumpkins, scotch bonnet peppers and American corn – perhaps that was why he was on a farm. Once he had married Sarita, the flow of information from her mother dried up.

It had always seemed to Leigh that little was required of her mother – she slept late with a mask over her eyes, lit a cigarette as soon as her eyes opened and was never seen outside her bedroom unless fully made up and attired in the latest fashions. She had been exasperated by her dishevelled tomboy of a daughter. No man will want you, she used to say, tugging at Leigh's hair with a brush.

Leigh piled her sopping laundry into the empty concrete tub at the side of the house and threw the dirty water onto the vegetable patch, now with a crop of tomatoes. Conrad's pumpkins had been reaped, eaten and the surplus given away. She refilled the tub for rinsing, and tried to get the soap completely out of her clothes. The sun was waning, but her exertions had made her sweat. Now the clothes she was wearing would need a wash. Her mother had told her that she was her swan song, her last hurrah, her surprise blessing. She had thought Andrew would be her only child, and she had so wanted a daughter – unspoken were the words, but not a daughter like you. Aaah mother, even your beauty was not enough to keep your husband, Leigh thought, as the water finally began to show fewer suds.

She hung her clothes on the line, then sat for a moment on the back step, savouring her solitude, wishing she could eat toast in her bedroom for supper, without conversation. She needed to think. Why had she come back? Had she given it any thought at all? In some ways it seemed she had never left. While she moved around the United States, Jamaica had occupied her mind in a way it had not done while she had lived there. She had lived on a hill. Better houses were always on hills, elevated in all the ways that mattered. You were above the people who lived on the flat, your house caught the cool breezes, the view from your verandah was not obstructed by other houses, the verandah went right around your house and you could see the mountains, the coast and the sea – all of which you owned with your gaze. Anyone who wanted to see you, perhaps to sell you a crocus bag of clattering live black crabs or a foot of yellow yam had to climb the hill with their eyes either downcast to the stony driveway or raised to the house silhouetted against the sky.

She had not had to do chores, had never called anyone "Miss" or "Master"; she had books, a bicycle, a dog and a dinghy; her parents had owned the edge of the sea. She had been friends with the daughter of a maid, but once she left, had not contacted her. As a child she could not have been expected to question her world. She had been too concerned with her own young difficulties, mainly her family's disintegration, to notice anyone else's lives. Her life had been warm, comfortable and protected – until her father left. Being born in Jamaica was merely an accident; it had no particular meaning – a person had to be born somewhere. Still, she had carried a dwindling collection of seashells with her as she moved, each move resulting in one more shell reduced to powder. She dreamed about the land she left. She lost track of her friends, but had sent for tourist board posters showing Little Island in San San Bay, the deep, green Rio Grande, landscapes empty of people or context or history, and she rolled and unrolled her posters in each new place, trying to smooth their creases as she placed them on the walls. Posters and shells had eventually been lost over the years.

She had tried not to think of her mother's frequent pronouncement with its many layers – *I can't deal with you now, Leigh,* but could not put aside the knowledge that she had been raised by other people's mothers. When her first college roommate had asked about her life in Jamaica, she had mentioned Nanny Ros and saw her roommate's surprise. "So," she had said, "you're rich then?"

"No. Not rich. Everyone in Jamaica had maids. It's nothing," she said, embarrassed. But the questions continued: Were the maids black, did they sleep with you, did they have their own children, did they smell different? I would not like a maid to help me bathe, they really helped you bathe? Only then had she begun to consider certain facts. She knew Nanny Ros had her own children, three of them, Donald, Jacob and Ardent, children she had seen only infrequently. She had began to wonder what this had meant for Nanny Ros's children. Her Jamaican life began to seem shameful and best left behind.

Now, sitting on the back step of the Libbey's house, she remembered Nanny Ros had lived in one room at the side of a house on Market Street in Port Antonio with a big common mango tree in front, much like the house she now occupied. Nanny Ros and her children had lived in a single room. This

Vineyard Town house was small in comparison to Fairlight, much closer to the neighbours, and there was no high view of coast and sea, but the similarities between this house and Fairlight were greater than the differences. Maids lived in outside rooms and houses were run by maids, who were to be regarded with caution. Leigh had heard many conversations about Beryl's shortcomings and they always ended the same way: "At least she's honest," Phyllis would say.

"Huh," Conrad would answer, "As far as we know."

Could Nanny Ros still be alive? And Zoe – what had happened to her? Her father had said they had different futures. It seemed it was all to do with how people had come to Jamaica, most without choice, but some finding their place. Like her great grandfather, perhaps. She had loved the island but had left it, had embraced the anonymity of America, had told herself she was at home anywhere. When she walked an American street, no one made remarks about her colour, she was not a target for panhandlers, no judgments were made before she opened her mouth. In Jamaica, people like her had the freedom of an abundant land, but in America she had the freedom to be one of the people.

She began the search for her school friends, working backwards from the most recent. Her move to a boarding school as a teenager had cut her off from younger friends, and the election of a socialist government in the 1970s had resulted in widespread middle-class emigration. The day she had told Zoe she was leaving for boarding school they had been sitting on the top of the Little Island, in a grove of bamboo, the fallen leaves scratching their bare legs. It was early and the sea had been calm enough to row around Alligator Head. She was not sure they would be able to get back, but that was fine with her. The tiny island had once supported a white man, a hermit, so the stories said, who had lived on coconuts and fish until he had been swept away in a hurricane. Later, it had become a Valentine's Day present for a princess. She liked the idea of taking up residence on the island, but it was within easy swimming distance of land and she was sure her parents would find them. Her parents. Her *mother* would find her, her father was gone.

She'd looked out between the bamboo fronds at the white

villas built on the land opposite the island. Her father had been offered one of the building lots, originally intended for cabanas or boathouses for the big houses on Goblin Hill behind. "A lot?" he had laughed. "Those places are just somewhere to put your back step." Now the coast contained many back steps.

It was quiet. The sea made no noise; the waves were so small they did not break on the reef. Soldier crabs rustled in the dead leaves and the wind whispered in the bamboo and willows. It was cool, so early in the morning.

"Where you going boarding school?" Zoe asked.

"Hampton. In St. Elizabeth. Near where Andrew was."

"Me hear of it."

"I have heard of it," Leigh corrected.

"When you going?"

"Soon."

"School don't start 'til September," Zoe said.

"Yes. But they're selling Fairlight and my mother is going to Kingston. I have to go with her."

Zoe hugged her knees to her chest. "You too big for a nanny anyway."

Leigh had not thought of this. Nanny Ros would lose her job, as would everyone who worked at Fairlight.

"Never been to Kingston. Me, I hear it is a bad place."

"Maybe you will come and visit." They both knew this was a lie. "And I'll write."

"Sea breeze soon come up," Zoe said. "Time to go."

"Not yet. We have time." They sat and watched the people who worked at the villas begin their work, raking the beach, putting out lounge chairs, opening doors. A white child ran onto the beach, carrying a bucket and spade. His black nanny held his hand, her uniform crisp and white against her skin. She sat on the edge of one of the lounge chairs, glancing up at the first floor balcony, as if she were afraid of being caught in some transgression. The blonde-haired boy wore a large orange float on his back; if he went into the water when no one was looking, the float would buoy him up and he would bounce along on the surface of the water like a man o' war jellyfish, until he washed up on San San Bay Beach. He dug enthusiastically in the sand.

Zoe stood up. "Me gawn." She did not entertain castaway fantasies, Leigh knew. Her dreams were of a concrete house on its own piece of land, with an inside bathroom and kitchen, piped water and electricity that flowed from a switch on the wall, and a small plot in the back for bananas and gungo peas. She disappeared down the steep path, her bare feet sure on the exposed tree roots. When Leigh jumped from the path onto the small beach, Zoe had already pushed the dingy into the shallows and stood beside it. They got into the boat and Leigh rowed for Alligator Head. It was still calm. The blonde boy waved from the beach and Leigh waved back.

"I have something for you," she said to Zoe, after the boat was moored in the cove at Fairlight. "Come up to the house with me."

"I wait here," Zoe said. Recently, she had started avoiding Fairlight. She sat on the end of the jetty, her skinny arms braced against the soggy wood, her feet dangling, gazing out to sea. Leigh left her, ran up the hill to Fairlight, the house full of half-filled cardboard boxes. She pulled her fishing tackle box from under the kitchen table and went back down the hill. The sun was well up now and the heat was expanding. She came round the last corner of the track and could see through the mangroves to the end of the jetty. It was empty.

She contacted Hampton School for Girls by telephone, introduced herself to the secretary and asked for the contact information for Carol Parsons and Felicity Mitchell. The information would take some time to find, she should call back in an hour.

Carol had been her best friend at Hampton, because she too had been a new girl at the time. She was the only black girl in their class. These two facts had made her an outcast and the subject of the other girls' talk, as they sat at tuck shop tables or on benches under the huge cotton trees that dotted the campus. She's black, Felicity Mitchell would insist. Felicity was the whitest girl in school, with hair so pale you could see her scalp through it, the epitome of good hair without wave or curl, and pale blue eyes that also looked entirely colourless in certain lights.

She's brown, another girl would say.

41

If you've got any black in you, you're not brown, you're black, Felicity would reply.

So who is brown then? someone else would ask.

There is no brown, said Felicity.

Leigh befriended Carol, sat with her when she saw her alone with her head bent over a book, because Leigh's own hair was not blonde or straight and the conversations of the other girls made her wince. Carol was the daughter of a lawyer and a nurse; people, Felicity said, who had got above themselves. Carol did not welcome Leigh's overtures at first, but in time they struggled together over French verbs and the poetry of T.S. Eliot, talked about the boys from Munro College they liked, studied their changing, imperfect bodies and stood guard for each other in the showers, to make sure none of the other girls played pranks on them.

But Leigh never visited Carol's home in school holidays. She had met her parents at open days at Hampton – her father settled the brown/black question as he was unquestionably black. It was blonde Felicity she saw in the holidays; Leigh's mother knew Felicity's parents, and Leigh escaped to the Mitchells' luxurious house in Jack's Hill whenever she could. There, she experienced the privilege of those several social rungs above her family: the elevation of the house, the city spread out below, the formal meals, the Mitchells' art collection. She heard the dinner conversations about the dangers of the Manley-led socialist government, the racism deliberately introduced by Manley and his army of communists, because everyone knew that before him Jamaica was a melting pot of racial harmony. It was Manley who had told Jamaicans that it was black man time now and made it dangerous for people of a certain class and colour. His government had made Jamaicans refuse to work and the economy was being destroyed by handouts. They were throwing their weight around with the state of emergency and soldiers on the streets, but they weren't stopping the violent crime directed at the middle and upper classes. It was against the law to hold foreign currency. Those who could leave were leaving. In Jack's Hill, dozens of shipping containers were parked in front of the gates of lavish houses.

Had she liked Felicity? Leigh couldn't remember. She had enjoyed the comfort and beauty of the Mitchell home; the orderliness, the lack of strife. She had disliked the steel bars on the windows and the Dobermans, who were only ever let out at night. The only person who could handle the guard dogs was the Mitchell's gardener, whose name she did not know. She remembered greeting Carol more enthusiastically than was merited on their returns to Hampton, feeling guilty that she had not seen her during the vacation, asking her about her Christmas celebrations or Easter holidays, and pretending not to notice Carol's monosyllabic replies.

She discovered she was unlikely to find either of her friends. Felicity, she learned, had gone away to college, married an American and never returned to Jamaica. Her parents had migrated. Hampton did not know what had become of Carol – the last address they had was c/o a travel agent in Ocho Rios, but when Leigh contacted the firm, Carol had resigned more than six years earlier. No, they did not know where she worked. Carol's parents no longer lived at the address in the telephone book.

She had no idea how to go about a search for Nanny Ros or Zoe. That would have to start in Portland. When she thought of the Junction Road, the journey across the mountains, her chest tightened. She was afraid of what she might find at Fairlight. Perhaps she needed to find her father first.

She found her address book and turned to "M". There was her mother's last address. Yes, it was in Montego Bay so it was likely that was where the crash had occurred. Her father was bound to know the details.

Leigh had never got the full story of her parents' rift – she knew the basics, the existence of another woman, the lack of discretion on her father's part. Her mother's ire was mostly about money – she had not got the settlement she deserved. Most nights, she paced around the small apartment's living room, cursing the day she had set eyes on Robert McCaulay. There was talk of respondents and correspondents. April McCaulay had never remarried. She had a contact at the United States Embassy and a sister in Tampa whom Leigh had never met. Within a year, Fairlight had been sold, the Kingston apartment vacated and the family furniture shipped. "I don't want to g-go," Leigh stammered to her mother as they boarded the Pan Am jet at Palisadoes Airport, four days after her fifteenth birthday.

"Leigh. Do not. Make a scene. And tuck in your blouse."

"I hate you! My father wouldn't have left me! It's *you* he left. As soon as I'm eighteen, I'll be back and you can't stop me!"

"When you're eighteen, you can do whatever you want."

But despite her promise, she had not come back. Her mother had, though. For reasons Leigh did not know, April McCaulay had returned to Jamaica eight years before.

She crossed out all her mother's addresses, and the sound of the pen on the paper seemed loud. She looked at her father's address: Edinburgh, Queen of Spain's Valley, Trelawny. She squinted at the phone number – was that a five or an eight? Perhaps she had been calling the wrong number. She dialled using the eight. The phone rang only twice before it was answered. Immediately, she knew it was his voice.

"Dad?"

"Leigh?"

"Yes. It's me."

"You heard about your mother then. I'm sorry about… I didn't know where to…"

"Thanks." She did not want her father's pity. "I'm here."

"Here where?"

"In Kingston."

"I thought you hated the place."

"Yes. No." I hated the summer after you left, she wanted to say. "Anyway, I'm here."

"So will I see you? I'm in Trelawny on an old plantation. Running a tourist attraction."

"I know. Yes. The lawyer told me you have some of Mom's personal effects – I need my birth certificate. Do you have it?" *A tourist attraction?*

"I don't know. I do have a box, but I never…"

"Could you…"

"Why don't you come and stay for a while, Leigh? What are you doing in Kingston? When will you go back?"

"I'm working. At a homeless shelter. I'm not going back. At least not for now."

"*Really?* So will you…"

"I'll try to get some time off to come and see you, go through the box."

"When?"

"I don't know. Soon. I'll call you again. Is Sarita… never mind. We'll talk when we see each other." *You're an adult*, Leigh reminded herself, hating the stilted conversation.

"Fine. It's good to hear your voice, Lee-Lah."

The forgotten nickname caused a sudden pricking of tears. "Thank you." She hung up the phone. *Dad*. Her father had taught her how to fish, how to row, how to be on the sea, with the sea. She thought he had loved her, perhaps he had, but he had left her.

"Brought you a sweetsop," Danny said. He handed her the lumpy green fruit. He was evidently trying to educate her on all things Jamaican. At first, she had gently pointed out she had grown up in Jamaica, but he had looked so downcast that now she didn't have the heart to tell him that she was well familiar with a sweetsop. "Thank you, Dans," she said. "How do I eat it?"

"It not ready yet. Keep it outta the fridge for about three more day, just when you see the skin start crack. Not too long, though, or fly will take it up. Then just split it and eat it. It have nuff seed."

"Sound good. Where you get it?"

"Tree over in Fletcher's Land. Most of them pick by now, but this one was high. Me get it for you." He stared into her eyes and she turned away, making herself busy with her register. "Later?"

"Later."

They had fallen into a pattern of leaving work together several times a week. She told the Libbeys that she was having supper with a friend and she knew they thought she meant a woman. Sometimes she and Danny went Uptown for ice cream at Devon House – he had guava, she had coconut, and they would sit on a bench under a big tree, eating their cones. The ice cream kiosk was called I-Scream, which Danny thought was hilarious. He loved the movies and they often went to the Odeon to see whatever was showing. Most of the films were violent and Leigh spent much of the time with her eyes closed or covertly watching

45

Danny. Like many others in the audience, he would warn the actors in the film out loud and laugh at the most tragic moments. He watched leaning forward, his elbows on his knees, and she envied the uncritical way he gave himself up to the world of the film, seeing none of its flaws. At such moments, she felt indulgent towards him and much older. She paid for his tickets, bought his ice cream; he brought her fruit and ground provisions from Coronation Market.

After the movies, they often took a bus to the waterfront, to the asphalted area where Danny told her the Myrtle Bank hotel had stood before it burned down some years before.

"How you know about that?" she asked.

"My mother take me to watch the fire. People glad it burn."

"Why?"

He shrugged. "Black people not allow in there. Only to clean and cook and pour drinks."

"A long time ago?"

"Not so long," he answered. "Not so long."

Once, she had asked him to come with her to look for her grandmother's grave; the streets of Kingston were easier to navigate with him at her side. They went to St Andrew Parish Church in Half Way Tree. "That's so ugly," she had said, looking at the venerable church, desecrated by a new bell tower. Danny said nothing. Leigh explained her business to a woman in a small office and asked if there was a plan of the graveyard. The woman shook her head. "You just have to look," she said, staring at Danny.

They walked through the jumble of graves, old and new. The inscriptions had worn off the oldest graves, now just pitted marble slabs. Some were cracked and holes gaped underneath. "Goat shit," Danny said, pointing. Leigh saw the small round pellets everywhere and heard the bleating of goats in the bush. Grass and weeds obscured most of the graves, but a few were tended, edged with blooming flowerbeds. The noise of traffic on Eastwood Park Road made reflection impossible, but even with its closeness, the graveyard seemed to her a dangerous place, where armed men could appear and harm them.

After an hour, she gave up. "We'll never find it." There was no order, no system to the cemetery's layout.

"You never come to the funeral?" Danny said.

"No. I was too young."

He pursed his lips and she could see he wanted to say something. She remembered that as a child he had witnessed the murders of his brothers. She had been shielded even from the rituals of death, never mind death itself, while he had faced bloodied bodies. She had not seen her mother's body. Had she been mangled by the car, or bloodless and white in death, the injuries all internal? She touched Danny's shoulder and together, they left the cemetery.

After work, they often sat together on a crumbling bit of wall, overlooking Kingston Harbour, watching the sun set and night fall. They sat there on dark nights and moonlit ones, nights with clear skies and stars, nights where clouds hung low and a few fat raindrops fell into the sea. They rarely spoke, but Leigh felt Danny's presence hum beside her in the dark. They sat without touching, without speaking, but she knew she wanted to lean against him, to have his slender arms embrace her. Not to kiss, she lied to herself. Nothing like that. He was too young for anything more than friendship. But it had been so long, too long, since a man held her. Every time they went to the wall, she tried to sit a little closer to him. She fidgeted, bouncing into him by accident. She felt the heat of his skin, of his blood, across the narrowing space that separated them. He never seemed to notice, never looked sideways at her. She did not know what he was thinking and only the bare bones of his life. When she began to feel sleepy, she would stand and say she had to be going. He never argued, never tried to persuade her to stay, walked with her to where the taxis waited on Harbour Street and bade her good-night. When she was in bed at Waverley Street, she stripped naked, and as soon as her fingers parted her legs, as soon as she touched herself, she came.

The mental list she had made on her first night home was forgotten. There was no rush to do any of it – to see her father, to get her birth certificate, to sort out her inheritance, to find out the details of how her mother had died, where she was buried. That burial place was sure to be a mess, too. She hoped her mother had not been at fault in the accident; that alcohol had not been the cause of injury to anyone else. Surely, the lawyer would have known that at least. Perhaps her mother had lost control of the car and run into a light pole. Or the sea. That ushered in images of her mother drowning – no, she did not want to face any of it.

She telephoned her father once a week and their conversations became more stilted, not less. She learned that her stepmother, Sarita, had multiple sclerosis. Bet you didn't bargain for that, she thought, as she uttered her sympathies. The tourist business was booming. The plantation was gorgeous. When are you coming, Lee-Lah? When will I see you? Soon, she would respond. Soon.

She gazed through the glass door at East Street, rippling in the wet September heat. She turned the sweetsop over in her hands, feeling its fecund weight. It would be good to go to the country. She was ready. She would ask Father Gabriel for a few days leave. "Danny!" she called. "Do you have a road map?"

She discovered it would be difficult to get to Edinburgh Plantation. The nearest coastal town was Falmouth, which was simple enough to get to on public transport, but no one seemed to know where the plantation was, exactly, how long it would take from Falmouth, or what it would cost. Danny had never heard of Edinburgh Plantation. They pored over the road map together and could not find even Queen of Spain's Valley, although Danny said he had heard of that, because he had a cousin who worked on a sugar plantation there. Leigh knew he wished she would take him with her.

In the end, she had a brainwave. If there was a tourist attraction at the plantation, then surely she could take a tour. She telephoned the Holiday Inn in Montego Bay and discovered that yes, she could indeed book a tour to Edinburgh Plantation. No, she didn't have to be staying in the hotel, but she would have to be there to make a 9.30 a.m. departure. It was expensive, but Leigh decided to do it. She would pose as a tourist, have a look at the place and, if her nerve failed her, could simply return to the hotel at the end of the day and go back to Kingston. Maybe if she didn't tell her father she intended to visit, she could avoid him.

But she knew this was neither likely nor sensible. She needed to see him; she wanted to go through her mother's effects, and there was the practical matter of the birth certificate. But if she decided to stay at the plantation, then she would have paid a huge sum for a one-way journey, and would then have the challenge of finding her way back to Kingston. It probably wasn't possible to stay overnight on this visit, no matter what happened. She could always return, once she had seen the lie of the land. At least the tour was a feasible method of getting to the plantation, and she liked the idea of seeing her father's world anonymously. The drive along the island's north coast – where she had not been since childhood – was something to look forward to.

Father Gabriel approved her three days off and she took the road map home. That night, she stared at the place names, tracing the roads with her fingers. She saw herself in various places in no particular order – here she was older, there younger. A school trip to Dunn's River Falls two days after her first period; a rainy family weekend in Oracabessa where she had curled up in a window seat and read *The Lion, the Witch and the Wardrobe* from start to finish; the blinding white sands of Doctor's Cave Beach, where she got her worst sunburn ever, and the wide empty beach in Negril, where mosquitoes bit even during the day and the crabs came out at night and everyone talked about how badly Negril needed development.

There were many more places she was sure she had never seen; mostly in the interior of the island. Christiana. German Town. Albion. Kellits. Duanvale. Mile Gully. Ulster Spring. Fortress. Sitting in her small, hot bedroom, she suddenly wanted to see them all, wanted to travel every road and track and a cane piece interval in Jamaica, to lay claim to it, to know it perfectly. She saw herself in a tank top, shorts and hiking boots, a short cutlass in her hand, a bandana around her neck, her legs muscled, going wherever she wished to go. There, on a hill, there in a valley, and over there, floating in the sea, arms outspread, in the shallows of the north coast. If anything conferred ownership, shouldn't that be birth?

She fell asleep holding in her mind the names of the places she had never seen.

Danny introduced her to a friend, an unsmiling man called Spoon, who operated an illegal taxi. They agreed a price and before dawn on the day of the tour, she left Kingston in an old Lada. Her efforts to find the reason for his pet name elicited only a shrug.

The streets of Kingston were empty and they left the city quickly. The sky lightened by the time they reached the Rio Cobre gorge. As they drove over Flat Bridge, Spoon broke his silence. "Flat Bridge have one dangerous duppy," he told her. "River Mumma live under the bridge and sometime she hungry-hungry." Leigh remembered Nanny Ros's stories and remembered Flat Bridge flooding and the road being closed, remembered her father pointing out the stone marker high on the vertical hill that formed one side of the gorge showing the highest point the river had ever reached. Now she looked upwards and thought she caught a glimpse of it, still there in the bush.

Bog Walk was wreathed in mist until they began to climb the flanks of Mt. Diablo, where the road switchbacked its way into St. Ann. They drove through the undulating hills of Moneague with its low stone walls and soon were descending through the dappled light of Fern Gully to Ocho Rios.

Leigh gasped when she saw Ochie – it was unrecognizable. The construction of hotels on the beach had begun just before she left; since then the old fishing village had been obliterated. The skyline was a row of buildings – not the medley of vegetation at the side of the beach that she remembered. She wanted to stop at Dunn's River Falls, but feared she would miss the plantation tour's departure. She put her head through the car's window as they drove past Dunns River, so she could hear the falling water.

They drove through the old cane fields of Richmond Llandovery, which fell away to the coast. Here, at last, was the sea, the reef with its curling waves and the horizon. Where were the coconut trees that had lined the coast in groves, with their curving trunks and hard-to-reach nuts?

"Lethal yellow," Spoon said when she asked.

"What?"

"Some kinda disease. It kill every tall coconut, except dis one place at di bottom a di Junction Road. Dem start planting dwarf coconut now. Dem better. Easy fi reap."

The road hugged the coast at Salem and the sea was right there, licking the low wall that tried to fend off the ocean. Again, she wanted to stop, to walk on the sea wall as she used to do when she became carsick on long journeys with her family, the smell of the salt air easing her nausea. Today was calm and the sea slid over small patches of beach and low flat rocks. They did not stop.

At Pear Tree Bottom, she took in the flat marshes that stretched to the hills in the south. Where the road crossed a river, a graceful blue heron took flight as the car approached. Leigh had to get out of the car. "Please stop," she said to Spoon. "Just for a minute." He turned right onto a small beach and parked under a big almond tree. She jumped out.

There was a rickety shop on the beach with a hand-painted sign: "Mama's One Stop." The door was padlocked. Three canoes were pulled up on the sand, their paint faded and chipped. Leigh sat on a rock, took off her shoes and rolled up her pants. She waded into the shallow water, the sun hot between her shoulder blades. The water was as warm as Sunday night's cocoa tea, left too long before drinking. Ticky-tickies swarmed around her feet and she felt a bubble of joy expand in her chest until it broke and she laughed out loud. She scooped up seawater in her hands and splashed an invisible playmate. The place smelled of old fish and rotting vegetation and wet sand – smells that instantly rendered her young. She saw Zoe, wearing a washed-out dress, passing the fishing tackle box. This was where her youth was – past, yet not past – at the edge of the Caribbean Sea.

She heard the noise of an engine and saw a fishing boat come round the western point of the bay. The paint was fresh on this one, bright yellow, and the registration numbers were clear and painted with a stencil. Yellowbird. A fisherman man sat easily in the stern, with his fish pot resting on the gunwales. He wore no hat and squinted into the sun. He guided the boat through the shallow rocks, cut the engine and lifted the propeller from the water. The boat drifted onto the sand and the man carried his pot onto the beach. Leigh waved to him and a poem she had learned in school suddenly came to her. She could not remember the author, but she remembered the words the whole class had learned in a singsong chant:

51

Across the sand I saw a black man stride
To fetch his fishing gear and broken things
And silently that splendid body cried
Its proud descent from ancient chiefs and kings,
Across the sand I saw him naked stride,
Sang his black body in the sun's white light
The velvet coolness of dark forests wide,
The blackness of the jungle's starless night.
He stood beside the old canoe, which lay
Upon the beach; swept up within his arms
The broken nets and careless lounged away
Towards his wretched hut beneath the ragged palms
Nor knew how fiercely spoke his body then
Of ancient wealth and freeborn regal men.

The man lifted his hand in acknowledgment when he saw her
and she returned the salute. She saw the glint of his catch in the
fish pot as it gasped and flapped, and she remembered the feel of
caught fish in her hands, the way you had to hold down the dorsal
fins to stop them cutting your palm, and how to wrench the hook
from the mouth, and how, if it was a big fish, you hit its head
against the side of the boat to kill it. She had been unsentimental,
quite able to scale and gut the fish she caught and hand them to
the cook for frying.

Leigh thought of the poem again and of Zoe whose fate she did
not know. Then she got up and turned away. She did not want to
think any more about the loss of her childhood friend who had
fished with her, nor the struggles of the suffocating fish, nor the
reality of the fishers who brought them to shore and, least of all,
the past of freeborn, regal men.

The Holiday Inn was typical 1970s architecture – concrete,
rectangular, unimaginative. It squatted on the coast, surrounded
by undeveloped land. A security guard stopped them at the
entrance. He peered into the car and saw Leigh sitting beside
Spoon in the front and it was clear he found this arrangement
suspect. "You checking in?" he asked Leigh.

"No," she said. "I'm not checking in. I've come to take a tour.
I've booked and they told me it was all fine."

"Well, you get out here then, Miss."

"Why can't my driver take me inside?"

"Is your driver?" Spoon stared straight ahead.

"Yes."

"Why you never say so? Him want wait for you in the car park?"

"Spoon, will you wait here, or you want go and come back?"

"Mi go into Mo Bay. What time mi mus come back?"

"Give me a minute. I need to ask the tour company. Guard, I need to go inside to find out what time the tour will return."

A car horn blew behind them. "Welcome to Holiday Inn," said the security guard, stepping back.

Spoon parked under an almond tree and Leigh went inside the hotel. It was not yet nine o'clock. She found the tour desk, but it was unmanned. A small cardboard sign announced that the tour to Edinburgh Plantation would leave at ten, not nine-thirty as she had been told. She sighed, saw a gift shop off to the left and went inside. A young woman leaned on the counter, listening to the radio. She looked at Leigh but did not greet her.

"'Morning," Leigh said. The woman did not respond.

"Do you know what time the tour desk opens?"

"No. Nine. Maybe nine-thirty."

"Do you know what time the tours come back?"

"No. You have to ask them." She examined her nails.

Leigh was irritated and hungry. She imagined food in the hotel would be very expensive, but perhaps she could have just a cup of coffee and a slice of toast. "Which way is the restaurant?"

"Down by the beach." The woman's body language indicated she thought this an idiotic question.

"Thanks." Leigh went back to Spoon's car, but he was not in it. She looked around, but did not see him. The guard was watching her. She felt she was losing control of the day. She went back inside and walked through the lobby, towards the beach.

She was not sure she had ever been in a big hotel in Jamaica, although she did have a blurred memory of a lobster cocktail eaten on a balcony overlooking the sea. She saw the beach was raked and swept and not a single strand of seaweed marred its surface. Danny would say the beach was under manners. She wished he was with her. She sniffed, but even the smell of salt was somehow missing;

53

it was a sterile place compared to the beach at Pear Tree Bottom. White wooden loungers were arranged in lines, some in the sun, others under round thatched cabanas. Small sailboats were pulled up on the sand, their brightly coloured sails hoisted, offsetting the multiple blues of the sea. She saw the dwarf coconut trees Spoon had mentioned. Few people were on the beach at this hour.

She turned and went back to the restaurant. A waitress in a pink uniform with a white apron arrived, her smile as wide and empty as the bay. "Coffee?" she said, offering the pot. Leigh could not ask the cost – if she sat in this place, she had to be prepared to buy a cup of coffee at least. "Yes, please."

"Milk and sugar?"

"Neither. All I want is two slices of toast and some jam. Okay?"

"The buffet over there." The waitress poured the coffee and pointed with pursed lips to a long sweep of table, swathed in a tropical fabric. "You help yourself. See the bread in that basket and the toaster next to it? Or you want me get it for you?"

"No, that's fine. I'll get it. Thank you." The coffee at least was strong, but she felt conspicuous, wrong. She was not staying here, with her room key thrown carelessly on the table and her eyes puffy from last night's excesses. The guests would know she did not belong, as did the waitress. Not foreign; not Jamaican. She stared out to sea and the glare off the beach made her squint. She wondered if the tour people were at work yet.

She made herself toast, helped herself to small packets of butter and a spoonful of guava jelly. The buffet was crammed with fruit, pastries, eggs, pancakes and even ackee and saltfish. She sat back down, ate her toast, and asked for the bill. When it came, it was for eight American dollars.

"But all I had was two pieces of toast and a cup of black coffee!"

"You did have the buffet."

"I didn't have the buffet! I had a cup of coffee and two pieces of toast."

"You never tell me you did want order from the menu."

"Why can't I tell you now?"

"Bill write up already."

"Well, then, I'm going to have the buffet."

"More coffee?" the waitress said.

54

It was almost nine-thirty before Leigh had finished eating a large dish of ackee and saltfish she had not wanted. It was lucky she had carried enough money to pay the bill. She hurried over to the tour desk and was relieved to see a woman there and a group of tourists gathering. "Excuse me?" she said to the woman who seemed to be registering names.

"Yes?"

"I'm Leigh McCaulay. I booked for Edinburgh plantation."

The woman consulted a typed list. "Yes, Miss McCaulay. You're here. You can pay now."

"What time will the tour be back?"

"Oh about four. Jamaica time." She laughed. "Bus will leave outside about ten."

"I thought it was leaving at nine-thirty?"

"Jamaica time."

Leigh paid, took her ticket and went outside to look for Spoon. The Toyota was gone. She would hate to be stranded here. The security guard was watching her. She walked over to him.

"You see my driver leave?"

"Him leave, yes. Him say him come back roundabout three."

"Oh, that'll be perfect. Thank you. The tour will be back about four, I'm told. Would you mind telling him that for me?"

"Mi tell him." The security guard gazed over her shoulder. "So wha' you can do for mi, Miss?"

"Excuse me?"

"You know, a little drink money. Times hard."

"When I come back," she said. The man kissed his teeth and turned away. Spoon would get no message from him.

She waited in the lobby, wishing she had brought a book. The tourists all seemed to know each other; they were telling stories about meals they had disliked, how much alcohol they had consumed, and the trips they had been on. They glanced at their watches and said "Jamaica time" with what-can-you-expect shrugs. A fat woman rubbed suntan lotion on a reddened expanse of skin. A young couple held hands; the man looked disgruntled. "We should have tried water skiing instead. A *plantation* – I bet it'll be boring."

"Don't you want to see something of the island?" the woman cajoled.

"Why? Beach and pool, sun and sand, all the food and drink paid for already. Bet it's gonna be a long drive on a bad road, some boring talk, nasty island food and then another long drive back."

"The brochure says there's a river. That should be nice."

"Whatever. Too late to back out now." The man turned away; Leigh could see a relationship unravelling.

The tour desk woman stood and clapped her hands. "Everyone for the trip to Edinburgh! Your bus is loading now. Don't forget your stuff. Have a wonderful day!"

"Sure," grumbled the young man.

Leigh followed the tourists to the bus. Ten of them. Four older people, travelling together and speaking in English accents. The young American couple. A family of four with two bored looking teenagers, probably American. The fat woman, who wore a Disney World T-shirt, so probably American. And herself. She would not be all that inconspicuous in this group.

They headed back towards Falmouth. The bus driver introduced himself as Dervol and said, in a mixture of American twang and Jamaican, that they were in good hands, he had been driving for years, although he'd only bought his driver's license yesterday. The Americans laughed, the English people didn't appear to get it. Leigh stared out the window. Did all tour operators feel they had to be clowns? Now that she was wearing the disguise of a tourist, she felt even more uncomfortable, as if she, too, had become a visitor. No, I live here. I was born here.

"So where y'all fram?" Dervol shouted.

No one answered right away. Then one Englishman said, "Leeds." The other said, "Coventry."

"Di mighty British Empire!" yelled Dervol.

The English quartet exchanged glances. Leigh wasn't sure herself if they were being insulted. "Where you fram, mi lady?" he asked the fat woman, looking into his rear-view mirror.

"Dayton," the woman mumbled.

"Dayton! Where is dat, eggzackly?"

"Dayton, Ohio," the woman said. "Don't you think you should watch the road?"

"Eyes in di back a mi head, mi lady. Eye-dem inna di head back. Welcome to you, fram Daytonohio!"

"We're from New York," said the man who wanted to water ski. "Our first time in Jamaica. We're on honeymoon, actually."

"Yang l-o-v-e-r-s!" yodelled Dervol. Was this going to continue all the way to Edinburgh? "I'm Leigh," she said into the momentary silence. "I live here. Born here. Just came home. Dervol, does this bus have music?"

"A RETURNIN RESIDENT!! Welcome home, dawta! Music? No mus! Wi has music! Wi has reggae, soca, ska, mento, rock steady, dancehall? What you want, dawta?"

"Bob Marley," said the fat woman.

"Wi can all sing along. Oonu know di words fah 'One Love'? No mus! See it here, Bobmarley. You know sey him dead of a rotten toe?" He inserted a tape into the deck.

Leigh was relieved. The music was louder than was comfortable, but better than Dervol shouting. She watched his back move in time to the music as he flung the bus around corners.

"The other couple didn't get to introduce themselves," the American wife whispered.

"For God's sake, don't start him up again," said her husband.

They left the coast at Falmouth and drove into the hills, the bus now lurching from pothole to pothole, raising clouds of dust on the better-maintained stretches. They drove through small villages of unfinished buildings and by roadside piles of marl and rusting zinc fences, through small farms growing skellion and yams, past low-roofed schools and bars and old men on donkeys. In the centre of little towns, women sat under blue tarpaulins selling the usual fare of soft drinks and beer, cigarettes and snacks. A few children shouted at the bus as it went past. Leigh wanted to know the names of the towns, but few were signed.

In the towns dilapidated buildings stood alongside blocky modern structures. Cars jockeyed with goats and cows for space on the road. Young men sat on walls and glared at the bus.

"How much longer?" shouted one of the teenagers over the music, now repeating songs.

"Eeh?" said the driver. "What you sey?"

"Please don't start him up again," moaned the American wife, but not loudly enough for the driver to hear.

"How much longer?" repeated the teenager.

"Maybe a fifteen minute. JAMAICA TIME!" Dervol shouted, turning off the radio.

"Oh God," said the American wife.

"I told you we should have tried water skiing," said the new husband.

And the villages became fewer and on one side of the road, Leigh saw cane fields bounded by low hills. The hills appeared to float like islands in a green sea. The bus passed a flat pond and a ruined windmill and low, crumbling stone walls crisscrossing the land. The road narrowed and rose and they drove through a tunnel cut in the rock, through which the roots of trees curled, searching and failing to find fertile soil, yet still persisting and even thriving. The trees shaded the tunnel and she felt that civilization had been left behind. Everyone in the bus was quiet.

Finally, they drove through gates in a low stone wall, though these walls had been secured with new cement, and past a wrought iron sign announcing "Edinburgh Plantation". The driveway was asphalted and the visitors perked up and stared up to an imposing house. One field close to the house was planted in cane, but most of the other fields were scrubby ruinate. Leigh saw two horses grazing in a field of guinea grass; off to the right, a line of large trees, she guessed, hid the river. She had never ridden a horse in her life, but suddenly it seemed the perfect way to see the land, slow and high and quiet and somewhat unpredictable. On a horse, she would not be confined to the roads. She saw herself picking her way through overgrown paths in a dense forest.

She felt nervous. It was just a stupid tour. She probably wouldn't even see him. She suddenly wondered if Dervol was going to be their tour guide. That would be unbearable.

They parked in what looked like a stableyard. "WI REACH!" Dervol bawled. "Evy'bady out! Take you bags. Dis bus leavin at tree-tirty, nobady mus late. If you stay a night at Edinburgh, duppy will GET you." Leigh reached for her backpack and was first out of the bus.

The stableyard was deserted. Low buildings enclosed the space on three sides and the ground was spread with raked gravel. A strange wooden structure, like an oversized door frame, stood in the middle of the open side of the square, next to an empty water trough. Some of the buildings were obviously stables, with painted half-doors, the top halves fastened open. The doors to other buildings were closed, probably offices or storerooms. There was a large stone ruin to one side and, further away, she could see the remnants of a mill with a huge rusty water wheel. She walked out of the yard and strolled a short way down the road, past the bones of old fences, mostly stone, some with wooden fence posts, leaning every which way, festooned with coiled barbed wire. The canepiece was perfectly fenced with a new stone wall.

She felt small, standing at the centre of the plantation, cupped in the valley. The land stretched away to the hills and she tried to imagine its conquest, the moment when someone crested a hill and looked over the valley and said – *I'll have this*. What would it have looked like – would the valley bottom have been covered in forest, would the trees have been huge, what kinds of animals would have roamed the land, would Tainos have been here? And before? She tried to imagine the island rising out of the sea, and settling down to become what it had become. She imagined people arriving in droplets and then in waves, beating themselves on the land, being absorbed by it, fighting for roots and fertile soil, then finally, overwhelming it like a muddy river in spate. What would it be like to possess a valley like this, to look over it at daybreak, to fence it in and order everyone else out?

"Aii! Miss! Yes, you! Tour a start. Come over here!" Leigh turned and saw Dervol waving. The tourists were huddled in a circle and there was a young woman standing with them, dressed in a long, bandana skirt, an off-the-shoulder white blouse, gold hoop earrings and a red head tie. She had rounded cheeks and full lips and her shoulders curved in the sun. Leigh walked over and the woman dropped an awkward curtsey.

"Welcome, Miss."

"Leigh," she said.

"Miss Leigh," said the woman. "My name is Grace and I am your tour guide. We are pleased to welcome you to Edinburgh

Plantation. Our tour will begin with the Great House and environs, then we will go to the ruins of the mill and factory. After that, we will go to visit some graves. Then we will go to the river for your swim and a picnic lunch will be served. Does anyone need to use a rest room before we begin?"

"Yes, please," chorused the English quartet.

"Let's go," said the honeymooning man, staring at Grace's shoulders.

"Were you really born here?" Leigh realized the fat woman was speaking to her.

"Hi. Yes. I was."

"You don't look Jamaican."

Leigh responded mildly, "I know. But I am Jamaican."

"It's cool."

It *was* cool, up in the hills. "Yes. Might get hotter as the day wears on, though."

"No, I mean it's *cool*. Jamaica is cool. The music and all, and the way things are slow and nobody cares. I wish I'd been born here. I'm Jody, by the way." She held out her hand which was slippery with sweat and sun tan lotion.

"Leigh." It was inevitable that the only other single woman would gravitate towards her.

Grace led the small party up the hill to the Great House. Once they were out of the shade, she said, "Please put on your hat if you have one. The sun in the tropics is very strong. When the first white people… ah, I mean the *Europeans*, when they came here, they found the heat very hard." Everyone rummaged in their bags and took out hats.

Grace stopped in front of the Great House. It cast a wide shadow and, for a moment, Leigh felt dizzy and perhaps a little carsick. "This is the plantation Great House," said Grace. "This is where the owners lived, while the slaves toiled in the fields below." As she spoke, she gestured with movements that seemed choreographed, like a pretty wind-up doll. If she had hoped to learn something about the history of this place, Leigh doubted it would come from Grace. "The Europeans tried to copy the lives of wealthy people in England," Grace continued. "So they built stone houses in the Georgian style and they brought with them many luxuries. The furniture you are about to see is mostly reproduction, but there are a few original pieces I will point out to you. Please stay within the roped areas. Follow me." She turned and led the way up the steps to the half open front door.

"I'm feeling a bit faint," said one of the English women.

"It's the walk," said the other. "Maybe we can get cup of tea."

"A rum punch would be better," said the water skier. "Can't believe I missed a day on the beach for this."

"It's beautiful, though, don't you think, honey?"

"Huh."

Leigh turned and looked at the valley laid out before them. The land shimmered. It was green and restful to the eye, the pale blue sky arched overhead. Leigh felt as if she floated between land and sky.

"Please Miss Leigh," called Grace from the doorway. "Come this way. The group has to stay together."

They walked through the Great House with its marble floors and thick stone walls, its faded tapestries and glowing furniture. It had obviously been modernized at some point; there were electrical light fittings and modern glass windows and some of the floors were concrete. Leigh let Grace's commentary flow over her – it was full of dates and rebellions and names – and wondered where her father and stepmother lived. It seemed impossible that anyone could reside in such a lavish, ghostly residence.

Grace led the way through upstairs bedrooms with small four-poster beds, commodes and tables holding pitchers and basins. Leigh noticed an elegant dressing table made of a light wood with a fine grain. "Is that mahogany?" she asked Grace.

"No, Miss. Yacca."

"Never heard of yacca."

"Used to be found in the Blue Mountains. Most of it was cut down to make furniture like this. This is one of the old pieces I told you about."

There were now modern bathrooms, but Grace told them that in the old days the slaves would have been responsible for emptying the commodes. That is what wealth means, Leigh thought. Never having to deal with your own bodily wastes. She

61

imagined sitting on the wooden commode over the ceramic pot, letting down the hinged wooden top after, and then just walking away, leaving the contents for someone else to deal with.

The second-floor bedrooms all had sweeping views of the land, and Leigh imagined waking to such vistas. She saw herself lying in bed, staring through the windows, awaiting the dawn sky, and then watching as the landscape was illuminated.

They toured the large outside kitchen with a replica of a cast-iron stove with an oven big enough to hold a man, and then the ruins of another building Grace said was the house slaves quarters. "Of course, the house slaves regarded themselves as better than the field slaves," Grace explained. "The lighter skinned you was, the more likely you was to be chosen as a house slave."

"How did they get to be lighter skinned?" Jody from Ohio asked.

"Oh, the masters all took slave woman as their concubines and had many children with them," said Grace. "In fact, some slave women encouraged their daughters to seduce the masters." The would-be water skier was watching Grace hungrily. "When are we going to the river?" whined one of the teenagers.

Outside again, they were met by a shaded jitney, pulled by a tractor. A bareheaded elderly man wearing faded overalls was in the driver's seat. A younger man wearing a white shirt, vest and khaki trousers sat in the jitney. He jumped out, fixed a smile, and extended his hand to help them into the vehicle. "Welcome," he said. "We go to see more of the plantation and the river."

"Finally," said one of the teenagers. As Leigh took the man's hand to help her up, his vest gaped and she saw a hand gun stuck in his waist. He was their security guard. Had the tour been held up by gunmen at some time or another? The Libbeys had told her that crimes against tourists were generally hushed up.

The jitney started down the hill, enveloping them in diesel fumes. The English quartet took out handkerchiefs and covered their noses. "I can't breathe," said the woman who had wanted tea.

"The smell will soon go away," Grace said.

As they came down the hill, the jitney headed away from the light wind and the fumes enveloped the driver instead. He seemed unconcerned. They drove down gravel roads and the fields stretched away on either side, some dotted with spreading trees.

"What kind of trees are those?" Jody asked Grace.

"Guango. The rain tree. After emancipation, Edinburgh was a cattle farm. The owners planted them, because they have pods which can be used for animal feed."

"Why the rain tree?" Leigh asked. She had not heard this name before.

"Because is always greener under a guango tree, Miss." It was true, the grass in the shade of the guango trees was green and thick.

"That tree over there, now, that is a cotton tree," Grace continued, pointing to another large tree with a grey, buttressed trunk and small canopy. "Slaves were buried under cotton trees and sometimes they were hung from them. Not on Edinburgh, though. This plantation used a gibbet and the place where the gibbet was hung is still in the stableyard where you came in."

"What's a gibbet?" said one of the teenage children, perking up.

"A gibbet was a device used to torture the most rebellious slaves. It looked like a cage made in the shape of a person. The slaves were put in the gibbet and left to die of thirst and their bones were left there as a warning to other slaves," said Grace.

"Cool!" said the teenager. "Can we see one?"

"There is a gibbet at the Institute of Jamaica in Kingston. It was found in Half Way Tree and the bones in it were thought to be those of a woman."

"So there's no gibbet here, then?" said the teenager, disappointed.

"No. Just the place where it was hung."

Leigh recalled the rectangular structure in the stableyard, the wood weathered like driftwood.

"Now those trees over there are cedar trees," Grace resumed. "That's where the planters were buried."

The group fell silent. It was after midday and very hot. The jitney bumped along and every now and then, the visitors got a whiff of the diesel fumes. Leigh felt more and more carsick and wished she could walk. The jitney wound its way through fields, past fallen trees which lay on their sides, their roots sticking up at one end, with a new trunk rising at the other.

"Why are those trees like that?" one of the English women asked.

"Hurricanes," Grace said. "Blown down in hurricanes. But if some of the tree roots still in the ground, the tree don't die, just send new branches straight-straight up."

Leigh smiled to herself; she liked the idea of that. A tree tested in this way would surely survive future hurricanes.

The jitney stopped at the grove of cedar trees that Grace had pointed out previously, and the man with the gun jumped down and extended his hand to the visitors. Everyone climbed out and stood in the shade. There were a cluster of marble headstones under the trees and Grace began a long, uninteresting account of the various owners of the plantation. Leigh longed to be free of the tour. She wanted to retrace her steps to the cotton tree and see where the slaves had been buried. She wanted to look again at the place where the gibbet had hung. She wanted to see where her father lived. She wondered if she would recognize him or he her. They had seen only people acting parts – the plantation nothing more than a stage. Apart from the two horses, they'd seen no animals. And the canepiece was obviously planted as teaching aid. Here the Great House, here the graves, there the cane that killed them all.

Leigh walked over to the driver of the tractor. "'Morning," she said. The driver looked down at her. "Mawnin, Miss." His face was grizzled, his eyes lost in wrinkles.

"You from this area?"

The man nodded, but did not elaborate.

"What's your name?"

"Banjo."

"How long you been working here?"

"Since mi a bwoy,"

"You always drive the tractor?"

The man shrugged. Leigh saw he was uncomfortable with her questions. She would probably never know his story, at least not today. "Sure is hot," she said, and she heard the American twang in her voice.

They reboarded the jitney and left the graves, heading down a shaded path towards the river. The tractor pulled up on a cleared and marled area and the visitors got out. Grace led the way down the path and Leigh heard the sound of water. Her spirits lifted. She was glad to escape the weight of the plantation – surely a swim in a river would bring some release. She began to walk faster and rounded a corner ahead of the others. There she saw the people of Edinburgh Plantation, all dressed for the part in bandana prints, all smiling, presiding over a mown lawn under an enormous tree, the curving river as backdrop, standing behind a table spread with a white cloth and covered with food. Three men sat on stools, one with a drum, one with a banjo and the other with a bamboo flute. As the visitors came into sight, they began to sing:

"This is my island in the sun
Where my people have toiled since time begun..."

Then Leigh saw her father, wearing a busha's hat, just as she had imagined, dressed in a white shirt, jodhpurs and riding boots – riding boots! – holding his hands wide in welcome to the tourists. His eyes met hers and, instantly, she knew he recognized her.

"Lee-Lah?" he said, dropping his hands.

"Dad," she answered.

BOOK TWO

GENESIS

1786
Port Glasgow to Montego Bay

Zachary heard the lookout's call: "Land ho!" He opened his eyes.
The deck rocked gently. It was so dark, he wondered how the
lookout could see anything. Perhaps it was only dark in the small
space he occupied, the one place on *Prospero* that was mostly
private. It was a cramped space under the fo'c'sle he had found by
accident, running one day to escape the icy rain from a sudden
squall, a day out of Port Glasgow. He had not yet gained his sea
legs, and as the ship leaned into the wind, he had stumbled and
fallen full length on the heaving deck. Just then, the deck canted
sharply and he felt himself sliding towards the weather rail. He saw
himself slipping over the side into the black sea, not even able to
utter a yelp of surprise. No one would miss him for days – perhaps
not until they made landfall in Jamaica. A cry would go up: Has
anyone seen young Macaulay? There would be a search of the ship,
down to the rat-infested, stinking depths of the hold, where the
cracking sounds of a wooden ship tearing through the sea banished
thought. They would find no trace of him; Zachary Macaulay,
sixteen, lost at sea. Aye, and he'll be sorry, Zachary thought,
picturing his father's twisted face the last time he had seen him.

Then the ship had steadied, his slide was slowed and he
grabbed a half-hidden cleat behind a coil of rope. He pulled
himself gasping into the small, sheltered space, where it was
warmer if not dry, and wedged himself there to wait out his first
winter storm. Gradually, his nausea left him and although his
muscles ached the next day, and his limbs were bruised, he vowed
not to return to his airless cabin for the rest of the voyage.

Two months had passed since that day and while he had not
forsaken his cabin entirely, sleeping behind the ladder let him
smell the air, taste it on his tongue and mark its changes from north
to south. For the last two weeks, he had worn only his singlet and
trousers – the feel of wool on his skin was unbearable. He had worn
and re-worn his few linen shirts. He knew his sea chest contained
almost nothing suitable for the climate he was entering. Even now

the heat made him fight for breath, though out on deck the wind cooled the sweat on his skin and the warm, wet air slid more easily into his lungs.

He crawled out from behind the ladder and stretched. Yes, dawn was sliding across a calm sea. He stood at the weather rail and squinted, trying to see the island he had been banished to. He could see nothing but the sea, empty in every direction. He heard the sounds of the ship coming to life around him and the lookout shouted "Land ho!" again. The sky lightened and then Zachary saw it – a dark green mass, still hours away, rising from the haze at the horizon. Jamaica.

Hours later, *Prospero* sat, hove to, off a small town. "What place is that, Sir?" Zachary asked the first lieutenant, as he hurried by.

"That there is Montego Bay."

He was suddenly desperate to get off the ship. He remembered his first sight of it, how small it had seemed, how unlikely that it could cross an entire ocean. He had considered running away – his father would never know if he did not embark. He could travel down to England and find work somewhere. He knew next to nothing about the West Indies. He had read in the newspapers that men died and men made fortunes there. He was going to work on a sugar plantation called Bonnie Valley. He did not know what a sugar cane plant looked like. Was it a tree, a shrub or a tuber to be dug from the ground? Not a tree, he had decided. He had settled on a root like a potato that would be dried and then crushed, its flesh transformed into something granular and sweet and expensive.

Prospero had been one of the last ships leaving Glasgow before the hurricane season. It was well known that the Indies were wracked with storms between June and November, storms no ship could survive. Zachary's father, the Reverend Macaulay, had marched him to the port, implacable. "Perhaps the Indies will make something of ye," he spat at his third-born son. "God knows I cannot." The Reverend turned on his heel and left Zachary standing in the Scottish drizzle, beside his sea chest. Zachary looked up, close to tears. The ship's rigging seemed to scrape the sky. He knew sailors had to climb those masts to set the sails. He saw them, skylarking on deck. They were about his age. That gave him courage and he hailed a stevedore, slipping him a coin to put his chest on board. He was welcomed by the captain, a slovenly man who gave him no confidence. A ship's boy was hailed and he was shown to a tiny cabin below the waterline, not much bigger than the cot it contained. He was immediately claustrophobic.

He saw the jolly boat had been launched and the passengers had been gathered on deck. Zachary had not spoken much to any of his shipmates on the voyage; he feared unwelcome questions. They were all men – four of them – a pastor, still clad in his robes and sweating in the heat, two rough-looking men who drank themselves into insensibility most nights, and a studious Englishman wearing spectacles and never seen without a book. Zachary knew their surnames; that was all. He nodded at them when he saw them and they exchanged stilted observations about the weather and the monotony of the voyage.

The jolly boat bumped against the ship. "Look!" the bookish man pointed; Zachary followed his gaze and saw the glossy water break into spreading circles. He could not identify the large head that broke the surface of the sea. "Sea cow," the bookish man said. "Good eating." He smiled. Zachary looked away.

The four men said farewell to the captain and the officers of *Prospero,* who were lined up at the entry port as if in a reception line. They clambered into the jolly boat. Zachary was last. The boat lifted on a low swell and Zachary tripped. "Steady on there, young 'un," the bookish man said, grabbing his arm. Zachary shook him off. The man shrugged. "Do as you please." Eight sailors were stationed at the oars and as soon as Zachary found a seat, they began to pull for shore.

Zachary stared ahead, squinting in the bright light. He wondered why he had rejected the older man's helping hand and felt ashamed of his bad manners. He saw a bay with a strip of white sand at the water's edge, and in the distance, low hills rising. As they got closer, he saw strange plants behind the beach with roots growing downward from the branches and, behind them, palm trees of various kinds. Off to the left – port, he corrected himself – waves broke on a line of rocks. The jolly boat edged into the bay, avoiding large rocks that lay just beneath the surface. Zachary stared down into the water to the sand bottom from which the strange coloured rocks rose. The rocks were crowded with fish and turtles breathed at the surface. He had not known turtles lived in the sea. He looked up and saw the town to one side of the bay. He could see the mouth of a river, flowing green into the sea.

The sailors docked the jolly boat at a wooden jetty and moved quickly to unload the passengers' effects, obviously anxious to be gone. As soon as the boat stopped its forward motion, Zachary felt the weight of the sun on his head. His collar was too tight. He thought there was a hat in his chest, but did not want to search for it. His trousers were loose – he had lost weight on the voyage. Suddenly he was starving. He wanted fresh food, meat and potatoes, and a glass of ale. He stood beside his chest and stared at the town of Montego Bay. He had no idea what to do next. He knew the Bonnie Valley plantation was about three days' ride away. He needed help to carry the chest, but he did not want to leave it on the jetty. He stood, irresolute. "Come on, young 'un, I mean you no harm. Macaulay, isn't it? You look lost. First time in the Indies, I'll wager. Where're you bound?" It was the bookish man. He had loosened his collar and was wearing a hat.

"Bonnie Valley Plantation." His voice sounded strange; he had not spoken full sentences in months.

"Aah, Bonnie Valley. Lovely spot. You'll be needing a horse. I know a man. Hi, you! Yes, you! Watch this chest 'til we come back."

"Massa." Zachary saw a black man, naked to the waist, dressed in rough pantaloons, walking up to them. He stopped beside the chest. He did not meet their eyes. He was thin and muscular, barefoot, and his skin shone. "Thank ye," Zachary said. The man did not answer.

"Come," the bookish man said. "Soon midday will be upon us. Better to be indoors at midday. Do you have money, lad? My name, by the way, is Manning. Trevor Manning. I know your name. Are they expecting you at Bonnie Valley? You'll enjoy Charles Monmouth and his children. I think he has a son about your age. You'd be what, seventeen?"

"Sixteen."

"Hmm. You'll do well, I'm sure. Bonnie Valley is famous for its parties."

"I'm going there tae work. I'm tae be the book-keeper."

Manning inclined his head. "Really? Well, now, I wish you every success with that, my young friend. See, that building over there? That's the tavern. We can refresh ourselves there and see about a horse for you."

"Why d'ye help me, Sir?" He had heard of men who preyed on boys. They stood on the jetty, the black man still as stone beside his sea chest. Manning did not have a sea chest; two soft bags that could be made into saddlebags sat at his feet. Zachary realized the chest was going to be impossible to transport by horse.

"Why? Why not? Because I too came here as a young man, sent away from my family. Got in trouble, didn't you? They've sent you here to make your fortune. Well, some do, some don't. I'll not harm you. But please yourself – I'm going for some grog." Manning tipped his hat and walked away.

"Wait!" Zachary took his first step to follow and the jetty seemed to rise to meet him. He fell to his knees as the solid wooden surface rolled like the sea. He heard Manning laugh. "Not regained your land legs, young Macaulay. Never mind. Here. Give me your hand. A little food and drink and you'll be a new man. You!" he shouted again at the black man, "Don't move an inch. It won't go well for you if things are not to my liking when we get back."

Zachary noted the black man was a full head taller than Manning.

The tavern was not marked by name or sign. Two saddled horses were tethered outside and a black man was holding a pair of horses harnessed to a buggy. He was dressed in black trousers, a white shirt with too-long sleeves and a vest, trimmed with pearl buttons; his feet were bare. Zachary and Manning went inside.

The tavern was cool and crowded. Zachary saw his two rough-looking shipmates. The floor was dirt, packed hard. Small wooden windows with slats were propped outwards, letting in narrow bands of sunlight. The walls were of thick stone with remnants of plaster clinging in places. Tables were scattered about, most seats taken. Many were well on their way to drunkenness.

"There. Two seats." Manning led Zachary to a table occupied by two white men. "Good morning, gentlemen. May we join you?"

"Help yourself, Sir. We're leaving now." The men were dressed in expensive cotton clothes in pale colours, their boots polished and, though they wore wide-brimmed hats, their faces were reddened and peeling.

"So, Zachary, I presume you have enough money to get to Bonnie Valley?"

"Sir, I am grateful for your kindness, but my father telt me it is unwise tae gie such details tae strangers."

Manning laughed. "Your father was right, lad. You seem to be well schooled – your English is excellent. He did well by you. From Scotland, are you?"

"Aye. We came from Inverary tae Glasgow."

"There are many Scots in the Indies."

"How long have ye been here, Mr. Manning?"

"How long? Oh, close on ten years. I go back and forth every few years. It's a long trip, but the climate suits me. It doesn't suit everyone. Now, what shall we eat?"

A woman approached their table. Her skin was rich brown with copper lights and her hair was hidden under a bright blue headscarf. "You gentlemens havin the turtle stew?" she said, eyes averted. Zachary had to listen closely to understand her.

"Turtle? I've no eaten turtle."

"Sea turtle," said Manning. "Very good." He looked up at the woman. "That sounds capital. And a flagon of your best grog." The woman nodded and left them. Zachary remembered seeing turtles from the jolly boat, their brown and tan shells glistening and he wondered if they would taste like fish.

"So how do you plan to get to Bonnie Valley?" Manning asked, removing his hat and stretching his legs.

"I dinna ken, Sir." Zachary felt stupid. "But I believe I hae enough money to buy a horse. How much would a horse cost?"

"That depends on the horse. We'll go in search when we've eaten. Everything will look different then. I suggest you sell your sea chest. It will be too difficult to transport."

"There are things o' value in it."

"Then we'll have to find someone with a carriage or buggy going your way. You may have to stay here for a while."

Zachary said nothing. Some of the men in the tavern were

becoming louder. He saw a couple of them grab for the brown woman. She wriggled from their grasp, her eyes downcast, and put two steaming bowls on a nearby table. The men crowed with laughter.

"Is she a slave, Sir?" Zachary asked, nodding at the woman.

"Probably. She could be one with more than six children, so no more labour in the fields. She could also be free."

"How dae slaves become free?"

"All manner of ways. She could have purchased her freedom. Her master could have granted it. She looks like a mulatto; maybe a quadroon – perhaps she has a white… ah, protector and he bought her freedom."

"A mulatto?"

"Child of a white man by a Negress. A quadroon is the child of a mulatto mother, with a white father."

Zachary found himself excited. The tavern had an atmosphere of danger and licentiousness, of rules discarded. He understood Manning's euphemism – protector. Lover, he thought. Lover and bidie-in. Lover and slave. He thought of the parlour at their house in Inverary, with its faded carpet and solid furniture, where his sisters sat in the afternoons, doing needlework or reading the Bible to each other, practising scales on the piano. None of his sisters would have been allowed to see a man without a chaperone. Martha, of course, had ignored the rules and now she was in confinement and he was in the Indies for concealing her transgressions. But the brown woman, the mulatto, she was a different kind of female altogether. She might be free or still a slave, but he was sure any man could have her. He imagined her laughing, with her head thrown back and her breasts bare. He squirmed in his seat.

Soon she returned, bringing their food. He wanted to pull her onto his lap and slip his hands under her skirt. His erection was insistent. He tried to meet her eyes, but she avoided him. She set the tray down and unloaded two large bowls of a rich stew. There was a platter of round golden cakes, cut into quarters, and a flagon of an amber liquid. The brown woman set down two mugs and the cutlery. She bowed her head and left them. The smell of the food was intoxicating. He felt he had wandered into a place where the pleasures of the flesh held sway. God, give me strength, he prayed, although despite his father's tutelage, he was not sure he believed in God.

The two men ate. The turtle stew was peppery and nourishing. The meat had a faint greenish cast. "What is this thing?" Zachary asked of the fried cakes.

"Cassava."

"What's that?"

"A root. If not properly prepared, it can be poisonous. It's what passes for bread here. Flour doesn't generally survive the sea journey, although a few people bring it in from the northern colonies."

The grog burned Zachary's throat and his head swam. "Rum, water and lime," Manning said.

They finished everything on the table. Exhaustion overwhelmed Zachary. He had not slept a full night in months, nor eaten such delicious food. Although harsh and potent liquor had been available on the *Prospero*, he had not touched it. Now he was in Jamaica where the sea gave up turtles, the land cassava and rum, and brown women who had to do what he said. Perhaps it would not be so bad to stay in Montego Bay for a few days. He felt his eyes closing. He wanted to succumb to the demands of his body.

"Falling asleep, young 'un? Only to be expected. I intend to stay the night here and set out early tomorrow. Shall we see if rooms are to be had in the town?"

Zachary allowed Manning to take charge. A small lodging house was located with rooms like cells, but each had a bed covered in rough white sheets, and a table with a basin of water and a jug. Two black boys placed his chest at the end of the bed. He tore off his clothes and splashed his face with water. Naked, he lay on the bed in a tumult of sexual arousal and masturbated. Then he slept, his body washed in a sheen of sweat, his hand around his penis and the semen dried crusty on his stomach. When the mosquitoes found him at dusk, he did not stir. He slept for fifteen hours straight.

"D'ye ken the name o' the river?" Zachary asked.

"Martha Brae," Manning said. "It runs through Bonnie Valley. Soon we'll head inland." Zachary felt a jolt hearing his older sister's nickname. His present surroundings made him feel his beloved sister was someone from his babyhood, someone who had spooned mush into his mouth and held him on her shoulder until he burped. He tried to see her face in his mind, but could not.

"Who was Martha?" he asked.

"There's some legend about an Arawak woman who led Spanish conquistadores to their death in a cave. They drowned."

The two men had left Montego Bay the previous day and had spent the night in the busy coastal town of Falmouth. Zachary had bought a sturdy bay mare, broken, the dealer explained, both for the saddle and the carriage. He had also purchased a harness and a small wagon for the sea chest, which the mare drew behind her. "That'll make for slow going, to be sure." Manning had shaken his head. "Still, you'll be able to see the countryside. I'm going in your general direction; I'll ride with you to the turn-off to Bonnie Valley. Then you're on your own, but the road is easy to mark and you'll find your way."

Zachary had found his coolest clothes and his hat. He was covered in mosquito bites. Manning had laughed when he saw him. "It's a rite of passage," he said. "You'll get used to them. Ask your employer for a mosquito net and tuck it under your bedding. And get a slave to fumigate your room before you retire – mosquitoes don't like smoke."

Zachary was happy to be astride the mare after the confinement of the ship. The freedom of his journey, the adventure of it, made him want to laugh out loud. The road followed the contours of the coast and when it rose, he could see over the coastal vegetation to the sea. He had not seen water of such varied colours. Though he could not swim, he wanted to throw himself into it.

"See where the waves break?" Manning had said. "That's the reef. Many ships are dashed to pieces on those rocks. Let's try a trot, see if that wagon of yours turns over. If we don't go faster, you'll have to sleep in the bush tonight." Zachary kicked the mare into a trot and he was pleased when she broke into a long, low stride that would eat up the miles. What would he call her? He thought of the *Prospero*. Back in Scotland, he had read some Shakespeare. The mare would be Miranda, he decided.

It was cooler the faster they went. Zachary watched how

Manning took advantage of the shade, guiding his horse from one side of the dirt road to the other, where it was lined by huge trees. "D'ye ken the name o' that tree?" Zachary pointed to a large tree with a peeling bark.

"No," Manning said, uninterested.

The road began to leave the coast and the forest was dense. The surface of the track became rutted and their progress slowed. A flock of bright green parrots exploded from the tree tops. The horses bolted and before Zachary could bring Miranda to a halt, the wagon tipped over. The sea chest was strapped to it and Miranda reared against the sudden dead weight. Zachary jumped off, holding her bridle and speaking softly to her.

Manning whistled. "I'll wager that's not the last time you'll be righting that wagon. You'd best do it on your own, lad. I'll not be with you much longer."

Zachary threw the tethering rein over Miranda's neck. She was still snorting and stamping. "Whisht! Quiet now." He walked behind her and tried to right the wagon. He could not move it. Within seconds, his clothes were drenched with sweat. Mosquitoes gathered around his head in a cloud. He wanted to cry.

"Think, lad. There are few to help on the road."

Zachary sat on the bank. It was hopeless. He could not even get himself from the ship to the plantation. Manning waited, still mounted, under a tree with a large grey trunk, small canopy and buttress roots. "I know the name of this one," he said, conversationally. "It's a cotton tree. The slaves say they're haunted."

Shut yer mouth, Zachary thought.

Miranda put her head down and strained to reach the grass, but the wagon held her immobile. Her flanks were dark with sweat. Zachary heard his father's voice: *You will amount to nothing. I wash my hands of you.*

He got up and unhooked the harness. He led Miranda to the bank and tethered her, allowing her to graze. He unstrapped the sea chest and it fell out of the wagon. He heaved the wagon upright and reharnessed Miranda. Then he unpacked the chest, laying his possessions in the dust and weighting them with a stone. He dragged the chest to the wagon and inched it up over the side. "Whisht," he said again to Miranda, as her head flashed up. He waited. She flicked her ears and after a while, lowered her head to the grass. Zachary pitted his strength against the chest and it slid into the wagon. He collected all that he had brought with him and repacked the chest. He replaced the straps that held it fast. He checked his knots and shook the chest. Then he untied Miranda and swung into the saddle. For a moment, the world flickered black and yellow and he feared he would faint. His muscles had wasted on the long sea voyage, and the heat was punishing.

"You brought books," Manning observed.

Zachary said nothing, still breathless from his exertions.

"And what does a young lad like you read?"

"I was reading Voltaire, but Virgil and Horace are my constant companions. Mr Thomson's *The Seasons* gives me much pleasure."

"Horace, eh? The golden mean. You might need to pay heed to that where you are going. And I wouldn't mention Thomson; his views on slavery are well known, though I doubt there's much poetry read on the Bonnie Valley estate. But Horace; I wouldn't have seen that as a young man's book."

Zachary sensed that Manning found him amusing, and did not reply.

"Let's go, then," Manning said and they rode on.

When the sun was high, they stopped under a tree with spreading branches, festooned with vines and orchids. Zachary noticed a huge spiky plant in the branches of the trees, shaped like a flower, the leaves thick and waxy. Manning followed his gaze.

"That thing can save your life."

"What, that plant up in the tree?"

"Yes. It holds water. If you get lost in the bush without water – climb a tree and look for one."

"I thought the island had many rivers."

"It does. But there are parts – near Bonnie Valley too – where the water runs underground. No surface water. Want some dried herring? Slave food, but that's what we have." He offered Zachary a small bundle, wrapped in a well-washed cloth, oil showing through. Zachary was more thirsty than hungry and he realized he had embarked on this journey without water. There had been places to stop for refreshment along the coast, but once they had turned inland, there was no sign of habitation.

They tied the horses to a bush and sat in the shade of the tree. The mosquitoes swarmed. The strip of exposed skin between Zachary's long sleeves and gloves was red. He pulled off his gloves and saw the sun had burned his wrists. He hoped his hat had shaded his face. The herring was wrapped in cassava and the salt had soaked into the cake. It was dry and tasted only of salt. He was thirstier when he'd finished.

"D'ye hae any water?" he asked Manning.

"We do, lad. But that's another lesson for you. No long rides in the bush without water and food."

Why was this man fathering him, Zachary wondered again. He watched Manning eat. He was fastidious, eating with dainty bites, even as he sat in the forest. He wiped his fingers on the grass, then rummaged in his saddle bags. He brought out two pewter canteens and threw one to Zachary. "Keep it," he said. "A present. For your new life."

"I couldna, Sir. But thank ye. I'm grateful for all ye hae done for me."

Manning laughed. "At least drink the water. You'll have fainted and fallen off your horse long before you get to Bonnie Valley if you don't." Zachary tipped the canteen to his head and drank the warm water.

"Don't finish it," Manning warned. "We still have some way to go." Zachary capped the canteen. It had a long strap and he slung it over one shoulder. It would bounce against his hip as they rode, but he wanted to have the water close at hand.

"How much longer?"

"About an hour to the turn-off. After that, I'm not sure. I've not been to Bonnie Valley in many years, not since Monmouth bought it. Four, maybe five hours. If you keep going you should make it by nightfall."

"We must go then." A night in the forest did not appeal.

An hour later, the road forked and Manning drew rein. "This is it," he said, pointing to a faded wooden sign, the words "Bonnie Valley" carved into it.

Zachary drew up beside him. "You never telt me anything about yersel, Sir. Where are ye going? Will I see ye again?"

Manning held out his hand and Zachary took it. "I don't know, young Macaulay. It's possible. White society in the colony is small. Good luck to you." He turned his horse onto the right hand fork of the road.

"Wait! How dae I find ye? I want tae thank ye... I want..."

"I'm going to Barton Park. Everyone knows it. We'll be in touch, I'm sure. God speed." Manning kicked his horse into a canter and was gone.

"Wait," Zachary said again, but quietly to himself. He stood until he could no longer hear the sound of Manning's horse. Then he urged Miranda down the road to Bonnie Valley. He still had Manning's canteen. He would have to find him to return it. Aye. That's what he'd do. He chirruped to his horse and she broke into a trot. "Watch out for ruts, Miranda," he said, just to hear his voice.

The road crested a hill and Zachary stopped. Miranda was blowing hard. Zachary had never been so hot, so tired or so tormented by insects. It was late afternoon and the hard light had softened. Below, a green valley was laid out before him, ringed by low hills. He saw buildings and, on one of the hills, a substantial house. Large trees drew a curving line through the green fields that he thought must mark a river. This must be it. Certainly a bonnie valley. He started down the hill. His spirits lightened and he felt a mixture of excitement and relief. He had found his posting.

He rode up the driveway. The front door was shut, but lit on either side by lanterns. He dismounted slowly, wincing as he hit the ground. "Well done, lassie." He patted Miranda's neck. It was foamy and her head hung low. The mare snorted and spattered his trousers with snot and sweat. He hesitated – he was in no state to meet genteel company. He supposed he could retrace his steps and try to wash up in the farm buildings he had passed, but his clothes would still be filthy. He shook his head, walked up low stone steps and hit a brass knocker on a solid wooden door. Nothing happened. He hit it again. If no one came, he'd have to sleep right there on the steps.

The door opened. A black man stood there, dressed in a white shirt and black trousers. "Massa?" He looked amazed.

"I'm Zachary Macaulay. I've come tae take up a position here."

"Who is it, Sutton?" a voice said. The black man did not answer but held the door wider. Zachary had an impression of grandeur – a black and white stone floor and a chandelier with dozens of lit candles hanging from a high ceiling. A young woman walked into the light. She was heavyset, pale and her skin was peppered with mosquito bites. "Don't just stand there, come inside. You're letting in the mosquitoes."

"I'm very dirty and tired, Ma'am," Zachary said, remaining on the doorstep. "I'm Zachary Macaulay. My father wrote tae Charles Monmouth – I'm tae take up a position here."

"Come inside. I'll get my father. We're just having dinner. Sutton, call Morgan. Tell him to care for the young massa's horse – a thorough rubdown and some corn. Turn him out in the north paddock. What is that, a wagon?" she said, peering into the night.

"Aye, Ma'am. It holds my sea chest."

"Take out the chest, Sutton. Take it to the back room. Penzance should have cleaned it this week." She turned to Zachary. "We weren't expecting you for another week."

"I'm sorry," he said. He swayed.

"You're dead on your feet. I'm Charlotte Monmouth. Come with me. I'll show you to your room and see you get something to eat. You can meet my father in the morning."

"Thank ye, Ma'am." He stepped into the hall and the door shut behind him. For a moment he worried about the safety of the contents of his chest, but he was too tired to care. Only his books would be of value to him here.

He followed Charlotte Monmouth down dim corridors. She opened a door at the back of the house on the ground floor and stood back to let him enter. She followed and set the lamp on a simple wooden table by a window. It held a white enamel basin and jug. There was a wooden rack next to the table, with a towel and blanket folded over it. He was surprised to see the blanket; perhaps it was much cooler here. A narrow bed was pushed against another wall with a mosquito net coiled above it in a large knot. A night table stood beside the bed. There was a rocking chair with a cane seat and a small bookcase. Zachary put his hand against the massive stone wall – it was damp to the touch.

Charlotte Monmouth lit two candles on the wall and he could see the room better. It looked like a cave and he liked that. It felt hidden and safe. "There's water in the basin. Chamber pot under the bed. The privy is through that door at the back." She pointed. "Food will be sent to you. Shell-blow is at six."

"Shell-blow?"

"Work starts. Sutton will knock on your door at five. The food won't be long. Don't forget to extinguish the candles before you go to bed, Mr. Macaulay – we don't want a fire." She bustled out, her grey skirts brushing the stone floors.

Zachary remained standing. He was too dirty to sit on the bed. He did not have his chest; he could not change his clothes. The candles flickered and he shivered. He listened to the sounds of the night: the rustles of vegetation and the squeaks of unknown creatures. He longed for familiar people, for home. Were there snakes in Jamaica? Why had his father sent him to this godfor-saken island?

There was a quiet knock on the door. He opened it and the black man stood there, carrying his sea chest. What was his name? Sussex? No, Sutton. "Put it there," he said, indicating. "Thank ye." Sutton did not reply. A woman, walked through the door carrying a tray. "Massa," she said, offering a scant curtsey. She put the tray on the table, pushing the basin aside. "I come back for the tray soon."

Zachary pulled the rocking chair up to the table. The tray held a jug and a plate covered with a cloth. The plate contained thick slices of warm ham and a chunk of a doughy bread. Bonnie Valley must be one of those places that imported flour. He ate hungrily, licking his fingers. He drank all the water in the jug.

When he had finished eating, he took one of the candles off the wall, so he could see his way to the privy. Outside, frogs jumped out of his way. A small, shining moon rode high in the sky. When he went into the privy, cockroaches scampered. He held his breath and used it quickly. When he came back to his room, the tray was gone.

He took off his filthy clothes and washed with the water in the basin. He let down the mosquito net and tucked it under the bedding, as Manning had counselled, leaving a space on one side from him to crawl into bed. He blew out the candles and the walls disappeared. He groped his way to the bed, but could not find the space in the mosquito net he had made. He cursed and struggled through the net, as if he were making his way through forest undergrowth. He could not tuck it in very well once he was on the bed. The bedding rustled like the bush outside and he wondered what it was made of. He lay in the utter darkness and listened to the whine of the mosquitoes as they came to find him.

When Zachary woke, the room was light and beginning to warm. It was well past dawn. His employer must have decided to give him the day off. He stretched and gasped at the pain in his muscles. He eased his legs over the side of the bed and stood. He walked to the window and tried to peer through the wooden slats. They were angled downwards and outwards; he could see only the grass. He heard noises – intermittent shouts, a rhythmic chant, and every now and then, a loud crack, like the branch of a tree breaking. He was ravenous.

He pulled back the bolts and slid the window outwards. He saw there was a brass fitting designed to hold them partially open, but he held it as high as he could. His room did not face the way he had come; he looked out on a gentle slope of rough-cut grass, like a grazed pasture. The field fell to below his line of vision, but in the distance he could see a forest and higher hills. The sun turned the tips of the grass to silver. He thought he had never seen such a beautiful place, but it had a rawness that was unsettling. There was nowhere to hide; the relentless cast of sunlight would find any fugitive; it covered the land like a tightly woven net of shining steel.

He walked gingerly out of the back door, his muscles protesting. The grass was soaked with dew and he almost lost his footing. He walked around the side of the house and saw a scythed lawn. A large tree with spreading branches shaded a white wooden bench, which faced the land below. There was a swing hanging on thick ropes from a low branch.

He stood, looking over the cluster of buildings and green fields, swaying like an inland sea, stretching to the valley's edge. Sugar cane. So it was a plant like a reed or a large grass with a thick, ridged stalk. Not, after all, a tuber. He saw a line of black figures moving in the nearest field in a wavy line. They were the source of the chanting. They moved slowly, more or less together, and he saw they swung large knives, which flashed in the sun. They advanced like an army and the cane fell behind them. These were slaves. Then he saw the source of the sharp reports he had heard. Other men walked behind the slaves and cracked their whips. He saw men mounted on horses. They too had whips, but they were coiled and hooked to their saddles. A second line of black men followed, picking up the stalks of cane and stacking them in carts.

Zachary knew about slavery. He had heard of the case of Joseph Knight, the former slave whose right to freedom in Scotland had been recognised about a decade ago, and his student friends in Glasgow had told him of the preaching of William Robertson. But then he had read the great philosopher David Hume who had declared that Africans were only a little higher than apes. There had been debate in Scottish newspapers, with the churches declaring Africans had souls like any other human being – though this was something his own father doubted – that they should not have been torn from their homelands and sold like cattle. Others said that black people might indeed have souls, but they were not like white people, and needed the discipline of being owned. He really did not know what to think. It was too uncomfortable a subject and he could not articulate the arguments for and against. He was just there for a job.

He heard a door bang behind him. Charlotte Monmouth stood on the small porch at the front of the house, wearing a complicated dress in shades of purple. She must be so hot.

"Mr. Macaulay!" she called. Zachary felt pleased at being accorded a title. "Come and have some breakfast. My father wants to meet you." He walked over to her.

"Good morning," she said. "I trust you slept well?"

"'Morning. Aye, I did, thank ye." He saw she was older than she had looked in last night's lamplight. Maybe even thirty. She'd said her name was Monmouth – she was unmarried then. She seemed to be running the household. He wondered about Mrs. Monmouth.

"The land, 'tis beautiful." He gestured to the valley.

"Sometimes it is," she said. "But it's April. You've arrived at a good time; not too hot yet, not time for storms, some rain, but not too much. Wait and see what you think in August after a hurricane, or in October, when the walls spring mould after all the rain." Her face was set in downward lines and he thought her unhappy. "You won't be staying in that room. I'm sorry, I should have made that plain last night. We were not expecting you quite yet and I saw you were exhausted. Your lodgings will be in the valley with the others." She pointed at a cluster of cottages; one of them a fairly substantial house. "You'll be in Bell Cottage."

"I see."

"I'm sorry." She lifted her chin. "This way. Today, you'll have a late breakfast and then Paul will show you around the plantation."

"Paul?"

"My brother." Zachary remembered Manning had mentioned a Monmouth son.

"How many are ye, Miss Monmouth?" The question sounded over familiar and he regretted asking.

"Five," she said "My father, mother, Paul, my sister Sarah and myself. I'm the eldest. Follow me, please."

He followed Charlotte through the entrance hall. His impression of wealth and taste was confirmed. A black and white stone floor – perhaps even marble – flowed through an arched opening into a parlour furnished with upholstered chairs. From the parlour, tall wooden doors with shining brass fittings opened onto a verandah at the side of the house. Zachary followed Charlotte through it. He saw a square table with six chairs, a little too large for the space. One place setting was undisturbed – perhaps some member of the family had not yet eaten. An older man sat with his back to the wall, looking outwards. His face was ruddy with sunburn. A retriever lay at his feet.

"Father," Charlotte said. "May I present Zachary Macaulay? He's the new book-keeper. Arrived last night. I let him sleep in today, as you instructed."

"Sir," Zachary said.

Charles Monmouth looked him up and down. Zachary felt ashamed of his muddy boots and wrinkled clothes.

"I knew your father. Is he well?"

"Aye, Sir, he is. I bring ye his compliments."

"You look younger than I thought."

"I'm seventeen, sir," Zachary lied.

"Have a seat," Monmouth said, gesturing to the set place. "Charlotte, ring for some food. Coffee alright? Our coffee is an acquired taste it's best you set about acquiring right away." He resumed looking over his land. Zachary sat and followed his gaze. He tried to imagine what it had taken to carve this valley from the surrounding forest; what it had taken to fence it, cultivate it.

Monmouth drank his coffee in silence. The woman who had brought Zachary's dinner arrived with a tray. She set a china coffee cup at his left hand.

"On the right, you damned dolt," Monmouth snarled.

"Sorry Massa, sorry," she stammered and moved the cup. She poured Zachary's coffee, her hand trembling. She left and returned with a platter, which she placed in the centre of the table. There were boiled eggs, more sliced ham, the doughy bread and another fruit like a large banana, cut into slices and fried.

"Plantain," Monmouth said, gesturing.

"Sir?"

"That," he pointed. "Plantain. Eat it at near every meal. Better get used to it."

The woman put a bowl of fruit slices on the table.

"Guavas," Monmouth said. "Help yourself."

Lastly, the woman set down a large bowl of brown sugar. Whatever else might be in short supply, there was no shortage of sugar on Bonnie Valley Plantation. Zachary helped himself to the crystals that had made fortunes for men.

Zachary mounted Miranda and gasped at the pain in his backside.

"Something wrong?" Paul Monmouth grinned.

"No, nothing. You lead the way."

Paul was about twenty-five, Zachary reckoned. The sun had burned his skin to a reddish brown, and when he smiled, grey-green eyes disappeared into creases at the corners of his eyes. He was perfectly dressed in a white shirt with tan breeches tucked into polished boots. He had a whip coiled on his saddle and carried a short riding crop as well. His tack was carefully tended, the leather supple and well oiled. Two small saddle bags lay on either side of his mount, an iron-grey gelding that topped seventeen hands. His mane was pulled, his tail banged and no trace of mud or stain marred his muscled flanks. He looked as if he had been bred, schooled and groomed for a show ring.

Zachary felt like a poor relation as he sat in his cracked saddle, taking his weight in his stirrups. He carried only Manning's canteen, slung across his chest. A little black boy in the stables had brushed Miranda hastily, and she still carried traces of caked sweat on her neck where he had not been able to reach. Still, her eyes were bright and she walked jauntily out of the stable yard, her ears flicking back and forth. She wanted to break into a trot and Zachary held her back, trying to protect his painful muscles.

"Ten o'clock," Paul said, consulting a pocket watch. "A bit late for a ride – it'll be hot. But you'll see most of what there is to be seen." He kicked the gelding into a canter and Zachary had no choice but to follow. He was grateful Miranda's gait was smooth.

Paul led the way through narrow tracks cut in the cane fields, the cane high above their heads. "These will be cut soon," he shouted over his shoulder. "You've come at crop time, so you'll be busy." The grey gelding was increasing speed and Miranda was falling behind.

Soon they were galloping, going too fast to see anything but green rushing by. Zachary's eyes watered and he let Miranda have her head. She began to gain on the gelding and he realized he was being challenged to a race. He leaned forward and urged Miranda on. To his surprise, she began to catch up quickly. He saw Paul sneak a look over his shoulder and then he hit his horse. They surged away briefly, but Miranda's long strides bore her onwards and soon her head was level with Paul's boot. Zachary heard Paul curse and then he kicked at the mare's head and she shied. For a moment, Zachary thought she would fall and he gripped her mane, but she regained her footing and galloped on. Paul's face was twisted in anger. He was cursing and applying his riding whip again and again. Just as Miranda edged in front, the path took a sharp right turn. Paul's horse wheeled into the turn, but Miranda skidded to a stop. Zachary sailed over her shoulder and crashed into the canefield. His head hit something hard. Just before he lost consciousness, he heard Paul laughing.

He opened his eyes in a long room with several beds. His head hurt and he felt nauseous, then ashamed as he remembered what had happened. He had fallen off his horse on his first day, in front of his employer's son. He flexed his hands and feet, moved his arms and legs; nothing seemed broken. He tried to sit up and the room swayed. He fell back, dizzy. His head pounded and his throat was parched. "Water," he said, closing his eyes to block out the swirling room.

"So you're awake, young Macaulay," a man said. "Here, drink this." Hands supported him into a sitting position and held a cup to his lips. Zachary drank thirstily; the water was cold and sweet. "Take it easy, not so fast," the man cautioned. Zachary opened his eyes. A middle-aged white man regarded him with a slight smile.

"So you've encountered Paul Monmouth?"

"Aye, Sir."

"Don't worry about falling off. Paul does that to every new-comer. That's a wicked turn, down by the South Field, if you're not expecting it. I hear your little mare nearly beat Thor – that wouldn't have pleased the son and heir."

"Where am I?"

"You're in the hot house. The hospital. You're lucky Bonnie Valley has one – many plantations don't. I'm Dr. Whitby. You hit your head on a rock, so Paul said, but I don't think you're badly hurt. A day's rest will set you right."

"How did I get here?"

"Paul threw you like a sack of corn over your horse and led you in. He was pretty worried. His father would not have been amused had his new book-keeper been seriously hurt."

Zachary closed his eyes against the light. "You should sleep," the doctor said. "I'll look in on you later."

When Zachary woke again, the room was dark. He must have slept the day away. He felt much better; his head clear. Perhaps he had been as much exhausted as hurt from his fall – the long sea voyage, the ride from the coast, the uncertainty. He swung his legs off the bed, realising he was in some kind of loose nightshirt. His riding clothes had been taken away. He looked around. All the beds in the room were empty, except one.

Its occupant moaned, a guttural rasp of wretchedness. Zachary walked over and saw the occupant of the bed was a black man; he felt surprised; he had not imagined a white man would ever have to share quarters with a slave, even in a hospital. The man lay naked, face down, a bloody linen sheet over his back. Zachary saw grey hair, ragged wounds on his neck, the back of his arms, his buttocks and a few on his legs. Flies circled and landed on the cloth and the man groaned again.

"Sam never can make it to the fields on time." It was Paul Monmouth. "I should have warned you about that turn. Sorry. Friends?" He held out his hand and Zachary grasped it, although he saw the amusement playing around Paul's mouth.

"Sam?"

"Him. Late several times a month; always gets 29, well laid in. You'd think he'd learn."

Zachary nodded. The sight of the man's back made him feel sick, but he would not show weakness. "Dae they get beaten often?"

"Pretty much daily. You can't keep them in line otherwise. They don't really care. I've seen them beaten to the bone in the field, and not five minutes later, they're up and back in their gang. They're not like us, no matter what the abolitionists and the churchmen say." He walked over to the bed and Zachary felt dread. Was Paul going to further harm the old man?

"Take this one. My father called him Sam when he came; he had some other name before. He wasn't young. Born here, though, not off the ships. He was sold off a plantation in St. Ann's. A good worker, cuts a lot of cane, but won't muster at shell-blow. Thompson has flogged his entire gang as punishment and he still comes late." He shrugged. "Thompson will kill him one day."

"Thompson?"

"The overseer. Anyway, get dressed. Time to be out of here – you should never have been put in this room, but there was a storm two weeks ago which took the roof off our ward. Let's get a drink and my sister will show you your quarters."

"Where's Miranda?" Zachary said, wanting to avoid the drink.

"Miranda? Oh, your horse! A good mare, that. Maybe I'll buy her from you.

"She's no for sale."

"Everything's for sale," laughed Paul Monmouth.

An hour later, Zachary sat on a narrow wooden verandah, looking over the valley. A duck pond shimmered in the setting sun. His things had been moved to this steep-roofed cottage on a small hill. The slight elevation meant it caught the breezes. He sat in a sturdy wooden rocking chair, resting his feet on the railing. Although his head still hurt and his muscles still pained him, he felt adult, resourceful, self-sufficient. He had navigated his first morning. He wondered where Trevor Manning was. He wanted to see him again, to thank him. He would write him a letter.

He was glad to be alone, free from the need to interact with others, to pick his words, to impress, to interpret what was being said. The cottage faced west and the sun was ending its descent directly opposite. A good time of day – it had cooled down, but was not dark. The mosquitoes were not yet out in force. The glowing light softened the undulating fields, stone buildings and trees, made them seem dreamlike. Horace had written about the simple pleasures of the rural life on his Sabine farm – surely there could be no cruelty or despair in such a landscape?

The cottage was called Bell Cottage because a large school bell hung near its front door. It was comfortable. There was a bedroom, much like the one he had briefly occupied at the great house, but without the stone walls. It had a commode of solid wood with a lid, concealing the hand-painted chamber pot inside. There was an outside kitchen, which he had only looked at briefly, and a large parlour. There was no separate room for eating, but there was a small table in one corner where he could take his meals. There were fat, creamy candles on tables and oil lamps hung on the walls, along with framed botanical watercolour paintings. He did not recognize the plants. When Charlotte brought him to the cottage, his clothes had already been put away and his books were displayed on the night table. He had checked quickly for the sketch of his sister in his Bible.

"Are you a religious man, then?" Charlotte asked.

"My father is a minister," he answered.

"And you read poetry," she said, fingering his copy of James Thomson's *The Seasons*.

"Aye," he said.

"And what is this? This isn't English." She pointed to his copy of Horace. "Did you bring slippers with you?" She replaced the book.

"Slippers? No. Why?"

"You must watch out for scorpions. Shake your shoes out before you put them on. The cobbler will make you slippers."

"Are there serpents?"

"Yes. But they're constrictors. There are no venomous ones here. Not that we've encountered, anyway. But they terrify slaves in the canefield, so we kill them on sight. "

He was to have his own servant, Olivia. She would look after his needs: cleaning, washing and cooking. Emptying the commode. He had not seen her yet. The evening meal was generally served at dusk, Charlotte had said, wiping a finger on a windowsill to check for dust. He was free to vary this as he saw fit.

He wished Miranda were turned out nearby. It could become his evening routine: he would lean on the fence and call to her, she would trot over and he would feed her a lump of sugar and rub her between her ears. There was a small field off to the left. He would ask about it the next day.

After leaving the hot house, Paul had strolled with him past the stables, a long stone building with wooden half-doors, painted dark green; and the tack room, as well equipped as any in Scotland. Paul had pointed out the gibbet, hanging from a high frame, where the ultimate punishment was meted out to the most rebellious slaves. He had seen the piggery and the dairy and the chicken run. He had seen the barbecue, where two kinds of beans lay drying. "We grow a bit of our own coffee," Paul had said. "But it's not as good as the kind that comes from the Blue Mountains."

"Which are the coffee beans?"

"The larger ones. The others are pimento."

He had seen the labourers in the fields, now he saw a few skilled men working in the carpenter's shop. One man had only two fingers on one hand. None of them looked up when he and Paul approached.

He had not seen the boiling house where, Paul told him, the cane was fed into the presses and the sweet liquid extracted. He had not asked what as bookkeeper he would count; The stalks of cane? It was a daunting thought – the cane seemed endless. Still, he was better than average at mathematics.

His stomach growled and he realized he had missed lunch as a result of his fall. He longed for a drink – a mug of that mellow grog he had tasted in Montego Bay – and thought about the woman. It would soon be dusk and he wanted food and drink. He began to feel irritated as the sun slid behind the forest. He was startled by a bright green reptile – a lizard, he guessed – running over the railing where his boots rested. He considered killing it, but he had no weapon and he was enjoying his rest. Then he saw the woman, Olivia, carrying a basket, making her way up the path. *At last.*

He watched her. She was not young, and her steps were slow as she came up the slight hill. She was singing a lament in a quavering voice. He felt guilty and then annoyed. She was housed and fed, wasn't she? She was not in the fields in the broiling sun, risking the lash. Why the dejected appearance? She raised her eyes and saw him on the verandah. She ducked her head and quickened her steps. He found himself disappointed that she was not like the brown woman in Montego Bay.

"You're late, woman," he said, when she stood before him.

"Sorry Massa. Ongle hear 'bout your dinner just now. Mi bring it." Her hair was mostly hidden under a rust-coloured head scarf. She wore a rough blue linen dress with a white smock over it. She wore ill-fitting shoes on large, clumsy feet.

"Bring the table out here. I want tae eat on the verandah." He wondered briefly if she could move the table alone. He forced the thought away. She was not a woman like his mother, his sisters.

"Out here, Massa?" she said.

"Aye. Out here. Right now." He tried to affect Charles

Monmouth's gruff voice. Olivia gave a barely perceptible shrug and went inside. "My name is Zachary," he called. "Mas' Zachary, I mean," he added, less loudly. Dealing with these blacks was going to take practice. He heard the dragging of furniture across the floor. He sat down again, stared over the darkening valley, and kept his back turned to her struggles. He heard a thump as the table fell over the low step to the verandah. He forced himself not to turn around.

The short twilight of the tropics began to erase the valley and mosquitoes rose from the bush. Zachary then understood the woman's reluctance to set his table on the verandah. He felt angry with her. She was stupid. Why hadn't she said something, warned him about the mosquitoes? She had lit the lamps inside the house and came to him carrying a candle. He flailed at the mosquitoes around his head. They landed on her bare arms and she made no movement to get rid of them. Different from us, he thought. He did not want to lose face by retreating inside, or to show weakness in the face of this assault.

"Massa, di mosquito, dem not goin' low you to eat in peace. Mi put di table back?" Her reasonableness annoyed him further. He nodded and went inside.

When he came out of the bedroom, the windows and doors were closed. The lamps blazed brightly and the interior of the house was smoky. Perhaps the lamps had not been properly lit and he opened his mouth to complain. Then he remembered Manning telling him to get his room fumigated before he went to bed because mosquitoes did not like smoke. He walked over to the small table, now covered with a white cloth, set with the proper cutlery and crockery, napkins, serving spoons, a glass jug of water, a pewter jug of what he hoped was grog, platters of sliced chicken and steaming root crops, yellow and thick, and fried plantain, and a small clutch of red tomatoes – what his mother would have called cooking tomatoes – and another bowl of a white fruit with a brown skin, cut into slices, and small bowls of sauces and dressings, pale green, and orange and a deep garnet.

"What is this?" he asked, pointing to the yellow roots.

"Yam, Massa."

"And this?"

"Coconut. Water a coconut water, but if you did want plain water, mi get it." Zachary shook his head, pretending impatience. The woman stood there. He did not know what to say to her, how to dismiss her. He sat and she stepped back and stood behind him, her back to the wall. "You can go," he said, anxious to be on his own.

"Yes, Massa." She left through the back door and he turned to the food. He was starving; the food was fresh and well cooked and he tried everything on the table: the watery orange sauce that burned his tongue and the thicker, sweeter condiments, and the heavy, dry yam, and the succulent flesh of the chicken, and the crusty, spicy chicken skin. Now he was alone, he put down his knife and fork and ate with his fingers, ate as if he was a condemned man and this was his last meal. His mother was not there to remark on his deplorable table manners. He ate everything on the table and pushed his chair back. He threw his napkin into the dirty plates and belly full and drowsy, went into his bedroom. The woman would be back to clean up. Tomorrow he would make her fill a tub for him – he had not seen a tub but she would have to find one – and he would sit in warm water and have her soap his skin. She would dry him with one of the rough towels hanging over the rack beside his washstand and she would rub his insect bites with soothing oils and massage his aching muscles with her strong, black fingers. He shed his clothes and fell into bed, forgetting to tuck in the mosquito net, and sank into sleep.

Zachary leaned on the fence of Cedar Paddock. Three weeks had passed and he had learned the fields of Bonnie Valley all had names. Miranda was now turned out in Cedar Paddock, near Bell Cottage. Each evening he walked to her in the fading light and fed her muscovado. She had gained weight; regular work had built muscle and her coat shone with thorough grooming. Her feet had been shod by Bonnie Valley's farrier, her mane was pulled into a straight line, her hooves oiled daily. As he watched her graze, she would sometimes startle and strut around the field, bucking and prancing in exuberance.

He had not found his work as a book-keeper hard, although it had nothing to do with books. His days were as long as the light held and often tedious. He had to count the plantation animals as they left their pens and were taken for grazing, feeding or work, and he had to ensure they returned each night. He had to keep track of the hogsheads of sugar leaving the boiling house, not by writing down the count, but by a wooden board with holes and pegs. He saw this as a device for someone who was illiterate.

He observed the crushing of the cane and made sure not a stick was stolen. The Martha Brae river turned a large mill, which did the crushing, fed incessantly by the labourers. The juice was sent along a gutter to the cauldrons of the boiling house, some boiling vigorously and others merely simmering. Other slaves had to skim the surface of the cauldrons with spoon-like implements and often the scum burned their skins and they screamed with their heads thrown back. Then the juice passed through another series of cauldrons until it began to granulate, after which it was placed in a trough. When the sugar had cooled, it was taken to the hogsheads. Holes in the bottom of the hogsheads allowed molasses to drain out and this was used to make Bonnie Valley's rum. Zachary soon found that Miranda loved molasses, too.

Sometimes he went with the overseer and his gang to the fields, and cast his eyes over their toil. He disliked overseer Thompson and stayed out of his way. He was a mulatto, the son of a slave woman and a white man. Despite his origins, Zachary saw Thompson regarded the blacks with loathing.

On Zachary's first morning in the fields, he had stood behind the line of canecutters watching their skins glossy with sweat, their arms wrung with muscles, their machetes flashing high and low, heard them chanting primitive songs with words he could not understand. He had seen their burns and their backs, furrowed and riven like the fields themselves, torn by the cowskin lash. He rode slowly down the line and could not see a single slave who had not been beaten. Paul Monmouth rode up beside him.

"You know the most common reason they're flogged?"

"Ye told me."

"For coming late to shell-blow. You'd think it'd be a simple matter to avoid a flogging – just get there on time. I tell you, Mr. Macaulay, they don't mind the beatings."

Even the children toiled, doing smaller tasks. They were not stripped to the waist, so he did not know if they were beaten. That first morning, he had wanted to dismount and borrow a machete and swing it at the cane. He wanted to see how difficult it was. The fieldworkers carried salt in bundles at their sides, to replenish the salt they lost. They were not allowed to cut even a single stick of cane for themselves, not allowed to strip the hard outer covering and suck the sweet juice. He thought of the lines from "Summer" in Thomson's *The Seasons*:

"… *and from the partners of that cruel trade*
Which spoils unhappy Guinea of her sons
Demands his share of prey…"

"You'll have to take a wife," Paul said, interrupting his reverie.

"A wife?"

"A slave wife. Everyone does it. I'll pick one for you, if you like."

Demanding your share of prey, are you, Zachary thought, but the image of the mulatto woman in Montego Bay also came to him.

"Who's your wife?" he said, embarrassed.

"I have a stable." Paul laughed. "Whoever I feel like, whenever I feel like it, wherever I feel like it. Canepiece, tool shed, my bed – it doesn't matter. I don't take them young as some do, though. See her there, the tall, brown one with the scar on one cheek and the brand on the other?" Zachary saw a rangy woman with a small boy at heel, like a hunting dog. She met his eyes for an instant and he saw they were fierce.

"A wonderful fuck," Paul said. "Spits and scratches like a cat. I gave her that scar." Zachary turned away, repelled and aroused.

On Sundays, when the slaves went to their own grounds in the hills, Zachary rode the cane intervals and paths of Bonnie Valley Plantation with a thin mongrel dog he had adopted. He saved his money. There was little to spend it on. His physical needs were better met than they had ever been in his life.

Sometimes he stood and stared at his reflection in the pitted looking-glass in his bedroom. He did not know if he had grown in height, but he thought so. His skin was tanned and his eyes stared back, unfriendly. His arms and legs were strong from his days in the saddle. He was lonely, but invincible. He viewed himself as from a distance, carrying out his duties in the counting house, indifferent to the daily injuries and cruelties he witnessed. He felt clad in armour and he was glad. His seventeenth birthday had come and gone without notice in May.

April and May had brought rain, the tropical storms Charlotte Monmouth had spoken about. He had not experienced such rain, the deluge pounding on roofs and drowning all other sound, raging down roads, turning fields into quagmires, making walls sweat, until they shone with oozing mosses. No one worked when it rained like this, and Zachary grew to love the days when the skies turned purple and swollen over the hills and the air cooled. Then the people of Bonnie Valley plantation looked to the skies and were expectant. Sometimes the rain was short-lived and white men and black huddled under the overhang of the farm buildings and waited it out. Other times, the rain poured without cease, the hills were obscured, and Zachary stabled Miranda and ran, laughing, through the walls of water to his house. Soaked but exhilarated, he kicked off his boots and shed his clothes and bawled for Olivia to dry his skin. Then, dressed in his loose nightshirt, he sat on his verandah and watched the duck pond rise and tree limbs bend under the weight of the water.

By July, the rain ceased. Crop was over and the fields were prepared for new plantings. Within weeks of the last downpour, the land began to dry, the flowers planted around the Great House wilted and the vegetable fields grew dusty. His favourite Sunday ride became a long canter through the interval cut in the South Field where he had measured his length in the canepiece that first morning, to the banks of the Martha Brae and then, picking his way through the dense bush to the Fontabelle Rising, where cold blue water welled from the earth. It seemed a holy place. The first time he saw it, he whispered Thomas Warton's version of Horace's words, *"Ye waves, that gushing fall with purest stream, Blandusian Fount…"*, but there was no offering of a kid's blood that he could make. These waves did not fall, but welled up, still as a painted surface, trembling only if a leaf fell, or he threw a pebble. Yet, under the surface, the strength of the water uncoiled and at one corner the water began to ripple and then to flow. He was fascinated by how it transformed itself from a subterranean welling into a river torrent. He imagined the water in a dark cavern under the earth, then coming up and spreading out, waiting for the moment when it would begin its rush to the sea. But that moment never came, because the water simply disappeared underground a few chains away.

His Sunday rides grew longer and he roamed widely. He left the tended fields of the valley and rode into the forest, up stony trails, festooned with vines and creepers, where the light was dappled and the mosquitoes were slow and fat and hung in the air all day. He wondered if these forests could shelter Maroons, but Paul told him they were now based much further inland. But how could they have lived in the forest? He saw no fruit, no water, no animal that could be eaten. He knew there were wild hogs and birds, but how to hunt them without a musket? Perhaps the Maroons had muskets; he knew little about them, except that they were fierce warriors, runaway slaves. He remembered Manning telling him of the spiky plants high in the trees that held water.

He grew to love the dim and humid forest; its drippings, its brilliant lizards. He saw soaring rock faces carved with the skeletons of the sea, the whorls of shells and the delicate backbones of long-dead creatures. The rocks were mostly white and full of holes; ferns and mosses of every shade of green found root in them. He saw caves with narrow entrances that echoed with the promise of large underground caverns. When he dismounted – holding Miranda's tethering rein tightly – he was sure being left on foot in the forest would be a death sentence – and stood at the edge of these caves, he could hear the sound of water far beneath his feet.

When he rode in the forest, he was careful to mark his passing by carving notches on trees with his knife, for the trails hardly existed and petered out without warning. Sometimes the going became too rough for Miranda and he would turn back, making an extra cut at the place of his retreat. The next Sunday, he would borrow one of the mules and the more sure-footed animal would find its way up and down the rocky hills that Paul told him were called the Cockpits. He had not so far made it through the tangled bush to the top of one of these hills.

One still Sunday in July, the air hot as an oven, he missed his turning and found himself entering a cultivated, circular valley. He did not recognize many of the plants and they were not grown in rows, but looked to him haphazardly spaced, with the bare, red earth showing through. Then he saw a handful of black women and some children, working the ground with tools obviously discarded by the plantation and roughly fixed. He knew the slaves were given Sundays to work on their grounds, to plant the food that fed them, and to take the produce to market. It had taken him more than an hour to reach the slave ground on horseback – perhaps it was a two or three hour walk, unless there was another route. He had, after all, lost his way. He wondered briefly about the length of the walk to market.

He rode through the ground, contemptuous of its untidiness, though when Miranda's hooves broke some of the plants he turned her to the edge of the ground. He could not call it a field; it did not have the discipline that term implied. The women heard his approach and turned to face him. The children stepped behind their mothers. They were thin and dirty and stared with expressionless faces. One of the women was Paul's brown-skinned, wild-eyed slave wife. He drew rein in front of her. She met his eyes and did not look away. The light-skinned boy he had noticed in the cane field stood behind her, gripping her skirt with his fist.

"I've lost my way," he said. "Point me in the direction o' Bonnie Valley."

"Back di way you come, but tek di path east to di river." She did not say "Massa" and he knew that was an affront. The sun beat on his shoulders and the brim of his hat was sodden from perspiration.

"Show me the way!" She did not answer right away. He knew his instruction would take her away from her work, but she had to do his bidding.

"Di path easy," she said. "You caan' lost."

"Did ye no hear me, woman? Do ye want a flogging? Come wi me and dae it now!"

The woman let her hoe fall to the ground, bent to the child and whispered in his ear; he left her to join another woman. She walked in front of Miranda and started across the ground. Her feet were bare but she walked in a long, free stride as if she did not feel the stones under her feet or the sun on her back. She did not look over her shoulder to see if he followed and led him directly to the path he had missed. As soon as Miranda's hooves touched the path, she turned on her heel and left him. Insolent bitch, he thought.

That night, he could not sleep. The cold nights of his first few weeks were a memory. The air was hot and wet and heavy and there was no comfortable position in which to lie. He longed for snow and ice. He recited from Thomson, his voice low in the dark:

> "...at last the flakes
> Fall broad, and wide and fast, dimming the day
> With a continual flow. The cherished fields
> Put on their winter-robe of purest white."

He wanted to shiver, then feel the welcome warmth of an indoor fire, to strip off woollen gloves and rub warmth into cramped fingers. The tropics were alien. He was in a constant state of arousal as if the heat brought his blood to the boil. He thought of the fierce brown woman, her body hidden under her faded, shapeless shift, but the strength of her limbs and the sureness of her stride excited him. He masturbated furiously; consumed with lust and hate. He was not sure whom he hated. He did not even know the woman's name.

It was not until August that he saw a slave truly flogged. He had seen punishment, of course, the cowskin whip cracked over the labourers all day, and found its mark on the back of any one who seemed to be slacking. He had seen slaves put into the stocks and left without water for a day or more. He had seen one slave forced to work in a leather mask, because overseer Thompson had seen him sucking on a length of sugar cane. Zachary's job was to prevent the slaves from stealing and he was proud when Paul told him that, since his arrival, stealing had been much reduced.

Bonnie Valley was one of the largest and richest plantations in Jamaica. Charles Monmouth was very far from being an absentee owner and while he was rarely seen in the fields, there was no question he ran the place. He was often in the infernal heat of the boiling house, or casting his eye over the never-ending building and maintenance that kept the estate going. He treated his slaves as valuable property, making it clear they had cost good money and were not to be brutalized. Zachary had heard him and the overseer in disagreement over Thompson's excessive use of the whip.

Today, though, a woman was to be punished for the crime of eating dirt. Paul had told Zachary that the slaves had to be prevented from doing this because it would make them ill or even die. They did it because they wanted to avoid work. At first Zachary thought this was another of Paul's jokes, but he soon saw it happen several times in the fields; a man or woman would palm a clod of dirt and eat it hungrily, frantically, before anyone saw. Eating dirt was another thing that set the blacks apart from white people.

Monmouth's orders were that slaves were not to be flogged for an offence at the time it occurred. It was a greater deterrent to spend a night in the stocks, dreading the punishment to come. Floggings were to take place at shell-blow, with all slaves present. Zachary had heard Monmouth had served in the British navy and he knew that all hands on British ships had to witness punishment.

Thompson thought this was nonsense. "If you lock up your dog 'cause you going beat him next day, you think him know?" But he was careful not to say this in front of Monmouth.

Zachary sat on Miranda behind a circle of workers and waited for the flogging to begin. He was anxious. He could see that slaves needed the whip to overcome their tendencies for sloth, but he was not indifferent to screams of pain and the blood that flowed from backs torn and torn again. He was afraid he would be sick or otherwise disgrace himself. He hoped it would be over quickly.

He heard a scuffle and saw two of the biggest slaves dragging the woman to face her beating. He saw it was the fierce-eyed woman. His dread increased. His heart beat faster. He saw she was fighting to walk on her own, rather than displaying reluctance. The gentle morning light was unseemly. Such a scene belonged in darkness.

Thompson walked forward, his whip in one hand, and the arm of the woman's child in the other. "Make sure he does not look away or close his eyes," Thompson said to one of the gang bosses and handed the child over to him. He pointed the whip at the child.

The woman's shift was torn from her body and she was thrown into the dust. "For dirt eating, they're flogged in the dirt," Paul whispered, moving closer. "For other things, like coming late, they're strung up." Zachary wanted to dig his heels into Miranda's sides, to force his way out at a gallop, to escape to the forests, to find his way to the coast and a ship waiting at anchor; to go home. He tightened the reins in case Miranda was startled by the sounds and others would think he had caused the mare to run. Thompson drew back his hand and the first blow fell. Zachary counted and his head swam. Time passed in fits and starts, marked by the crack of the whip.

The woman grunted as the lash fell and her blood flowed, but she did not scream. She turned her face into the dirt and lay like a fallen tree. After the twenty-ninth stroke, Thompson waited. Zachary saw her muscles relax. Then Thompson sent one last blow into her bleeding back, and finally, caught by surprise, she screamed. Thompson reached into his breeches and took out a handful of salt. He dashed it on the woman's back and strode away. The men holding her released her wrists and ankles. Zachary looked over at her boy – his head still held firm by the gang boss. Tears streaked his cheeks, but his eyes were open. Zachary's gorge rose and he swallowed hard. The only way to process this deed was to regard the woman on the ground as an animal, like the hog to be butchered for dinner that afternoon. Then unbidden, unwanted, came the thought: no hog would be beaten like that.

"What's her name?" he croaked to Paul.

"Who, her? Victoria. A good name. She got beaten last year for refusing to use it." He laughed. "You've gone quite white. Not going to faint, are you?"

Zachary forced air into his lungs and managed a laugh. "It's the heat. Your sister was right, August is a brute of a month."

He heard the shell blow and the men and women began to disperse to their work. The two men who had held the woman raised her to her feet. Her back was washed in blood and Zachary saw her bare breasts through patches of dirt. He wheeled Miranda away. He had to find something to drink.

Late that night, Zachary took one of the lamps and walked carefully down the hill to the hot house. The fireflies were out and their tiny, intermittent lights made him feel hopeful. The hot house door was shut, but not locked. He walked inside. Guttering candles gave a fickle light. At least four of the cots were occupied and he hesitated. He saw one figure lying still and he crossed to that bedside. He could not see her face, but he was sure it was Victoria. She lay on her stomach, her face turned away, like the man he had seen on his very first day at Bonnie Valley; a bloody sheet of linen across her back. He could think of nothing to say, but he wanted her to know he stood there, that he had left his house to stand at her bed. He squatted and the light from his lamp fell across her face. Her eyes were open and their light was undimmed. She raised her head and looked at him. He saw her cheeks move and she spat a small wet pat of dirt at his feet.

1885
Fortress, Trelawny Parish

Pastor John Macaulay stared at his church with keen disappoint-
ment. It was a small, stone structure and the interior walls were
shedding plaster in large flakes. The roof was thatched and he
could hear the rustlings of hidden creatures. There was a hole in
the thatch near the entrance and several planks of the wooden
floor were rotten. The uneven wooden floor was covered with
animal droppings – rats, he supposed, and lizards. Something
larger too – maybe a mongoose. He had read that the mongoose
had been brought to Jamaica to kill snakes in the cane fields. Each
wall of the church had a single sash window with pale pink glass
panes. The altar area was slightly elevated to the height of one
plank of rough wood and held a rickety table. There was no piano
or harmonium. A few solid, well-made pews were pushed back
against the walls. The church smelled of excrement and mould.

He had imagined a country church; small, yes; but neat and
clean, in the manner of rural Scottish churches. His daydreams had
himself as an avuncular saviour. He had been exhilarated at the
thought of the souls of the people, souls destined for eternal hellfire
until his arrival. His mission was to point those souls to heaven.

One of the double wooden doors at the back was stuck. It was
evening and the light was fading. He tried to open the door to let
in more light, but could not see what the impediment was. He
would have to investigate further in the morning. He walked
outside and gazed at the threatening bush at the edge of the
roughly cleared churchyard. The church could be claimed by the
relentless tropical vegetation. There will be no roses by the door,
he thought; climbing weeds, that's what I'll have to train to grow
over the entrance. He bit back laughter; afraid to hear the
desperation in his mirth.

He saw there were two graveyards, one on either side of the
church. He walked to the nearest one, which had imposing
marble stones. "Joan Patricia Moore, beloved wife of Rev. Peter
Moore. Not gone from memory. Not gone from love. But gone
to her Father's home above." Vases of wilted flowers stood on

some of the marble slabs. These were the graves of planter families, he supposed. He strolled over to the other side of the churchyard, slapping at mosquitoes. Here was the graveyard for the Negroes. There were no marble slabs, no bunches of flowers, no cherubs or angels. He counted only four graves, each marked with ordinary river stones, one with a wooden sign carved with a name: Abel. There were no dates to mark Abel's earthly time, no surname, no mention of any relatives.

He had been in Jamaica for three months, most of it spent with his brother, Bruce, in Kingston at the Baptist College at Calabar, awaiting their respective postings. Their principal, Angus Ross, was a thin, disapproving Scot with a bad skin condition. He told the new missionaries they were part of a growing movement to provide salvation for the former slaves and he talked about the legacies of Wilberforce, Knibb and Lisle. Sam Sharpe he did not mention. John daydreamed while the Principal pontificated in his disappointed voice. He was not interested in events that had already passed. He wanted to be part of events now, to make his mark. He longed to be on the road to his mission. Lord, grant me patience, he prayed, as he sweltered in Kingston's heat.

John Macaulay was thirty; he felt already middle aged. He was unmarried, the survivor of an early, protracted and unsuccessful engagement; he hoped he would meet a woman in Jamaica, a softly spoken, capable woman who would make his home, cook his meals, mend his clothes, and sit opposite him while he prepared his sermons in the evenings. She would ask if he needed a drink, and he would smile and say, "Whatever you're having, my dear." She would get up, settling her skirts around ankles that he alone knew were finely made, and she would return with a cup of tea, perfectly brewed. She had silky brown hair and blue eyes, not so beautiful as to inflame the thoughts of men, but pretty enough. Obedient to his will, but able to butcher a yard fowl and ride a horse. Strong enough to bear children. Devout. Then he felt guilty over the specificity of his requirements and reminded himself he, too, had to cultivate obedience to the will of God.

John and his brother, Bruce, had grown up hearing stories about Jamaica – an island of great beauty, strange fruit, cold rivers and colourful birds. Their grandfather, the Reverend Arthur Macaulay, had been born there, but had left when he was still a baby, in circumstances that had never been fully explained. He had not returned and his family had grown up in Glasgow, but he spoke often of an old man with calm grey eyes and skin ruined by the tropical sun who had visited him when he was a boy, given him a pewter canteen, and told him stories of drama and adventure. The old man had been an abolitionist, one of those who fought for the freedom of the slaves, and had even been the governor of some African country. John understood this old man – Zachariah was it? – was probably not a relation, but a guardian to Arthur. The man had died, of course, long ago – it was thought during the very year the slaves had been granted their freedom. His stories, however, had survived and both Macaulay boys vowed that as soon as they were old enough, they would find their way to Jamaica.

So here he was, Baptist minister for the village of Fortress. His dreams had seen him traversing the ocean while a young man, hot of blood and ready for anything. It had not turned out that way. When he was just past his twentieth birthday, his mother had become consumptive. The task of caring for her fell to him. His father travelled widely in Scotland, preaching the word of God and was rarely home. Bruce was ten years younger and still at school. John learned the duties of the sickroom: holding an enamel bowl for his mother's pink phlegm and laying cool cloths on her brow when her limbs were wracked with fever. He loved her, but as his youth slipped away, he wished for her death. He came to hate her skeletal frame, sodden coughing and, most of all, her gasping words of gratitude.

When he was twenty-five, his father agreed to the employment of a nurse for a few hours each day. Nurse Duncan was a young woman of working-class background, clad in the stern, white uniform of her profession, which failed to conceal her brimming sexuality. Within weeks, John was locked in a passionate but unconsummated love affair; the nurse was a young woman of a practical nature and had no intention of allowing herself to be seduced outside the bonds of marriage. For a full three years, they exchanged glances and brief touches as they encountered each other in the rambling Macaulay house.

John fell into a stew of guilt over his lascivious thoughts about

Nurse Duncan. He rubbed his penis raw at night and abraded his knees in prayer afterwards. He was unsuited to the life of a clergyman, but he could not bear that thought and thrust it away. He sprang from a line of churchmen and had never considered any other profession. Enslaved by his body's urges, hating its intractability, tormented by his unruly thoughts, he wished for the Roman Catholic ritual of confession – how easy it would be to visit a priest hidden behind a panel and pour out the filth of his desires and then to hear the priest's easy absolution. He had no one to talk to. It was unimaginable that he should discuss his confusion with his father, his brother was a child and his mother was drowning in her illness.

John's mother died when he was twenty-eight. Before that, the affair with Nurse Duncan had progressed to whispered declarations of love from the nurse and promises of marriage from the minister's son, as soon as, they both agreed, Mrs. Macaulay's health could withstand the news. They waited for the woman's death. When finally her breath took on a scraping, industrial sound, Nurse Duncan told John the end was near. Each night, he kneeled at his mother's bedside and begged God for forgiveness. "Please, Lord. Take my mother into Your kingdom. You, who are all knowing, know my thoughts. I am unworthy. I…" He could think of no way to end the prayer. He watched his mother's chest rise, hitch and then fall in three shuddering exhalations. He thought each breath her last, but each time, she would draw in the dank air of her sickroom and her chest would rise again. Die, he thought. I'm tired. I want to go to sleep. I want to awake to a different life. I love you, mother, but it's time for you to go. Was this true? He did not know. Please Lord, take her now. And then… not my will, but Thine.

His father had been sent for and had come home. He too waited, pacing his study, smoking his cigars, filling every room in the house, even those he did not occupy. The three Macaulay males ate silent meals together and sat silently in the parlour, while the Reverend read his Bible and made notes for future sermons.

"What will you do after she dies, father?" John asked as they stood in the corridor, outside her room, taking a break from the dangerous vapours of the sickroom.

"What will I do? I will go on as before."

"Will you keep the house?"

"I imagine so. Presumably you boys will be in it."

"I plan to go to the Indies, father. I have put my name down. So has Bruce. We are awaiting our postings."

"Where did you get the money?"

"I've saved a little. Our passage will be paid for by the Baptist Missionary Society and once we're aboard, we'll get a stipend."

"The *Baptists*?"

"The Baptists," John said.

The Reverend made a dismissive gesture with his hands. "You've been saying this since you were a child, John. You're too old for the Indies. It's hard out there, the heat, fevers, the natives. No, much better to find a posting here in Scotland. Even here in Glasgow would be better." He stopped, apparently in painful thought. Then he said, "Perhaps Bruce can make it out there; he has the right spirit. But why the *Baptists*?"

"The Baptists have been making history. And you've never been out there. You don't know what it's like."

"It's well known what it's like. And you'll have to be baptised again."

"It's already been done," John said. "Both of us."

There was no more to be said.

The funeral was held on an unseasonably warm and sunny afternoon; the church was filled with friends and neighbours and members of his father's congregation. John could not keep his thoughts on his dead mother. He stood with his brother and he had to fight to keep a smile from his face as he imagined the night when, finally, he would lie beside Nurse Duncan – Alice – his wife, her body his.

But Nurse Duncan proved unexpectedly elusive; a decent period of mourning had to be observed. Although she no longer had any duties, the Reverend continued to employ her, but all John saw of her was her white uniform disappearing around corners in the Macaulay house as soon as he walked into a room. She smiled at him, but their conversations consisted entirely of polite greetings. The Reverend, against expectation, was still in the house.

Then one evening, Nurse Duncan joined the Macaulays for dinner and John saw his father reach across the table and clasp her hands. John saw her drop her eyelids in the demure way he had come to know, and then lift them to reveal a frank and womanly stare. I will if I want to, that stare said. The Reverend revealed that he and Nurse Duncan had fallen in love and would shortly marry. He asked John for his blessing.

"My blessing? You could be her father!"

"I am a man in the prime of life," the Reverend said, and John knew Nurse Duncan had allowed his father to remove her starched, white uniform: the cap, setting her golden hair free, the bib, releasing her breasts, and her skirt, allowing him access to the smooth skin of her inner thighs he had only dreamed about. He pushed back his chair and left the table.

Six weeks later, the Macaulay brothers had left Glasgow. John took a temporary teaching position at a school in Aberdeen; Bruce took work in a bookshop nearby. John prayed each day for his posting to the West Indies to be granted. It was, and on a chilly March morning in 1885, the brothers boarded the steamship *Abigail* for Kingston, Jamaica.

John locked the church door and looked down over the village to a few small farms clustered around simple dwellings, with rounded hills in the distance. As he walked across a sloping, grassy field to his house, he wondered how Bruce was doing. He missed Bruce. As boys they had never been close because of their difference in ages, but the tiny cabin they had occupied during the six-week journey across the Atlantic had brought them nearer. Even though John had turned out to be the better sailor, and often left Bruce moaning in his cabin while he walked the rolling, spray-soaked deck of the *Abigail* alone, they talked more than they had ever done before. Bruce had been sent to a larger town called Cave Valley in St. Ann's. Perhaps his church was in better shape than the Fortress Baptist Church. He would have to wait for a letter.

He let himself into his house and lit a lamp. The wick was damp and the flame faltered. He had hoped the generous meal he had eaten while on the road would be enough, but his stomach growled. There was no food in the house and the lamp gave insufficient light by which to read. He had already unpacked. He stripped and dressed in his nightshirt. The sun had only just gone down, but there was nothing else to do but go to sleep. The hours stretched emptily ahead. He thought back to his baptism in the cold murky waters of the Clyde and wondered if he really had the makings of a Baptist missionary.

He lay on his hard cot and stared guiltily at the pewter canteen he had brought with him. He had not asked his father if he could take it. He supposed he had stolen it. He closed his eyes and said his prayers. The familiar words failed to quell his loneliness.

It was still dark when the rooster started crowing. John lay with his eyes closed, hoping it would stop and he could go back to sleep, but he was wide awake. The bird crowed on and on. He groped for a lamp and matches, stubbing his toe on the bed. When he had the lamp going, he looked at his pocket watch. It had stopped. He held the lamp high and considered his small bedroom – a bed, one sash window, a table with a jug and basin, filled by someone he had not yet met, a set of wooden hooks on the wall, wooden floors with wide planks, a tin roof. There were no attempts at decoration, no pictures, no curtains, no rugs on the floor. Only his canteen hung from a bent nail he had found hammered into the wall.

He peered through the window, but he could see nothing, not the faintest glow of a street lamp, nor the flicker of lamps in other houses, nor the flare of the coming dawn. His bladder urged him outside. He eased his feet into his shoes, felt a pricking sensation and then a sharp pain erupted in the soft cleft under his toes. He dropped the lamp and the fuel spilled and flames began to lick at the wooden floor. Was he going to begin life in Jamaica by burning down his own house? The pain in his foot swelled and he was afraid. Perhaps a snake had bitten him and he would die. Which would be the easier death – snakebite or the flames? He tore the sheets from the bed and smothered the lamp, beating the flames with his unprotected hands. The fire burned his palms and he groaned, caught between the pain in his hands and spiralling pain in his right foot, but he continued beating at the burning sheet, until the red of the flames was gone. The room smelt of kerosene and smoke. He collapsed on the bed. There was no one to call. He would just have to wait to see if whatever had bitten him would kill him. He did not have the energy to wash his foot or burning palms, but his bladder was insistent and he lurched over and relieved himself in the basin. The rooster crowed at short, regular intervals and he thought of his mother's breathing, in and out, up and down, in and out, up and down. The rooster was the only thing alive in Fortress. He lay in bed and gave himself up to his injuries and the whining mosquitoes. When dawn began to lighten the sky, he realized that for the first time in his life, he had forgotten to pray.

The pain in his foot ebbed, but his hands hurt more and more. The rooster still crowed but his squawks now came from a distance. He sat up and studied his blistered hands. They were painful but he was not seriously injured. If he could avoid infection, he would be inconvenienced for a few weeks; nothing more. He looked at his foot. His toes were swollen; the nails sinking into his flesh. He saw an angry red mark at the base of his second toe. He searched for double puncture marks, but there were none. Not a snake then. His tongue felt heavy and large in his mouth. He heard the sound of a key outside and a door creaked open. Caught between embarrassment and relief, he sat on the bed and waited.

He heard the sounds of someone moving about, but the door to his bedroom remained closed. He would have to let whoever it was know he was awake. He limped to the door and opened it. The living room of his small house was flooded with light and he squinted. He saw a black woman dressed in a long skirt, white apron and red head scarf. She was opening his windows. He did not know how to greet her. He cleared his throat.

"Mercy!" she said, spinning around. "Pastor, you did frighten me!" Then she took in his appearance and her eyes widened. "What happen? What that smell?"

"I had an accident," he mumbled and indicated the room behind him.

She brushed past him and went into the bedroom. "You lick over di lamp! Mi clean it up. Don' worry." She made clucking noises, as if speaking to a not very bright child. "You bring any provision? Me tell dem over a di church, dem mus tell me di day before di new pastor coming, so mi go market. Mi tell dem and tell dem. But them don't listen." She turned to look at him, standing on one leg in the doorway. "You mash up you foot, Pastor?"

"What?" he said, struggling to understand her speech.

"You hurt you foot?"

"Something bit me."

"You see is what bite you? Mosquito?"

He was annoyed. His foot was grotesquely swollen and the woman was suggesting a mosquito. "No. Not a mosquito," he said. "Something that was in my shoe."

"Prob'ly a scorpion. Lemme look." She bent down and shook out his left shoe, and then his right. A large but maimed scorpion dropped out, tail held high to ward off the new threat. The woman reversed the shoe in her hand and squashed the scorpion with a swift, accurate blow. Its curdling body fluids shot out.

"Is a hot bite, don't it, Pastor? You wash up. Mi mek you a dressing for you foot; will bring down di swelling. You bring food wid you?"

"No," he said to the repeated question, wondering how to broach the matter of the urine in the basin.

The woman shook her head and made more clucking noises. "Mi tell dem an' tell dem an' tell dem…"

"The basin," he said. "I was ill… I couldn't…"

"Wha' happen to di basin?" She strode over to it. "Oh, you pee pee inna it." She threw her head back and laughed.

"The scorpion bit me and I couldn't walk."

"Awright, Pastor. Listen mi, now. You go sit inna di big chair outside. You just sit there. You like cocoa tea? Mi bring some. You just sit there." She shooed him from the bedroom.

"What's your name?" he said.

"Irene."

"Irene. Thank you." He limped to the chair. Outside, he could smell stale sweat, kerosene and smoke on his skin.

In no time, Irene had set the bedroom to rights. The kerosene was cleaned up, the burned sheets disposed of – lucky we have more, she observed out loud – the offending urine dumped outside on an invading vine running over the back fence. From where he sat, he could see into the outside kitchen, joined to the house by a covered walkway, where Irene was moving about, lighting the wood in a black iron stove, boiling water in a dented pot, all the while singing in a high wavering voice songs he could not identify. He yearned for a cup of tea. Irene went out into the yard and returned with a handful of plants. She poured the boiling water into a mug and stirred it. Then she set the plants in the dented pot and covered it. She brought the mug to him.

"Cocoa tea," she said. "Drink up. You feel better." In his fantasy a blue-eyed woman made him real tea, perfectly brewed. He took a cautious sip of the dark brown liquid and winced at the hot, bitter taste.

"You soon used to it," Irene said, watching him.

He sat, sipping from the mug. His stomach churned with hunger, his palms throbbed and his foot ached. His tongue, at least, was returning to normal size. Irene returned with a hot, wet mass of leaves in a cloth. "Show me di place," she said.

"No, no, it's feeling better, it's quite alright."

"Come on Pastor, scorpion bite need attention. Put you foot up here." She pushed over a wood and cane footstool and he acquiesced. She slapped the wet leaves on his foot – he gasped at the heat – and wrapped it tight with the cloth. "Now show mi you hand." With his palms upturned he felt like a schoolboy at St. Andrew's, waiting for the blow from the schoolmaster's tawse.

She clucked again. "You have to careful with dis. Burn can get infect. Right hand worse dan left. Mi soon come."

"Where are you going?" he said, suddenly anxious.

"Get some sinkle bible for di burn. Mi soon come."

She returned with a succulent, spiky plant from which she squeezed a clear jelly. She spread it on his hands and he was surprised at its soothing chill. She wrapped his hands with long strips of a loosely woven cheesecloth. He felt helpless sitting there. Irene asked him for money and again she left the house, returning with a basket full of food. He heard the spitting sounds of frying from the kitchen and the smell of cooking increased his hunger. Irene brought him round, brown cakes – cassava, he learned – a small fried fish and more of the cocoa tea. She put a bunch of ripe bananas on the table and he ate three; they were small, soft and very sweet. He stopped her ministrations only when she attempted to wipe his face with a damp cloth, which smelled strongly of mint.

Pastor John paced the altar of the Fortress Baptist Church. It was his first Sunday and his first service. It was just past seven and the rooster that interrupted his sleep every night was still crowing. The service was meant to start at seven, but he was the only one present.

Irene had been cleaning; she'd banished the cobwebs, removed the animal droppings, polished the glass windows and set the pews in place. She had covered the altar table with a white cloth and borrowed one of the vases from the planters' graveyard and filled it with a plant with dainty white flowers and large, waxy leaves.

The scorpion bite was no longer troubling him, but his burned palms were still painful and inconvenient. He worried about infection, though Irene dressed his hands every day, washing them in stinging rum first of all and then reapplying the jelly. He asked her how to spell the name of the plant which had yielded the jelly, but she did not know how. He presumed she was illiterate.

Irene had collected the church's stipend from the post office in Fortress, and his house was now lightly stocked with food, much of which he failed to recognize. Food was short, Irene told him. There had been a drought and some problem with ships. He discovered he owned the rooster and there were hens in a small fenced area in the back. He had suggested the rooster might find its way into the stew pot, but Irene had refused. "Hen need rooster."

He walked to the back of the church and looked out. He liked the mornings – he experienced none of the reluctance to get out of bed induced by the cold, foggy Glasgow dawn. Having thrashed through the hot and mosquito-plagued nights, he was anxious to rise, to splash his face with water, to eat the fresh meals Irene prepared, and then to gaze from the small porch down to the village, with its neat, tin-roofed houses, front steps polished a deep red, encircled by the surrounding hills. He longed to explore, but judged it was best not to subject his foot to too much walking.

But what he was supposed to do as missionary for the people of Fortress was becoming less clear. After four days, he was bored.

115

He had brought a few books with him, but none held his interest. So far, his only contact had been with Irene and her clucking and chattering irritated him, even as he was grateful for her care. He wondered about her history. Perhaps she was old enough to have been born in slavery, but would have been very young at emancipation. He judged it inappropriate to ask.

He waited at the door of his church. Suppose no one came? Last night he had worried about the content of his sermon; now he worried that no one would hear it. God would, though. He would hear his words and, eventually, so would the people.

It was nearly eight when he saw a few people walking up the path to the church. They were all Negroes and seemed to be one family: a man, dressed in working clothes, a woman in skirt, head scarf and apron, and two girls, both under ten, dressed in identical tunics. The girls walked uncertainly and John guessed they were unused to shoes. Could this be his congregation? His stipend would be very meagre without regular dues.

As they approached the church, the family fell into line, the man at the front. "Preacher," he said, eyes downcast.

"Good morning, my... son," John replied, feeling foolish. The man was years older than he was. The family filed into the church and sat at the back, the empty pews a barrier between them. He was at a loss. Should he wait or should he start the service? How would hymns sound in a near-empty church, with no harmonium? What could he possibly tell these people? He walked out into the churchyard and looked down the path, affecting a bored impatience but feeling a rising panic. He faced the empty path. He took out his watch and looked at it. He would wait ten more minutes.

That first morning, he had a congregation of eight. There was no collection. Four more villagers had arrived; all women. Irene was not among them. His voice was unconvincing even to himself and fell like dust into the dusty corners. He read the familiar scriptures and his congregation made no response, not even a murmured amen at the end of a prayer. The two children sat without fidgeting. He turned to his sermon with relief; it was based on his favourite passage in the Bible, Ecclesiastes, Chapter Three: *"To everything, there is a season,"* he began. When he said, *"...a time to plant and a time to pluck up that which is planted..."*

heads were raised and he realized he was not speaking in terms the people understood. But he knew nothing about these people, next to nothing of their history or their present. Oh, he knew the basic facts of the slave trade, the millions of Africans traded and transported and murdered to build personal fortunes. His church had, after all, been prominent in the abolitionist movement. He had half-heartedly listened to his training lectures on the economics of the plantation, and more enthusiastically embraced the notion of black people with souls to be saved. The abolition of slavery was fifty years in the past – talk over the Calabar dining table in Kingston had suggested it was time to move on. Yes, conditions for the Negroes were still poor and there had been the Morant Bay Rebellion, and yes, indeed the response of Governor Eyre had exceeded reasonable bounds, but progress, the dinner conversation maintained, was being made. Now, as John stood at the front of his crumbling church, uttering the ancient words that pointed to the one true Way, with eight souls sitting stolid before him, eight souls two generations removed from the status of property, he was struck by his own unfitness for his mission. His words trailed off; still the people before him made no reaction. He felt sweat running down his sides. The people sat. He did not know how to dismiss them. Eventually, he repeated the last words of the selected reading and then he walked to the door and stood. The people rose and filed from the church, ducking their heads as they passed him. This Sunday and innumerable other Sundays stretched ahead of him.

That evening, he sat on his porch, pretending to read his Bible in the fading light. The words danced on the page as he stole glances over it to the villagers as they went about their business and hoped he would catch them watching him. But no one appeared to notice him. Then he saw a white man, the first he had seen since leaving Kingston, coming up the slight hill towards him.

The man came through the small wooden gate that marked his yard and stood at the bottom of the front steps. "Good evening, ah… Pastor?" His accent was English and educated. He was a portly man in late middle age. He removed a wide brimmed hat.

117

John stood. "Good evening, Sir. Pastor John Macaulay at your service."

"Henry Bannister. Magistrate. May I join you?"

"Please."

The man walked onto the porch and sat heavily in the only other chair. "May I get you some refreshment, Sir?" John said.

"I'm grateful. Do you have tea?"

"I'm afraid not. My maid has not been able to find any. Perhaps you can give me some advice in that regard?"

"Certainly. Essentially, you have to order the luxuries yourself. Has your maid introduced you to the local mint tea?"

"Not yet."

"Drinking that foul cocoa brew?"

"I quite like it."

"Ah well. To each his own, I suppose. Ask your woman for mint tea. I guarantee you will find it more to your liking."

Though he was grateful to see another white face, his visitor's imperious manner irked. He called to Irene, who arrived, wiping her hands on her apron. "Do we have mint tea?"

"Your Honour," she said to Bannister. "Yes, Pastor. You want some?"

"Aye. Two cups. Do we have any biscuits?"

"Biscuits?

"Biscuits."

"We have jackass corn." Though this sounded entirely unbiscuit-like, he nodded his assent. Irene left.

"So. Where are you from, Macaulay?" Bannister said.

"Glasgow, Sir."

"What brings you to Jamaica?"

"I'm a missionary."

"Well, yes. Obviously. But why Jamaica?"

"My grandfather was born here."

"Really? Where?"

"I don't know. He returned to England when he was a baby. But he told stories about Jamaica to my family and I heard them while I was growing up."

"Interesting. A plantation family?"

118

John shook his head. "I doubt it." This conversation was making him uncomfortable. "And yourself?"

"Born here," Bannister said. "Falmouth. Town on the coast. You'd have travelled through it."

"Aye." John remembered brick buildings in a dusty coastal town. "How long have you been in Fortress?"

"Coming up eight years."

"And before that?"

"Montego Bay, Kingston, St. Ann's Bay, Spanish Town." Bannister fanned himself with his hat.

John felt he was running out of conversation. There was much he wanted to ask this man, but his manner did not encourage intimacy. What is life really like here? Do you know any Negroes? Do they eat at your table? Where do you go to church? What was my predecessor like? Why were so few people at service this morning? What he wanted to ask more than anything was what he should do from day to day.

Irene returned with a teapot, two mugs and a plate of brown biscuits with crimped edges on a tray. She poured a pale aromatic liquid into the cups. "Honey, Pastor." She pointed to a small jug.

"Thank you, Irene."

The two men sipped their tea. Bannister added a generous dollop of honey to his cup and John followed suit. The biscuits were crisp with a taste he could not identify.

"Are there many white families in Fortress?" John asked.

"There's mine. My wife, Sally. We have a son, Walter, but he's at school in England. No others. There was a doctor, Dr. Morgan, but he died last year. Hasn't been replaced. "

So no daughter of suitable age… but John felt he must appear self-sufficient, unconcerned about social attachments.

"And yourself, Macaulay? Are you married?"

"No. My mother had a long illness and I cared for her until she died."

Bannister accepted the explanation without comment. "I imagine you'll find Fortress lonely, then. The nearest town of any size is Falmouth – a couple hours' ride, depending on the state of the road. My chambers are in Falmouth."

"Why do you live in Fortress?"

"Circumstances," Bannister said, but did not elaborate. John thought they were circling each other like dogs, each searching for signs of weakness.

"Won't you have a biscuit," he asked, taking another.

"Those? I thank you, but no." John felt rebuked.

"Where do you worship?" he asked, feeling this to be an appropriately ministerial question.

"The Anglican church in Falmouth. St. Peter's. If I may be frank, I'm not in favour of your sect. I've seen it foment rebellion and murder in the old days. And now with the *native* preachers…" He shook his head. But…" he continued, lowering his voice, "…the blacks love it. Keeps them quiet. As long as your sermons emphasize the benefits of accepting one's lot in life and the rewards in the hereafter, there'll be no trouble." He stood. "Perhaps you'll have dinner with us this week? Tuesday?"

"I'm grateful, Sir. What time would suit?"

"About this time. Dusk. Well," Bannister said, holding out his hand, "appreciate your hospitality."

"My pleasure. I'm glad you introduced me to mint tea."

They shook hands and Bannister walked down the steps. John realized he did not know where he lived. "Wait," he called, "where do I find you?"

"Of course. You've just arrived. Straight through the town and past the farrier's shop. The road takes you up a hill. Take the first right. The name of the house is Belmont."

"I'll find it."

"A very good evening to you, Macaulay." Bannister was soon lost in the twilight. He heard a sound behind him. Irene was standing in the doorway, her mouth pursed. "That man," she said, shaking her head.

"What about that man?" John said, uncertain whether he should entertain such a discussion with his maid.

"Nutt'n, Pastor. Brown stew fish for supper. You wash up now."

"The biscuits were good, Irene. What were they made of?"

"Coconut."

"Aah. What did you call them?"

"Jackass corn."

"Strange name. His Honour didn't seem to like them."

"His Honour think dem a slave food."

The sound of a torrent on the tin roof woke him from an afternoon nap. John's mind was thick with sleep and at first he couldn't make any sense of the noise. Then he heard the boom of thunder and realized the pounding on the roof was rain.

He put on his night shift and went into the living room. It appeared to be dusk, although a look at his watch confirmed it was only four o'clock. Irene was nowhere in sight, and all the windows were closed. He opened one, sat at his desk and watched sheets of water falling. Visibility was reduced to a few yards, but he could see a river of thick, brown water running down the path into the village. He feared the small houses would be swept away and understood why the better houses were built on hills. The sky was low and muddy. Here things did not stay in their proper places. Earth became sky and the sky came down to touch the hills and even the air was thick with water.

Then the rain stopped suddenly, the clouds cleared and the sun resumed its assault. He had to get out of the house. He dressed, making another mental note about the necessity for Wellington boots, and walked outside. He slipped in the mud, almost falling and haltingly made his way down to meet the people of Fortress, his people.

He stopped at the first house he came to; one of the poorer ones, with holes in the walls and no sign of any livestock. The front door was open. The house rested on large stones and was not entirely level. The roof was partly tin and partly thatch. There was no demarcation of the house's yard, which was half-flooded, but he was reluctant to walk up to the open front door. He stood on the road and called a greeting. No one came out, although he could hear movement inside.

"Good afternoon!" he called again. "Hello! Is anyone home?"

A small child came to the door; a boy, dressed only in a torn vest. He sucked his thumb and stared. His arms and legs were thin, but his belly bulged over his tiny penis. "Hello, young man," he said, feeling inadequate. "Is your mother or father home?" The boy made no movement or sound. John was about to leave, when arms grabbed the boy and he disappeared from sight. He heard the urgent sounds of speech he could not understand and thought he heard a slap. "Ma'am?" he called again. "I am the new pastor at the church. I mean no harm. Please…" His voice trailed off. He felt small stirrings of anger. Surely ordinary courtesy was not too much to expect?

A woman came to the door. Her face was set and sullen and her clothes were ragged. "What you want?" Children of different heights were gathered behind her like ghosts. One, two…four. At least five people lived in this tiny dwelling.

"I'm Pastor John Macaulay; the new pastor at the church. I arrived…" He stopped. He had lost track of the days. "…recently." What could he say to this woman? Are these all your children? Where is their father? Do you have enough to eat? "What is your name?" he asked. He wanted to give her a title of some kind – daughter, missus, madam – but none seemed appropriate.

"None a yuh business. We nah business wid white man church." She slammed the door and a large slice of mud fell from the front wall of the house to dissolve in a murky puddle. He heard the cries of the woman's children as he continued down the street. Please God, he prayed, help me to find the right words.

He walked from house to house, the afternoon's rain still present in the air. He met mostly women and children, all unresponsive to his greetings. The women were cleaning up after the rain, sweeping water out of their houses with thatch brooms and emptying wooden buckets set to catch leaks. Some closed their doors when he approached. Others were working on the land, restaking plants and picking up fallen fruit. They did not answer his call. The small shop in the village square seemed open and he walked towards it. As he passed an open door he saw a burly man with a sombre face holding the tools of a farrier. John greeted him and the man nodded in return.

The men of Fortress were in the square and in the shop. Some sat on a low stone wall outside and watched his approach with impassive faces. In the shop, others were leaning on a counter, drinking from brown bottles without labels. A woman stood behind the counter, laughing with the men. Silence fell when he entered. He saw that many of the shelves in the shop were empty. The men turned to face him, and he stood awkwardly in front of them, looking over their heads, studying the few goods on the shelves. He saw a plate with brown circular cakes, half covered with a cloth. He would buy something. That would legitimize his presence. Buying something from local people was appropriate.

He decided suddenly to admit his ignorance, and asked the woman, pointing, "What are those?"

She followed his gesture. "Bulla cake."

"What are they made of?"

"Coconut. Sugar. Nutmeg. Little flour. Flour short now."

"How much are they?"

"Penny farthing a piece."

"I'll take two." The woman tore off a piece of thick paper from under the counter and wrapped the cakes. He paid her.

"Thank you." She did not reply. "What do you have to drink?"

"Rum. Ginger beer."

"I'll have a ginger beer." She gave him one of the brown bottles. The liquid was peppery, sweet, not like any beer he knew.

"What is this made of?"

"Ginger," she said, expressionless.

"What is ginger?" The distance between himself and the woman might as well have been the Atlantic Ocean. If he could find a horse to buy, he would pack and leave the very next day.

"A root. It grow inna di ground. Wi dig it up, grater it, pour boiling water over it, likkle sugar, cover it, let it sit. Ginger beer."

"It's very nice."

"Farthing for di ginger beer," she said. He paid her again. Some of the men walked outside, making sucking noises he took to indicate rejection or even disgust, leaving him alone with the woman and a very old man, who sat on the only stool and rested his head on his arms. Something, though, made him stay and try to engage the woman's eyes; she looked back at him frankly and he wondered if her expression had lightened.

"I am the new pastor. For the church. Pastor John."

"Mi know."

"What's your name?"

"Prudence."

"Do you come to church, Prudence?"

"Sometime. Not all di time."

"Why not?"

She shrugged. She began to wipe the counter and the old man made a grunting noise. He was losing Prudence's attention, but this was his first encounter outside his own house that did not seem entirely hostile. "I would like…" He stopped. He had been going to tell her he would like her to come to church. She regarded him steadily. He would try another approach. "Is there a school in Fortress?"

"No. Preacher before you, him did sey him going keep school, but it never happen."

"Would you… I mean, would everyone like their children to go to school?"

Prudence stared at him. He could not tell her reaction. She was a tall, thin woman with very black skin. Perhaps about thirty. Her nose was wide and her lips thick; she had a long neck and wide shoulders; he could see her tilling a field or butchering a cow. He found her faintly repellent but pushed away the thought. She was a child of God. The silence went on. She was not going to answer him, and he turned to go. "Thank you for the cakes and the beer," he said, over his shoulder.

"Yes, Pastor. About the school. People want dem pickney fi learn to read."

He turned to face her. He wanted to see a hint of welcome in her face, even the wavering beginnings of acceptance. There was nothing. "Alright, Prudence. I'll see what I can do." He walked out of the shop and through the waiting men. He felt their eyes on his back as he walked up the muddy road to his house on the hill. He felt he had just survived something dangerous.

His first invitation to dinner at the Magistrate's had been postponed – Henry Bannister had had to travel to Falmouth for several weeks. A boy had brought a note setting the new date. Now as John dressed for dinner, his clothes felt damp. It had rained again that day and as soon as he had finished washing, he

124

began to sweat. By the time he climbed the hill to the Bannister's house, he would be drenched. He combed his hair in front of the small, oval mirror in his bedroom. He needed a haircut – his hair was curly and unruly and could only be worn very short. His skin, always swarthy, had darkened. His moustache needed trimming, but he was not an ugly man, he told himself. He would find a woman of good character. Perhaps not in Fortress, but he planned to explore Falmouth as soon as possible. Since his walk around the village, he had posted a letter to his brother, had explored the possibility of purchasing a horse locally with the farrier – there was no possibility – and found a piece of flat land where a small school house might be placed. He had written three sermons and prayed daily for God's guidance, fighting the recurrent thought that God had lost track of him. He was still undecided as to whether or not he could stay in Fortress.

But more recently, when he'd walked through the village, though he still encountered averted eyes, one or two people had nodded in acknowledgement.

On his way to the Bannisters, he walked past the flat piece of land he thought might be a good place to build a school. It would have been best to have the school on the field between his house and the church, but the land was sloping and construction would be more problematic. The piece of land he had chosen was just before the cross roads, on the left. It was high in grass and a donkey was tethered to a large tree. He stopped and looked over it. The school could be built in the shade of the tree, so it would be fairly cool throughout the day. The land appeared to be well drained, except for a marshy corner at the far end. He was suddenly excited about it – building a school would occupy him for many weeks, and then there would be the design of the lessons. As he stood, he saw Prudence walking along a track, which ran alongside what he was already thinking of as his land. She carried a machete in one hand and a large of bunch of green bananas on her head. He walked to meet her and stood waiting at the junction of the main road and the track.

"Good evening, Prudence."

Her skin glistened. The bananas rode easily on a coiled pad of cloth on her head – she did not steady them with her free hand

– and he began to realise the genesis of her graceful, erect posture.

"Nice bananas."

"Nah fit yet. But we 'ungry."

"I was thinking of building the school here," he said, indicating the land with a sweep of his hand.

"Here?"

"Over by that tree."

"Di guango tree?"

"That tree, there. What do you call it? Guango?"

"Umm-mm. Good for cow and pig. Wi use di pod for feed."

"What do you think?"

Prudence looked blank.

"Of putting the school here?"

"Mas Georgie leggo him animal in dere. Mas Devon cut grass for him goat. Dunno if dem going like a school to build dere."

"Och, the school wouldn't take up the entire place." He began to feel irritated. It was so hard to get people to see the right way. "We can cut a path through the grass and clear a space under the tree and the children will learn how to read and write and count."

Prudence shifted her weight and John thought she wanted to put her burden down. "I'll be getting on, then," he said. "We'll talk again about the school. Good evening to you."

"'Evening, Pastor."

He watched her, wondering if he would have been able to lift the bananas, never mind carry them on his head.

He walked up the hill, turned right as instructed, onto a rutted, potholed and puddled path. He squelched in the mud between buggy tracks until, after a short distance, he saw two square gateposts with the word Belmont painted on the right-hand one. The driveway was packed hard and without holes or puddles.

The large two-storeyed house sat square on the top of the hill. He felt a pang of envy, and reproved his covetousness. He climbed the front steps to a verandah that ran along two sides of the lower storey, kicking his boots on the last step to dislodge the worst of the mud. Large sash windows were open, but he saw no one. He leaned against the verandah railing and looked out over Fortress and the surrounding countryside. The land retreated in shades of green, with only an occasional spot of colour. He could see the glint of water running through a curving line of large trees. The air was clean after the rain. He walked around the verandah to the west side of the house. The sun was sinking behind the hills and the sky glowed orange and pink and pale blue.

"Reverend?" he heard a voice behind him and turned, guilty at being found lost in the view. Perhaps he should have remained on the steps until he had been noticed.

"Aye," he said. "I'm Pastor John Macaulay. Mr. Bannister invited me to supper. You must be Mrs. Bannister. I apologize for the intrusion... I should have waited... the view." He stopped. The woman in front of him could not be Mrs. Bannister. She was about twenty, with frizzy red hair and hazel eyes. She wore a plain black dress with a black arm band.

"Quite alright," she said. "We're expecting you. I'm Mrs. Bannister's niece, Lillian."

"Miss...?" John said, making a shallow bow.

"Miss Watt," she said. "Please, come inside."

He really wanted to sit on one of the wicker chairs outside, and watch the sunset until the last drop of light faded from the land, but it would be rude to say so. He followed Miss Watt inside the house.

"Please sit by the fire," she said, and he saw a stone fireplace in one corner of the room. He had not imagined it would ever be cold enough for a fire in Fortress. He sat in a large wing chair and waited for her to join him, but she remained standing.

"What would you like to drink? We have the local rum and even some whiskey, I believe."

"I'm not one for alcohol. Water would be fine."

"I'm having some soursop juice. Will you join me?"

"That would be very pleasant."

"Good. Make yourself comfortable. I'll call my aunt and uncle." She smiled and he saw her teeth were good. Here was a woman of marriageable age. He would have to learn more. What was she mourning? He cautioned himself to control his anticipation, but she was here and he was sure that was a good beginning.

"Ah, Macaulay. Glad you were able to make it. Apologize

again for the postponement, but duty called." Henry Bannister strode into the room, hand outstretched.

John stood. "Magistrate. Please don't apologize. I quite understand." They shook hands.

"You met my wife's niece, Lillian? Did she offer you a drink?"

"Aye, she did. I didn't realize your wife had such a grown-up niece," he said, hoping to extract some information.

"Her sister's last-born child. Lillian's always been a favourite. Tragic engagement to the son of a publican, if you can believe it. Killed in a bar brawl last year. She wasn't eating, so Merle – my wife's sister – sent her for a visit us. She's been here a month. I think she's quite bored."

"Are you talking about me again, Uncle?" Lillian came into the room with a tray. John stood again.

"Not at all, my dear. You've met our new... ah minister, I believe. Please..." he said to John. "Please sit."

Lillian handed him a milky juice. It was thick and sweet.

"Not a drinking man, then, Macaulay?" Bannister said, swirling an amber liquid in a glass.

"I like my wits about me, Sir. But tell me about this juice, Miss Watt."

"Soursop. You might have seen the fruit. Large, green, with prickles on the skin. We add lime juice and sugar and a touch of flour for thickening."

"Delicious," John said, although he thought the taste somewhat sickly and wondered if he would be able to finish the glass. He was hoping Lillian would join them, but she remained standing, her hands clasped in front of her.

"I'll tell Aunt Sally that Mr. Macaulay is here," she said.

"Yes, do that... Women," Bannister said, "tend to be unpunctual. If you've not been married, you're yet to discover this." There was a silence. Outside, the light had gone and the room in which they sat was warm and dark. John saw there were screens on the windows to keep out insects – his list of items to acquire was growing.

So," Bannister said, "how are you finding Fortress?"

"Quiet. Few people at service last Sunday. No horse available here – I'll have to make a trip to Falmouth for that, I'm told."

"You should do that as soon as possible. It's unseemly for you to be seen walking. You'll never gain the natives' respect if you're seen on foot too often."

"Is that so?"

"Indeed. I'm making a trip on Friday – market day – perhaps you would care to join me?"

"Thank you, Sir. I would. How…"

"My buggy holds two. Sally can miss the trip."

"Oh, I would hate to preclude Mrs. Bannister from her visit."

"Let me worry about that."

"Well, thank you, Sir. I'd certainly appreciate it. Will we return by Saturday evening? I have to be in Fortress for services on Sunday."

"No. You'll have to return on your new horse. I stay on for our own service at St. Peter's."

"Will I be certain to acquire a horse?"

"I would think so. If you don't, you'll have to miss your service."

"I couldn't do that."

Bannister shrugged. "Please yourself. The offer stands. So your church has been empty?"

"Not entirely. Ten or so. Did the previous pastor – what was his name? – have better luck?"

"Quinn. Marcus Quinn. I couldn't say. We didn't socialize. He was local, one of the native preachers, encouraging all kinds of departure from the Scriptures. We worship in Falmouth, as I explained."

"Perhaps Mrs. Bannister and Miss Watt might come to my service in Fortress, if I am forcing them to miss theirs in Falmouth? I myself am faithful to the doctrines."

Bannister laughed. "I must remember you've just arrived. Your church, Macaulay, adherence to doctrine or not, is for the Negroes and you'd do well to remember it. Your predecessor had a tendency to ignore the conventions to his considerable detriment. I hope you won't make the same mistake."

John was saved from having to reply by the return of the women. The men stood and Bannister introduced his wife, a bosomy woman in a dress of muslin trimmed with lace, her grey hair secured in a bun.

129

"Madam," John said, bowing over her hand. "Thank you for inviting me to your delightful home. What a view."

"Our pleasure," she said. "Dinner will be a few more minutes. Is it not rather dark in here? Pansy!" she called.

"Ma'am?" said a voice from the kitchen.

"The lamps," said Mrs. Bannister. "Bring the taper."

Dinner was plentiful, but indifferently cooked. There was a stew of tough, unseasoned chicken, with cassava, breadfruit and plantain, and some string beans boiled almost to mush. John stole glances at Lillian Watt. The lamplight was flattering to her, smoothing her freckled skin, making interesting hollows in her rounded cheeks. Her hands were square and veined with nails cut short. Capable hands. He imagined them touching him. She had none of Nurse Duncan's womanliness, though. She was a woman who would not inflame the thoughts of men. He wondered if he had been invited to dinner to meet her. She showed no interest in him.

"Tell us about your family, Mr Macaulay," said Mrs. Bannister. "What brought you to Jamaica?"

"My father is a minister, although not a Baptist. My grandfather was born here, but he left while a baby. His stories of the island became family stories. I grew up wanting to come here."

"So you come from a line of churchmen?" Mrs. Bannister said.

"I do."

"And how do you…" Mrs. Bannister was interrupted by Lillian.

"If your grandfather left when he was a baby, how could he relate the stories?"

She *was* listening. "There was a man, an old man, some kind of guardian – I never knew him of course, but he used to visit my grandfather and tell him the stories. He knew my grandfather from the time he was born. He was an abolitionist; quite well known in his day."

Bannister grunted and opened his mouth to speak, but Lillian interrupted, "Was he related to you?"

"Lillian," Mrs. Bannister interjected. "Perhaps Mr Macaulay would rather not be questioned."

"No, it's quite alright," John said. "I don't think he was a relation. We know little of him really. There always seemed to be some kind of secret surrounding my grandfather's birth in Jamaica. I don't think even he knew how it came to pass. His mother and father died in a hurricane, we understand, and this man, the abolitionist, brought him back to Scotland."

"So who raised your grandfather?" Lillian asked.

"A sister of the abolitionist. She died when he was quite young and he was sent to an orphanage. But there was money for his schooling and…"

"What an interesting story," said Mrs. Bannister, her manner indicating quite the opposite.

"The abolitionists doomed this island," said Bannister. "And the Baptists. No offence intended."

How he was expected to respond to this? A better man might excuse himself from the table, but he wanted to get to know Lillian Watt. "You agree with slavery, then?" he said mildly.

"Agree with it? You think the Negroes are better off since *emancipation?*" Sarcasm emphasized the word.

"I imagine any man is better off free," John said. The two women ate slowly, looking at their plates. Magistrate Bannister took a long drink.

"When you've been here a while, Macaulay, when you've seen how the Negro treats his children, how he treats other Negroes, when you've observed his work habits, then talk to me about men being free. They can't handle it."

"The village seems very poor," John said.

"Poor? They have more than they deserve. They won't work regularly. They spend their money on drink. They don't marry – that should bother you. The men don't live with their families and the children grow up wild."

"Where *do* the people in Fortress work?" John asked.

"Some have their grounds. They plant yam and bananas – even sugar cane. They take their produce to market in Falmouth. The women take in washing or sewing. Some Negroes work on the sugar estates – there's one at Hampden. The skilled ones do better. Cuba, the farrier, is probably a rich man."

John thought of the man he had met. He had been wearing

rough clothes and his hair was unkempt. He doubted he was rich.

"Have you had enough, Mr Macaulay?" Mrs. Bannister asked.

John realized she was referring to the food. "Aye, more than enough, Madam. A wonderful meal. I'm grateful."

"We have some sweet potato pone for dessert. Has your maid cooked that for you yet?"

"Not yet."

Mrs. Bannister rang a small bell at her elbow and the maid came into the room, her hands folded in front of her like a penitent. "You can clear, Pansy," she said.

"Here are some letters for you," a female voice said.

Zachary turned from the fence of Cedar Paddock. It was Sarah, the younger daughter. He hardly ever saw her or Mrs. Monmouth. Their domain was the Great House and the extensive gardens around the house. He had eaten dinner with the family only once since his arrival – a formal and tense meal of halting conversation.

Sarah handed him two letters. It seemed strange that there were people who could write to him and the letters would find him here, leaning on the fence, watching his horse graze, thinking about a slave woman with blazing eyes.

"Thank ye." He saw Sarah was carrying a basket, in which two puppies squirmed.

"Would you like a puppy? Damsel had pups and I thought you might like one for company. Much better than that mongrel I've seen you with."

Zachary smiled. "Aye, that I would." He reached into the basket and picked up one and held it at eye level to check its sex – a bitch. "I'll hae this one," he said, suddenly sad. He'd had a dog at home – a spaniel called Shane. He knew his mother would feed his dog – she did not abide cruelty to animals – but apart from that, Shane would be ignored as one of the throng of humans and animals fighting for attention in the crowded Macaulay household. For a moment he was back in the dripping morning mist of Inverary and desperate to read his letters.

"Make sure she does not breed with the mongrel," Sarah said. "Best to keep bloodlines pure." She regarded him steadily.

"Thank ye. Forgive me, Miss Sarah. I must go." He smiled to make his departure less abrupt. She inclined her head and he saw she was disappointed. Was she interested in him? She was at least five years his senior. But even though her brother would inherit Bonnie Valley, she would come with a fortune. But she was too pale, too thin, too lacking any defined character. She spent most of her time indoors. Outside, she wore a wide-brimmed straw hat that obscured her face – and carried a parasol as well. He had never seen her on a horse, never met her walking in the shady grove by the duck pond, never seen her among the cocoa plants or in the banana walk. He had never heard her laugh. "Good night, then, Mr. Macaulay," she said, and left him holding the puppy.

Zachary ran up the hill to his house. "Olivia!" he shouted as he mounted the stairs.

"Yes, Massa?" She was outside, in the kitchen.

"Get my bath ready. Come here first. Take the dog. Give her some milk and stale bread. Get a basket for her."

"Massa," Olivia said, hurrying onto the verandah, wiping her hands on her apron. "Where me must get a basket?"

"I dinna care. Find one. No ower big, wi low sides. It must be lined wi cloth. If the dog willna eat, you must feed her." He would name his dog Martha.

The light was fading rapidly; he would have to read quickly. He had twelve brothers and sisters, but he had been close to only one, his oldest sister Margaret. Martha was his secret name for her, a symbol of their closeness. She had shielded him from his father's rages and compensated for his mother's overwork. She had taught him to read. She was the only person in his family who needed him, who sought his company, who listened to his fears and desires. When he had learned she had a lover, he had helped her conceal her absences. Then she became pregnant and his father became aware of his complicity. Margaret was beaten and sent away to a place for unwed mothers. He still remembered one of the women there, in the last stages of syphilis. It was her image that kept him from taking a slave wife.

He opened the first letter, but it was not from Martha. It was from Trevor Manning. He set it aside and opened the second letter. It was from his mother. He liked to think he loved her, but he did not know her. She was a woman who was never still, never in repose, never free of a task. Did she miss him? Had she realized he was gone? One morning, over porridge, had she turned to her husband and said: "Where is Zachary?" He would make a trium-

134

phant return to Scotland as a wealthy man, a man who had seen and done much. A man resolute and unwavering, his transgressions forgotten. He smoothed his mother's letter and began to read.

His mother wrote of the weather, of his father's last sermon, of the debate on the abolition of slavery, raging an ocean away. She hoped her son would do well and make the family proud. The postmistress, Mrs. McNulty had died, and the service had suffered. She asked him to write. She did not mention Margaret. He crumpled the letter and threw it down.

He unfolded Trevor Manning's letter. It was short. Manning hoped Zachary was settling in, that he had found Bonnie Valley to his liking, that he should keep the pewter canteen. He was now in Kingston. He did not say what work he was doing. He said the abolition debate was raging in Kingston's salons. There was a fever epidemic and people were afraid to leave the low foothills. He hoped Zachary would keep in touch. That was all. As he turned over the envelope and saw the faded return address, he heard the puppy yelp. Blasted ignorant bitch – what was she doing to his dog? He strode to the kitchen, noting the lamps were unlit and the house unfumigated. That perfectly-cooked first-night dinner, transported from the Great House kitchen, had never been repeated. Olivia was a poor cook. He thought he hated her. In the smoky, sweltering kitchen, he saw his golden puppy tied to the leg of a table with a piece of twine. He backhanded Olivia across her face and she fell to the floor, staring at him in astonished terror. He looked down at her, surprised, as if his hand had acted entirely on its own accord. "I told ye to find a basket."

"Yes massa, yes. Sorry massa."

"Useless woman," he said, but his anger had ebbed and he felt foolish and ashamed. He wanted to reach out and help Olivia to her feet. He turned on his heel and left the kitchen.

"Mr. Macaulay?" Charlotte called. It was mid-October, the land still broiled under the sun and the October rains had not arrived. A constant haze obscured the distant hills. Zachary's Sunday rides were taking him only as far as the river, where he shed his clothes and slipped his sweating body into its coolness. He

135

managed a clumsy dog paddle, but he stayed close to the banks, holding onto a large tree root, remaining in the water until his fingers wrinkled. The water level had fallen and its movement was sluggish. Insects skittered on the surface.

He had just returned from his usual ride when he heard Charlotte's voice. He slicked back his wet hair and went outside.

"Miss Monmouth?"

"My father would like you to join us for dinner next Friday. We've invited several others – we won't be *en famille*. Dress is formal. Eight o'clock."

"Thank ye. It would be an honour." He cast his mind over his clothes for anything that might be considered formal.

"Oh. I almost forgot. Letters for you." She handed over the usual monthly letters from his mother and Trevor Manning. She lingered on the steps. Zachary realized he was being rude.

"Would ye like tae come in? Sit yersen down for a minute? It isna an easy walk in the sun, is it?" He wished she would go.

"Thank you. I would. It is indeed very hot." She mounted the steps and he pulled up a chair for her.

"Something tae drink?" He was sure that all he had was water.

"Some water would be wonderful. I can't face tea in this heat."

He bawled for Olivia and a jug of lukewarm water was brought. It tasted alive with growing things.

"How are you liking Bonnie Valley, Mr. Macaulay? We've hardly seen you up at the house recently."

"Well, my days are long," he said. "I'm finding thae autumn months hard. Although there are fewer mosquitoes."

"Do you miss your family? Did you leave a sweetheart behind?" She nodded at his letters.

"I dae miss my family. Nae sweetheart, though." Charlotte looked at him through her eyelashes. Was he being flirted with? Surely not. She was old, a spinster.

"Perhaps they will visit you."

"Aye, perhaps. But 'tis a long journey." Their conversation lapsed. Zachary gazed out at the sweltering valley. The heat would not ease until the early hours of the next morning. Often, he felt he had just fallen asleep when Olivia's knock awakened him. When he walked out into the early mornings, the soft shades of dawn were already long gone and the sun battered the land.

"You know, the rules here are not the same," Charlotte said.

"The rules, Miss Monmouth? I'm no sure I understand ye."

"The rules. Society's rules. They're suspended. Out here, you can do what you like." She stared at him and he felt uncomfortable. He thought if he reached across for her hand she would put his fingers to her breasts. Was he mad? This was his employer's daughter. He inclined his head, pretending to consider what she had said.

"Well," she said. "I must go and supervise dinner. How is Olivia working for you?"

"She's no a good cook and tends tae insolence," he said, immediately feeling this was unfair. Olivia was just old and slow.

"Really. You must flog her."

"D'ye think so?"

"They're not like us, Mr. Macaulay. You must have realized that by now. Perhaps a younger slave would be more to your liking?" Again her words seemed to have a double meaning. He thought of Victoria – perhaps she could be released from the fields.

"What about Victoria?" he ventured.

"*Her?* She's light-skinned enough, but would never be a house slave. She's one of those likely to run. Or be flogged to death one day. I'll find another house slave for you. Someone brighter. I'll sample their cooking myself." She stood. "Thank you for the refreshment. We'll see you next week."

"Aye," he said. "Please tell your parents I am honoured tae receive their invitation." She nodded and walked down the hill, pulling the brim of her hat over her eyes. He thought her a desperate woman. He turned to his letters.

He had been at Bonnie Valley for six months. In that time he had become used to mosquitoes, learnt to sleep when his skin was slick with sweat, regained his riding muscles, found his way around the plantation and then the countryside, learnt his job, adjusted to a solitary life after growing up in a large and boisterous family. He had been sick with fever twice, but Dr. Whitby had told him his bouts had been mild. He and Paul had never become friends. He thought of Trevor Manning often and wished he had not gone to Kingston. Manning wrote him each month, and Zachary wondered why. It was still not clear how he made his living.

He had never lived so much inside himself, with only his churning brain and his animals for company. He had little inclination to read, but his favourite passages often rang in his thoughts before he fell asleep after his evening meal. On his long rides, he thought. Sitting on his verandah, waiting for the right moment to visit his horse, he thought. Lying in bed at night, yearning for the onset of the morning breeze that wafted off the hills, he thought. Unlike the juice of the sugar cane in the huge coppers, his thoughts never crystallized.

He thought about Charlotte's statement that there were no rules in the colonies. He knew he could have her and no promises would be required. She was unlikely to have a venereal disease. He might lose his job, but most he feared a pregnancy. He did not want to think about fatherhood.

He was seventeen years old and had never lain with a woman; he lived alone, torn between a restless mind and a clamorous body. There were the slaves, of course, and he still remembered the brown-skinned woman in Montego Bay, a woman, he told himself, he would not have to rape. But he did not want to force himself on some cringing girl at Bonnie Valley, take the risk of a wasting illness, or face the inevitable mulatto offspring who would perhaps carry his features and his temperament.

Money was often in his thoughts. People came here for various reasons – fleeing crimes or creditors, seeking adventure and fortune, or banished by their families. Little as he had seen of the rest of the island, he knew there were riches to be had; he had seen it in the lavish dress of the men and women on the streets of Montego Bay, in the luxurious details of the Great House, in the expanse of Bonnie Valley's orderly fields. The sugar made its way to the tables of Europe. All who owned the land on which it was planted, who transported it, sold it and ate it were wealthy. Only those who grew it had nothing, not even the right to weariness.

He dressed for dinner. He remembered Trevor Manning telling

him that Bonnie Valley's parties were famous. He had found vaguely suitable clothes, though they smelled musty and needed darning. Olivia had hung them out in the sun and had sewn the holes closed. The white breeches had taken on a yellowish cast and were tight around his thighs, although they were loose in the waist. The cravat made him break out in a sweat, and the velvet jacket made him feel he would go mad, as it strained across his shoulders. He looked out at the Great House and saw it blazed with light. Carriages had been arriving for several hours.

Bonnie Valley Great House was always impressive, but now the fortune that had constructed it was on conspicuous display. Every candle in every chandelier was lit, the wall lamps were perfectly trimmed and cast a warm and smokeless light; the marble floors shone; vases glowed with orchids cut from the forest. And, born to this opulence, the white families swirled, dressed in velvets, muslins and brilliant coloured silks, their garments trimmed with lace and pearls, their hats adorned with ribbons and feathers. Peacocks, he thought. They are like peacocks with their tails spread. His clothes were at least two seasons out of date.

The Monmouth money could do nothing about the heat, however. Although every window was open and slaves stood in corners waving huge, woven fans, it was sweltering. Women carried their own painted fans and hid their faces. Everyone sweated and face powder ran, but the room rang with a frantic and determined gaiety. Zachary stood on the edge of the crowd and wondered if he would be missed if he left.

"You've come," Paul said, walking up to him. "No drink? Sutton! Bring this man a drink! Some rum and lime?" Zachary nodded, grateful that he no longer stood alone, his employee status obvious. Sutton, immaculate in gold-trimmed livery, brought him a glass on a tray. The outside of the glass was wet with condensation.

"Come and meet some people. The ladies especially. They'll be wanting new blood." Zachary followed Paul through a bewildering round of introductions: Miss Hazel Clarke of Barton Park – wasn't that where Trevor Manning had said he was going? – Miss Selina Boundbrook of Boundbrook Estate, Mr. Phillip

Douglas also of Boundbrook Estate – he's a book-keeper, like you – Miss Amelia Farquharson, all the way from Worthy Park in Lluidas Vale. He bowed over their thin, smooth fingers, met their bold eyes, and tried to remember the manners his mother had absent-mindedly enforced. He drank too much and spoke little.

"Mr. Macaulay!" Charlotte walked up to him. She was splendidly attired, her cheeks powdered, her hair coiled, dressed with combs that glowed with jewels he took to be rubies. "Are you enjoying yourself?"

"Certainly, Ma'am."

"You seem lonely. It's an overpowering gathering. Don't worry. These people are our closest neighbours, although some have ridden across half the island to be here. You're causing quite a stir among the ladies. But come and sit with me at dinner, won't you?" She linked her arm through his and he felt the stiffness of her undergarments, restraining her stocky body into a more pleasing shape. He could not refuse, although he would have preferred to sit with Miss Farquharson – a black-haired, green-eyed miss with swelling breasts and not a trace of a mosquito bite.

"Thank ye, Ma'am. Ye are very kind."

Sutton hit a huge gong and people dispersed into the massive dining hall, where two tables, each seating twenty, were set. Wood shone through lace tablecloths and an orchid spray graced every place setting. Tapestries hung from the walls except where an enormous gilt mirror took up most of one wall. Mrs Monmouth presided over her guests with a slightly exhausted air. Zachary was happy to find the dining room a bit cooler. Guests settled themselves in their seats and an army of house slaves ladled the first course of turtle soup onto gold charger plates.

The talk and laughter lessened as people ate. Course followed course: carved duck breast, braised beef and roasted yam, steamed callalloo, golden cakes of cassava, French beans, fried plantains. Wines and claret that was rather too warm flowed, and there was a milky fruit juice for the ladies who did not take alcohol. There were many more men than women.

During a lull between the main course and dessert, an overweight, red-faced man at the head of Zachary's table said, "Have you heard what happened to the Grandisons?"

"Jerome," said a woman to his left, presumably his wife. Her tone was reproving, as if she sought to divert his subject.

He ignored her. "The Grandisons of Canterbury Penn?"

"No, Mr. Cassidy," Mrs. Monmouth answered from the other end of the table. "We haven't heard about the Grandisons. Did they leave? Patricia has been threatening to go back to Salisbury for many years."

"No," the red-faced man said. His face was grim. "No, they didn't leave. They were murdered. All of them. Including Celia's baby. Well. The baby was never found, so it was assumed she was murdered. Probably raped and murdered, if you ask me. Possibly eaten too. Not yet a year old." Wine glasses clinked and guests drank hurriedly and looked away. A heavy silence settled on the table.

"Tragic. Just tragic," Mrs. Monmouth said. "Perhaps, though, the men might talk about this after dinner, Jerome. We don't want to upset the ladies."

"The ladies better damn well prepare themselves to be upset," Cassidy said and Zachary saw he was drunk. "They'd better understand what's going to happen when they free the negers. Rape and murder, that's what. Having those black sons of Beelzebub coming up to the ladies in the street and speaking freely to them. Well, it's clear what's going to happen."

"Jerome…" Mrs. Cassidy said again.

"Have you heard what's a happening in Sainte-Domingue, for instance? And France? The French are on the verge of declaring that negers have rights like anyone else. Damn the Frenchies…"

"Charlotte!" Mrs. Monmouth said sharply. "Mr. Cassidy is obviously unwell. Perhaps you and Mr. Macaulay could help him outside. I'm sure some fresh air would revive him." Charlotte rose to her feet and crossed to her guest. "Come, Sir, you are feeling the heat. Perhaps there will be a cooler place on the verandah." Zachary felt superfluous, but he followed Charlotte. He was surprised when Cassidy folded his napkin, placed it by the side of his plate and followed them meekly outside.

"Perhaps a short walk, Mr. Cassidy? It might clear your head." Charlotte led him down the steps at the side of the house.

"You think I'm drunk," he said, stumbling a little. "I've had a few. But what I said is the truth. The writing is on the wall, unless the planters fight."

"Fight whom, Sir?" Zachary asked.

"Oh, the governments," Cassidy said. He turned to face Zachary. "Do you know how many white people are presently in Jamaica?"

"No, Sir."

"Now, Mr. Cassidy, we all know the mathematics. People have been predicting disaster for years," Charlotte said.

"We may know the mathematics, but we pretend they do not matter," Cassidy said. "Around thirty thousand, young man. That's how many white people live on this stinking, disease-ridden rock in the sea. Another ten thousand free coloureds, give or take. And do you know how many slaves? Two hundred and fifty thousand! Six to one. If the slaves had any leadership, if they got together with the mulattoes, they could exterminate us in a matter of weeks."

"How is Matilda?" Charlotte asked. "I missed her tonight – Mr. Cassidy's daughter," Charlotte explained to Zachary.

"Matilda is back in Aberdeen, with her mother. God willing, I will soon be with them. I warn you, Miss Charlotte, get your father to listen. They'll soon free the slaves and even if there's no bloodshed, the plantations are finished. These *islands* are finished."

Cassidy bent over Charlotte's hand. "Give your mother my apologies. It's best I go on my way."

"Let me send one of our trusted slaves with you," she said. "You'll never find your carriage in the dark."

"I would appreciate that, Miss Charlotte. You've always been one of my favourites." Zachary saw his leer and felt repelled; he was a man twice her age.

"Wait here with Zachary. Did you meet earlier? Our new – well, no longer so new – book-keeper."

Cassidy nodded. They stood together, awkward. There was nothing to say. Zachary heard the screech of an owl; the slaves said owls meant death. It was ignorant superstition. He heard the rumble of wheels and saw a carriage detach itself from the others at the foot of the hill and make its way towards them. "Safe journey," he said.

Cassidy looked around for Charlotte, who was not in sight. "Say good-night to Miss Monmouth for me."

"Aye. Safe journey."

He watched Cassidy clamber into his carriage. He did not want to return inside to that crowded, sweltering room. Here the sky arched above, flecked with stars. He had never felt the air so still.

"Let's walk." It was Charlotte, back again.

"Won't ye be missed?" He did not want to walk with her. He wanted to throw her against the front steps of the Great House and kiss her until she gasped. He wanted to thrust his hand under her skirts. Yet he also wanted nothing to do with Charlotte Monmouth.

"Not immediately. Are you afraid of me, Zachary Macaulay?"

"Afraid? Why should I be afraid?"

"Because of this." She stepped in front of him, raising her mouth to his. He kissed her clumsily and felt her mouth open, slick and hot, and tasting of the meat she had eaten. This is a disaster, he thought, but his hands pulled her closer and he felt the whalebone of her corsets. A door banged behind them and they jumped apart. "Not here," he said, panting. "We'll be discovered."

"When? You don't have to be afraid. I won't tell anyone and I know what to do."

"Tomorrow night. Late." He saw her eyes shine and he was aroused past bearing. He could not go back to the company inside the Great House. "Leave me," he said, asserting his manhood.

She smiled and touched his cheek. "Tomorrow, then. Walk for a while and come back inside. If you don't, it will be noticed." She left him, looking over her shoulder, smiling.

A poor coquette, he thought, as he walked away from the circle of light cast by the house. He could hear laughter inside, the clink of glasses and the clatter of cutlery. He had to return; Charlotte was right; his absence would be noticed. He wondered who the Grandisons had been, whether they had been a large family, and who Celia had been, the one who had lost her baby and her life. Why would such a thing happen? Perhaps Mr. Grandison had been a brutal owner, driving his slaves to revolt. Perhaps he had not provided for their slaves; perhaps the slaves had been hungry.

Perhaps they had not been killed by slaves at all, but by a mad white man – he had heard stories of a white man who had built a castle and then had gone insane. From his property in St. Ann's, he had captured, tortured and murdered an unknown number of travellers.

But Cassidy had spoken the truth. It would be easy for the thousands of slaves to turn against their owners; the force of numbers were with them. But then, what? Would Charles Monmouth's slaves occupy the rooms of Bonnie Valley Great House? Would they work the plantation for their own benefit, make it a profitable business? Or would they burn it to the ground, destroying the place of their bondage and turn to the hills, to join those who already lived there? He knew the Maroon treaty required runaway slaves to be returned, but what if there was nowhere to return them to?

He could not imagine blacks in the Great House. They did not belong with glittering chandeliers and intricate tapestries, just as white people did not belong in the mean, wattle-and-daub, thatched-roof dwellings of the slaves with dirt floors and nothing inside but planks of wood for sleeping, only slightly softened with cut bush and rough cotton coverings. But then, did he feel at home in the Great House, and weren't there people in his own Scotland whose dwellings were little better than the slaves? It was all confusing. Perhaps it was just as it always had been: those who could conquer, did conquer. Those who built palaces needed servants. Britain led the world with her ships and her muskets and the courage of her men. Black people sold their own into slavery, and here these people laughed and sang in the fields, even as the long reach of the whip threatened, and then found its mark.

The plantation system could not continue without the slaves. Even if they became working gangs who received payment for their labour, they would not work when tired, they would not come to the fields at shell-blow, they would spend days under shade trees, drunk on rum, and turn to work only when starving. Well that was what his elders and betters said. The Great House would fall into ruin, rats and serpents would occupy its rooms, the cane fields would wilt and turn to scrub, the roads would become overgrown and a way of life would disappear. Bonnie Valley would lie in ruins, with neither whites nor blacks to cultivate it.

He shook off these thoughts. The night was the most oppressive he had experienced since arriving in the island. It was unusually silent. He walked further from the house until the sounds of the party were faint, yet he did not hear the usual buzzings and creakings of insects. No fireflies blinked on and off on the fences. He turned his back on the night and returned to the party.

It was not yet fully light when he was aroused. He had only been asleep for a few hours and his mind was foggy with drink. He stumbled from his bed and threw open the windows. Sutton stood there shouting, but Zachary could not understand his words.

"Sutton! What is the reason for this damned noise? Today is Sunday; why are ye disturbing our rest?"

"Massa, hurricane a come! You must get up and make preparation."

"What hurricane? What are ye talking about? Did ye get into the rum last night, Sutton? Thompson will skin ye alive," Zachary said.

"No, Massa, no rum. Hurricane a come."

"Sutton! What are you doing? Get over here!" Paul shouted from the road below.

"Coming, Massa! Me just a tell Mas' Macaulay." Sutton ran off. He was still in his party clothes.

Zachary dressed hurriedly. He had the devil of a headache and longed for his coffee but Olivia was nowhere in sight. He ran down the hill to the farm buildings, where he found every man and woman on the plantation engaged in battening down doors and windows, storing carts and carriages, bringing the animals in from the fields near the river, making preparations in the hurricane house, a solid square of stone with massive rafters and a shingled roof. He saw Thompson shouting orders.

"What can I dae?" he asked.

"*You?*" Thompson said. "Stay out of the way, is what." Women ran by, carrying stores of food and wooden buckets of water. It looked as though the plantation was preparing for battle. He saw Paul and his father standing at the edge of the turmoil and walked over to them.

"Good morning," he said. "Is there going tae be a hurricane?"

"'Morning," Monmouth answered. He did not appear worried and Zachary was heartened by his calmness. "It's possible. The weather signs are right. And a traveller brought news from a ship. It's best to be prepared."

"Father, we should send our guests home. We cannot feed them if there is a hurricane," Paul said.

"We cannot send them home. Those still here have too far to travel. We will not turn them out into the storm. Those are my *orders*." He turned to leave. "Mr. Macaulay, make sure your horse is turned out in a field a good distance from the river and one without large trees. Palisade Paddock is a good place. Bring your dog and yourself and whatever you consider your valuables to the Great House within the hour. You will wait out the storm with us."

"Thank ye, Sir," Zachary said.

Miranda was skittish and bounded away as he approached, but eventually, he haltered her. A light breeze was picking up and he welcomed its touch on his overheated skin. The headache hammered his skull. Perhaps the storm would not be so bad if it caused the temperature to fall. "Through the hushed air the whitening shower descends," he said out loud, and then laughed at himself. Could a hurricane be worse than a winter blizzard?

He vaulted onto his horse and cantered bareback to Palisade Paddock. Other horses were already there. He hoped they would not fight. He slid from Miranda's back and let her into the field, slipping off the halter. She shied away from him and bucked. He shut the gate and slid the bolt home.

The wind grew stronger as he walked back and he began to feel afraid. The sky had a yellow cast and hung low over the hills. He broke into a run. He thought about his valuables, as Charles Monmouth had called them. What did he own that was of value? He ran, panting, up the steps to Bell Cottage and whistled for Martha. She was hiding under his bed, her tail low. She whined when she saw him. He threw his books, his mother's Bible with the sketch of his sister, and his letters into a bag. He cast his eye around the room and saw nothing else that belonged to him. Then he ran out to the kitchen and grabbed Trevor Manning's canteen from its peg. He filled it with water from the jug that was always kept full in his kitchen. As he did it, he cursed himself for a fool. A canteen of water would be near useless in the face of a catastrophe and the river was nearby. But it was the only preparation he could think to make. He felt dirty and wanted a bath but Olivia was no doubt caught up in the preparations at the Great House. The last thing he threw into his bag was a change of clothes. Outside, the trees frothed in the wind, but there was no rain. He whistled to the mongrel dog he had never named.

Zachary ran up the front steps to the Great House, Martha leashed at his side, the mongrel following. The parlour was empty of furniture and he heard voices coming from the dining hall. In it he saw many faces from the previous night, although numbers were fewer. The tables were pushed back against the walls and chairs and carpets from the parlour crowded the room. The men looked tense and talked in low voices about their own holdings. The women sat together, comforting one woman who cried without restraint. It was the appealing Miss Farquharson; she was unrecognizable in her despair. He saw the guests were no longer in their evening clothes and realized they must have planned to spend at least a night at Bonnie Valley.

"Mr. Macaulay," Charlotte said, rising from the cluster of women. "Please take your dog to Sutton to be kennelled. When you return, find a place to sit. There may not be a chair, but this is the safest place in the Great House – few windows and a solid roof. We've weathered storms here before. There are refreshments on the table. Please help yourself. Once the storm starts, we will not be able to replenish stocks from the kitchen."

Sutton walked in behind him and without being told, took Martha's leash. The mongrel hesitated and Zachary swung his boot in his direction.

He wandered over to a table and helped himself to coffee, which was hot and strong and bitter. He sat on the floor, with his back against the wall. Although the room was full of people, he felt utterly alone. He leaned his pounding head against the wall and waited. Then he heard a roaring sound and the first burst of rain hit the walls of Bonnie Valley like stones, hurled with the force of a thousand catapults.

★

The hurricane lasted all day. The planters and their families, the white employees and the black house slaves waited together in the unnatural, murky light. The blacks stood like sentries and everyone else sat on chairs or on the floor. Overseer Thompson was not there. Zachary heard the cracking of fallen trees and the groaning of the Great House as it fought the storm. Water forced its way through the locked and battened shutters and slaves tried to clean it up, wringing their rags in buckets. The more familiar sounds of thunder and lightning were a relief, because he could not identify many of the other sounds. Every now and then, one of the men would try to peek between the shutters. Others would ask, "See anything?" The first man would shake his head.

At about midday, the gale stopped abruptly. Zachary thought he had gone deaf, so shocking was the silence. He stood, surprised no one else moved.

"It's the eye of the storm, Mr. Macaulay," Charlotte said. "It will not last long. The storm will return from the other direction." Zachary was revising his opinion of her. She had courage. She came nearer. "Would you like to go and see?" she whispered.

"Aye," he said and felt a sudden excitement. She took his hand and led him through a side door. No one appeared to notice them. He saw the floors were awash. She pushed open another door and they were in a large cupboard that held outdoor clothes. She shut the door and fell on him, her mouth devouring. This time he did not resist and fully clad and in the silent vacuum of the eye of the storm, he had her against the wall.

Afterwards, his body felt slack and his eyes heavy. He wanted to stretch out on a soft bed and give himself up to sleep. He found himself smiling; the hurricane must have gone. There was no eye; it was all over. And now he was finally a man – a man made in a stuffy cupboard with his employer's daughter. He had no idea what to say to Charlotte, who was cleaning her thighs with an old scarf and rearranging her skirts. She tucked the scarf deep into her bosom and smoothed her hair. She met his ebbing smile and patted his cheek. "Let's go and see if we can open a window."

The Great House seemed intact, although the floors were

flooded. They did not go upstairs. "The real danger is losing the roof," she said, "and afterwards." He did not ask about afterwards. He was still thinking about their encounter in the cupboard. She crossed to a window.

"Why don't ye open it?" he asked.

"I'm afraid I won't be able to get it closed again. The wood might have swollen. Or there could be debris. Let's go back. There's nothing we can do anyway; there'll be more than enough time to see." She sounded remote.

"Charlotte…" he said.

"No." He did not know what she was rejecting. "Let's go back," she said again.

In the dining hall, Zachary was surprised to find most people as he had left them. He thought they had been away for hours. No one looked at him. A few men were standing by the table, eating. He joined them, his face flaming, sure everyone knew what had happened. He helped himself to some cold chicken. He kept his back turned to the women.

There was no warning before the storm returned. Out of the dense silence, the wind hit the house with a solid blow and there was a tearing sound. "The roof," one of the men said. "It's gone."

"Perhaps not all of it," another said. The wind rose to a screech and the house shook. Zachary thought of his mongrel catching a rat; the way he shook it in his jaws until it went limp, and then discarded it, losing interest. He returned to his place on the floor and closed his eyes. Although the storm still raged, and Bonnie Valley's roof might have gone, he slept.

The storm eased at dusk, but rain still pelted down and it was agreed it was too dangerous to go outside. They would have to wait until morning to see what awaited them. The dining room had stood up to the hurricane, but they knew the house itself had been damaged. The men began to make jokes and light cigars. The women fanned the smoke away. The slaves dried the floors.

"Should we at least open a window, gentlemen?" Charlotte asked. "It's become stuffy in here." Zachary watched her from the floor, his limbs heavy. His headache was gone. He looked around for Charles Monmouth. He stood with the men, smoking, his face serious. When his daughter spoke quietly to him, he put out his cigar and with a slight incline of his head, suggested the other men to do the same.

"I don't think so, my dear. There could still be flying debris. We may have an uncomfortable night, but we are safe here. Please," he gestured to the people in his dining room, "refresh yourselves. It has been a long day and will be a longer night."

Zachary felt the tension in the room abate. The rain still fell and thunder shuddered in the distance, but the sounds of destruction had stopped. Slowly, people stood, arranging their clothes, stretching, wandering over to help themselves to food. One of the slave women tried to light the wall lamps, but the wicks were damp, and she was too short for the task. Zachary took a step to help her and then stopped. He looked around for one of the male slaves, but they were not in the room. The woman kept trying to light the lamps. Zachary wondered what would happen if all the slaves took advantage of the storm to run away. No one would come to help with the lamps. The whites would stay in darkness forever, watching the slave woman trying to light their lamps. They would not help her. Then Sutton returned and took the tallow from her and the lamps' flames held.

The first glow of dawn shook the room awake like a gong. Led by Charles Monmouth, the men walked to the huge front doors. Sutton struggled to open them.

"Get out of the way," Monmouth said, and tried to pull back the brass bolts. They were stuck. "Break them down," he ordered.

"Massa? Me try again," Sutton said, working the bolts back and forth.

"Do what I tell you, you worthless black piece of shit," Monmouth said.

"Yes, Massa." Sutton walked away and returned with one of the pokers from the fireplace. He eased the end under the lower bolt and applied his weight. The bolt sprang free. He could not get the same leverage on the top bolt and it remained stuck.

"Break it down, I say," Monmouth said. Sutton hit the huge doors with the poker, but did no more than make dents in them. The other men looked around for wood and iron and, together, they splintered the carved mahogany doors.

Zachary followed the men into a grey, rainy morning. They stood on the verandah in a line, like troops preparing to repel a siege. The mist was low, the farm buildings obscured and the hills were lost. The giant cedar tree near the house was uprooted and thrown down, its roots pointing to the sky.

Then Zachary saw the devastation that surrounded them. The land had been laid waste. Every plant and tree had been stripped of its leaves, debris was piled against any fence that stood, but most fences were down. The river had burst its banks and, thick with soil, was spreading across the South Field.

They turned to look at the Great House. Half the roof was gone. They could see straight into rooms through what had been shuttered windows. Furniture was piled high, partly hidden by a mess of debris. Zachary could see that even the wooden door frames had been torn away. He could not imagine the force of a wind that would remove door frames.

"Macaulay," said Charles Monmouth. "Go back inside and tell the women they are to remain on the lower floor. The upper floor is unsafe. They are to ensure the slaves clean up and replace the furniture and restore the kitchen to working order."

"Sir," Zachary said. He went inside. The women were much as he had left them. He found Mrs. Monmouth in a rocking chair, bent over needlework. He delivered his message and she nodded. He thought she failed to recognize him.

When he went outside, the men had gone. He could see them picking their way down the hill towards the boiling house. He knew Monmouth was facing financial ruin and he was reluctant to join them. He circled the Great House, climbing over fallen trees, branches, doors, windows, the pieces of a chair, even the cauldrons used to cook large meals. The kitchen still stood, although the roof was peeled off in one corner. He looked inside and saw the house slaves, including Olivia, trying to restore order. The floor was covered with smashed crockery.

He walked over to Bell Cottage. The rain came harder, but the mist was lifting, and as if he were part of the audience at a stage play, he saw the mist rise to reveal his house an empty shell. The roof had gone. There were no windows or doors. All that remained were the walls. All his intact possessions were now in a bag in the dining room at Bonnie Valley. He stood at what used to be the front door and looked inside. Everything was filthy and destroyed and he could not recognize any individual piece of furniture. He saw the school bell had survived the storm. He rang it and the sound echoed from the roofless walls.

Numb, he ran to Palisade Paddock. He could hardly find his way; every landmark had been obliterated. He climbed over fallen trees. He saw a clump of drowned pigs. When he got to the paddock, the fence was down and every animal gone. He sank to his knees in the mud. No Miranda. No. Not the mare who had carried him safely to Bonnie Valley, not the companion who waited each evening at Cedar Paddock fence, not the horse with a big heart who had beaten Thor in a race.

The rain came in squalls and Zachary made his way back to the farm buildings. He passed the vegetable garden; it was destroyed, the plants flattened or uprooted. The fields of young cane were flat. As he approached the boiling house, he saw animals gathered and began to hope Miranda was among them. The visibility was poor and from a distance, he could not distinguish between horses and mules. He came closer: horses, mules and cows milled nervously, but Miranda was not among them.

It rained all day. Zachary abandoned his solitary wanderings and joined the men, who were assessing the wreckage to the plantation's workings with stern faces. It was not their first hurricane. Drenched, dirty, despairing, he trailed after them, listening for solutions. He wished he could go back to the women, to the lesser obstacles presented by the damaged Great House. There, a room still stood. Food graced a table. Outside, he saw a dead black woman and her child in the corner of the mule pen, barely visible through the mud. The woman's lifeless arms held her child close. Animals and machinery had been stored in the hurricane house, but there had not been enough room for the over four hundred slaves of Bonnie Valley and many had faced the storm unsheltered. Zachary realized he had not seen Thompson, whose brown skin had denied him the sanctuary of the Great House.

He continued walking; aimless, heartbroken, trying to assimilate the evidence of his eyes. He passed the slave village: every building had been destroyed. A few wattle-and-daub walls still stood, but there was no structure capable of providing shelter. Men picked over the wreckage and women held sobbing children. Zachary saw another dead body; a man lying in the mud, face up, head smashed, eyes open. He raised his eyes to the hills and he saw the distant mist had cleared. The hills looked like the unshaven stubble of an old man. Bonnie Valley was finished.

"My father instructs us to take a journey," Paul said. He stood at Zachary's door. The roof on Bell Cottage had been replaced. Basic furniture had been repaired or built. Even in the aftermath of the hurricane, Charlotte had kept her word to replace Olivia and Zachary's new housekeeper, Anna, was a much better cook. Olivia had been sent to the fields and sometimes Zachary saw her, labouring with the women's gang. She never looked at him.

"A journey?"

"A buying trip."

"What are we buying?"

"Everything. Slaves. Animals. Horses. Corn, if we can get it. Food is getting short here. We've eaten too many animals and our stores are almost gone."

"Where are we going?" Zachary asked.

"South coast. A place called Paradise. The owner is selling up."

"When?"

"Tomorrow at dawn."

"How long will we stay?"

"However long it takes. Not more than a few weeks, though. We need slaves badly; can't wait for the next sale."

"I'll get ready," Zachary said. It would be good to leave Bonnie Valley for a while, even in Paul's company. The weeks since the hurricane had been hard. Miranda had not been found; more than a hundred animals had been lost, and Zachary rode a temperamental mule named Hector. He mourned his horse and felt he did not want another. Charlotte had told him that this was not an option – white people had to be mounted on horseback, that he should look for a horse on the trip with Paul. It was a chance, too, to get away from her. She'd taken to visiting Bell Cottage every few weeks. She gave him no warning and he never sought to make an arrangement in advance. She came at night, often just as he had closed his eyes. He would hear her tapping her fingernails on his window and he would get up, trying to remember when last he'd bathed, and let her in. Their couplings were much as the first one had been: hurried, furtive, embarrassed. She never stayed the night. He had no idea what she wanted of him, but he craved her visits and since he feared her answers, he asked no questions.

Zachary considered his preparations for the trip. There was little to do because he had little to take with him. Mrs. Monmouth had given him some of Paul's old clothes. He ordered Anna to prepare field food: some dried herring so old and flaky it looked like weathered thatch, a too-green plantain roasted dry, a few cakes of cassava and a heel of roasted yam. He filled Trevor Manning's canteen with water. He wondered if he should bid Charlotte goodbye. She would know he was going. If she wanted to see him, she would do so. He slept fitfully, waiting for the tap of her fingernails on the shutters, but it did not come.

He got out of bed before dawn. Anna served him the last of the eggs he had been allocated. There was no fresh fruit, no bread, little meat. Even water had been rationed in the first week after the storm, because the river roiled with dirt. Charlotte had organized a bucket gang of slaves who dipped the muddy water from Bonnie Valley's tanks and strained it through stretched muslin into other buckets. Then the water was boiled in the huge sugar coppers. The one thing Bonnie Valley was not short of was wood.

Zachary was glad to be leaving the broken valley. As they rode towards the gates, he glanced at the downed cedar tree and thought he saw a faint green tinge among the dead branches.

They rode without stopping. They spoke little. One of the gang bosses, Hannibal, rode behind them in a small cart harnessed to one of the mules. A wooden barrel of water was lashed inside along with other stores. Zachary missed Miranda's long smooth stride; Hector's trot was choppy and his canter a test of endurance. When they came to the fork in the road, they turned away from the coast-path Zachary remembered from the day of his arrival, and they headed into the hills. The sign to Bonnie Valley was gone.

After three nights and four days, the forest lightened and the path widened. They began to see signs of cultivation and clusters of miserable dwellings with reddish front steps. "Who lives in those places?" Zachary asked Paul.

"Free slaves," he said. Zachary imagined trying to survive on the island without the cocoon of the plantation's wealth. He saw women come to their doors and immediately retreat inside when they saw the small party.

In a village called Abbey, they found a tavern with stabling for the animals and a barracks with rough beds. The tavern owner was a black man and Zachary wondered at his story. Mostly the freed men were mulattoes. They asked for lodgings and Paul decreed his price. The tavern owner did not argue and called them "Massa", ducking his head whenever he was spoken to.

That night they ate hot food: pepper-pot soup, spicy with bird peppers, thick with okra and the flesh of land crabs, served with cassava cakes and rum. The men who worked there watered and rubbed down the horse and the mule. There was no corn for the animals, but swaths of guinea grass were cut from a nearby hillside. A river was nearby and the water was cold and sweet. Dizzy with exhaustion, Zachary fell into a deep sleep as soon as he lay down. In the night, he was disturbed by grunts. He lifted his head. At the other end of the room, he saw Paul on top of a black woman, his hand across her mouth.

Finally, they saw the sea in the distance. They had followed the river and slept each night in taverns along the way. In a village called Barton they asked the way to Paradise Plantation, and within an hour, were riding down a long path lined with tall palm trees. The air here had a different quality; it was heavy and smelled of rotting vegetation. The mosquitoes were fierce. Zachary hoped no one in their party would get a fever.

It was just past noon when Paul walked up the steps of the main house and knocked. Zachary could immediately see this was not a wealthy plantation. The house was in poor repair; its roof was partly wood and partly thatch. There were no flower beds or lawns. The house sat on about an acre of cleared land and the bush waited to reclaim it. The cane fields were patchily planted and the rows uneven. He could see no evidence of work taking place.

A bleary-eyed white man answered their knock. He threw the door open. "Aye?" he said. "What in the name o' damnation d'ye want?" Zachary saw he held a young black girl by her wrists. Her clothing was torn and her face was streaked with tears. The man's face was florid with sunburn and drink. Zachary could not guess his age, but the girl was very young. His manner softened when he saw his visitors.

"Come about the sale, have ye?"

"Yes," Paul said.

"Go on with ye." He released the girl. "I'll be needing ye as soon as these men leave; make sure I don't have to look for ye or ye'll be pissing blood for a week. Get some refreshments for them," he added as an afterthought, and then to the travellers, "Come in. Your neger can take the animals to the stables."

"Our need is urgent," Paul said, remaining in the saddle. "You will have heard news of the hurricane that hit the north coast. We would prefer to see what you have for sale immediately."

"Aye, I heard. We were hit last year. This place never recovered."

"I'm Paul Monmouth from Bonnie Valley Plantation and this is our book-keeper, Zachary Macaulay."

"Bonnie Valley, eh? I've heard of it. Rich, resident owner. Not like this place; the owner of Paradise has never seen it." He hawked and spat to one side.

"You're the overseer then?" Paul asked.

"Douglas Maguire at your service, Sir." He made a parody of bowing.

"How long have you been here?"

"Too long. Coming on two years. After the hurricane, owner decided to sell up. Reap one more crop and then be shot of the whole thing. Aye, and I'll be glad to go. Only entertainment is fucking the slaves; or flogging them." He spat again. He winced as he walked past them down the steps. "Got a dose of the clap," he said, conversationally.

Two hours later, they had seen Paradise Plantation. It was

inappropriately named. Much smaller than Bonnie Valley, it was flat and ringed with swamps. The fields were planted on low hills Douglas Maguire called islands. "In the wet season," he explained, "all the bottom land is flooded and teeming with crocodiles. Aye, and 'tis a wretched place. The owner was sold a bill of goods, but will he hear that? Can't keep the slaves working; every month, two or three die of the fever." The buildings might once have been well constructed, but now were little more than shacks. The machinery was rusted and old. Zachary saw the overseer and book-keeper slept in barracks; there was no equivalent of Bell Cottage. There was no hospital. The slaves themselves were emaciated and disfigured from beatings indiscriminately applied to every part of their bodies. Zachary began to feel angry.

He saw a slave girl in the stocks. She was naked. He could not see her face, but he judged her to be no more than twelve. Her back was torn and bloody and her head hung low. Her legs were spread. "Her? She's dead," Maguire said, following Zachary's stare. "Had her myself before her flogging two days ago, though. Young black meat. Telt them tae bury her. No matter how much I beat them; they flout my orders. Winchester!" he bawled to an old man, walking around the side of a building.

"Did I not tell ye tae bury the verminous cunt? Do ye want tae join her in the grave?" Winchester did not answer, but walked over to the stocks and released the girl. She fell limp into the dirt and he squatted beside her, stroking her hair.

"His fifth daughter," said Maguire. "A good stud."

Zachary was suddenly desperate to get out of this fever-infested, disease-ridden place. He wondered at the good fortune that had brought him to Bonnie Valley instead of this hell-hole. Yes, the slaves there were beaten, but not in this arbitrary way. There were reasons. He started to list Bonnie Valley's attributes: the buildings were kept in good repair; every inch of the plantation showed evidence of a careful tending; the elevation rendered the air relatively free of miasmas; Charles Monmouth managed his workforce well, using punishment only when he thought it necessary; there was medical attention after punishment.

He watched the old man pick up his naked, violated daughter from where she lay in the dirt. He held her in his arms, her limbs lolling, his head bent to hers as if in silent prayer. He was going to bury her, bury his daughter, perhaps in a peaceful place, and he would say a prayer to his gods over her grave. He would visit his daughter's grave in the months afterwards, until he too succumbed to disease, overwork or torture. People said slaves did not have souls and were a step removed from people. Zachary watched the old black man in ragged clothes walk away with his dead daughter. In that instant, the differences between Bonnie Valley and Paradise became excuses, mere matters of degree, the difference between twenty-nine strokes of the cowskin lash and thirty strokes, the difference between a bed and a filthy floor after torture, between rape and rape, death now and death tomorrow. There was no difference. He thought of Victoria eating dirt, hoping, according to Paul, to hasten her own death. Perhaps a man would prefer to be in a place like Paradise with its earlier, certain end, than at Bonnie Valley, with its thin veneer of care.

They completed their mission hurriedly. Maguire brought out the slaves and Paul walked down the line of men, women and children, looking them over. "Tell them to take off their clothes," he ordered. Zachary closed his eyes. He longed for the forest; it was clean there, empty of this barbarity. He saw Hannibal standing in front of the slaves, a knotted end of rope in his hand. He was impassive as the Paradise slaves stripped to the skin.

Paul was decisive and his choices were quickly made. The youngest, strongest slaves were selected; six men and four women, one heavily pregnant. No children. One of the women wailed as a small child was taken from her. "Do, Massa, do," she cried, dropping to the dirt in a position of prayer, her hands raised. "Lemme take mi chile. Mi carry she. She grow big an' strong to work fi you. She do man work. In di name a Jesus. In di name a God. Mercy, Massa."

"Take the child away," Paul said, wheeling Thor around. "Chain them. What field rations do you have?" he asked Maguire. The woman's wails became shrieks.

"Wait," Zachary said.

"You have something to contribute, Mr. Macaulay?"

"She's a Christian. Someone must have baptized her."

"Quite possibly. I've heard there are missionaries preaching to these sorry creatures, imagining they have souls to be saved. But she and the child will not make it across the mountains."

"Send her with the stores. Ye said ye would send the stores by road."

"There seem to be few stores."

"We've no finished our inventory. Let us do that. Perhaps there will be enough and then this woman and her bairn can travel with them. She will be grateful to ye and a good worker, I reckon."

Paul laughed. "You have not been in the Indies long enough. Grateful? Loyal? These are not words these negers know. But let us complete our inventory and see. At the very least it will stop that infernal noise."

Zachary wanted to haul him from his horse and grind his smug, well-fed, good-looking face in the dust. Paul had striking eyes – grey-green like the Martha Brae River, but they were cold. Zachary had seen babies and children around Bonnie Valley with those eyes. "Thank ye," he said, his voice shaking, sorry the grateful words had escaped him.

"Don't thank me yet. This is business. Chain the slaves. Keep the child with the woman for the moment," he snapped at Hannibal. "Shut your useless mouth," he said to the woman.

Stocks of corn were found, along with packets of seeds, hogsheads in good repair, saddles and harnesses, tools, a few pieces of fine furniture.

"My mother will love this," Paul said, running his hands over a dressing table made of a light, glowing hardwood.

"It's yacca," Maguire said. "Comes from the Blue Mountains, so I'm told."

Hannibal loaded the wagon with some of the corn. They refilled their water barrel and purchased field rations: dried herring and cassava cakes. Zachary made lists and tallied up the amount owing. The slaves were listed by name, approximate age and identifying marks: Cyrus, approx. 30, brand TT; George, approx. 25, no brand, scars on face; Simon, approx. 25, missing little finger, left hand; Marly, 20, brand Triangle P; Samba, 25, lost left eye; Elizabeth, under 20, pregnant, burn scars on her breasts; Marilyn, 25, brand XX; Gail, 25, no marks, light skin, house slave? and Amy, 20, mother of Clarissa, female child, 2 years, brand &!, no marks. Zachary wanted to write: She fought for her child. Then another thought: so would a bitch for its pup. He shook his head. His thoughts buzzed like tormented bees.

Arrangements were made for the large items to be sent by sloop to The Rock on the north coast, and thence by carriage to Bonnie Valley. Amy and her child would be included. She was unclipped from the line of slaves and she scooped her daughter into her arms, covering her face with kisses.

"Get her out of my sight," Paul snapped.

It was nearly four in the afternoon. Zachary wondered if they would spend the night at Paradise Plantation. He was impatient to leave; the bush was infinitely preferable to this sweltering, brutal place. "We can make Barton by dusk," he said to Paul.

"Yes."

"How will ye make sure our stores are collected?"

"The trader is well known to us. The sloop should be on its way. Maguire would not dare default and risk the actions of my father." Zachary nodded, but privately thought it quite likely that Maguire would simply disappear with the money and leave Paradise to sink into the swamp: buildings, animals, slaves, all. He hoped for its rapid annihilation.

They left, straggling a little at first, but falling into an orderly line before they had passed through the row of feathery palms, Paul in front, Hannibal next with the loaded cart, then the eight ragged slaves, chained together at the neck. Zachary brought up the rear. He had longed to escape Bonnie Valley; now he yearned to see it as he had always seen it – the soft sea of sugar cane, the imposing Great House, the embracing hills in the distance. He longed for Bell Cottage, for his lost Miranda, for the occasional lavish meals at the Great House, for the sound of shell-blow at precisely the same time each morning and evening. All he could see was the father with his dead child. He found himself hoping that the shipment of plantation stores *would* be stolen and Amy and her girl set free; perhaps even to find passage on a boat to some other place. But what other place? Was there a small, unknown island, where a Robinson Crusoe-like existence would be possible, where the woman and the girl would grow strong and eat of the abundant sea and the fertile land? Wrung with emotions as violent as the hurricane, Zachary followed his employer's son and his employer's slaves back to the place he had once hoped to call home.

They had been gone only two weeks, but when they rode through the stone pillars, Zachary saw Bonnie Valley was recovering. Charles Monmouth's discipline and money had blunted the storm's impact. Roofs had been repaired, the slave huts had been rebuilt, new shoots emerged from the vegetable garden. The slave gangs were back in the fields, making rows, beginning to plant. And when Zachary walked into the stables and swung his leg stiffly over Hector's back, he heard a familiar whinny. He dropped Hector's rein. Miranda's head with the thin white blaze appeared over one of the stable doors. He saw she was thinner and her skin was scarred, but her coat was groomed and her eyes were bright. He walked over to her and she dropped her soft lips to his outstretched hand, nuzzling for sugar.

"We found her the day you left," Charlotte Monmouth said, behind him.

"Thank ye. Thank ye." He saw her dress was dirty. "I missed ye," he said, his voice low, wanting to give her something.

"Victoria found her. Victoria found her in one of the slave grounds. We ordered all their produce reaped; the plantation needed it. Victoria tried to escape with your horse. She was flogged. I think she's still in the hothouse."

Flogging and more flogging. Would there never be an end to it? Suddenly, he wanted the low, grey skies of Scotland, far from the blinding light of the tropics, far from a system that used human beings like beasts of burden. Yet, in Scotland, sugar graced tables; who was not complicit?

"Thank ye," he said.

"Let Sutton take your mule," she said. "Your horse – Miranda, isn't it? – she must remain stabled for now. The fence at Cedar Paddock has not yet been repaired. Come to the Great House for dinner tonight."

"Thank ye," he said again. "But no. I'm ower tired tae dae justice tae your hospitality. I hope ye will forgive me."

She nodded. "Of course. I'll be getting on then."

He laid his head on Miranda's white blaze. He yearned for the oblivion of ignorance. He would have to settle for the little death of sleep.

1885
Fortress, Trelawny Parish

John's brain seethed with plans. He designed his school in his mind. He thought of ways to influence the people. He would locate the few people who had come to church for his first service, befriend them; perhaps then they would invite others. He thought of Lillian Watt and hoped to see her as he went about his days.

Cuba, the farrier, had found him a horse and buggy for rent and John had travelled to Falmouth and attended a sale of effects from an abandoned plantation. He bought a roan gelding of obvious good breeding, a saddle, bridle and halter, two rocking chairs for his verandah, a stack of books, an entire chest of mosquito nets, blankets and other pieces of fabric, two chamber pots, two pleasant paintings, kitchen equipment and several kerosene lamps. He named the horse Friday, tethered him to the back of the buggy and paid for his other purchases to be delivered to Fortress. He wondered about the horse's previous owners, but no one seemed to know much. "Many plantations are selling off," the lawyer in charge of the sale told him. "Shame."

He pastured Friday in the field where he planned to build his school, forgetting what Prudence had told him about how the field was used. He added an afternoon ride to his routine, after his nap, and began to explore the countryside rather than the village – where no one spoke to him if he was mounted. He scouted for a river and found a charming spring nearby – Ulster Spring, it was called. There was a pool deep enough for baptisms, and he employed Cuba to clear a path to it.

Slowly, he learned the names of the people of Fortress. Prudence, who ran the shop, had no male partner and three children, all boys. Cuba lived with Ella and they had no children. Leroy and Patricia worked on Hampden plantation and had come to his first service with their children. They had both been born in slavery and had benefited from previous Christian instruction. His maid Irene had an adult son she had not seen in years. The woman who had refused to speak to him on his first walk was Icilda. She lived with her swarms of children and her ancient mother.

Then there were the men of Fortress, nine of them. They lived in an old slave barracks and hired themselves out as working gangs. They were thin, muscular and ragged and they congregated each evening in Prudence's shop and drank rum until they passed out. They smoked a sweetish-smelling weed they called ganja and were alleged to rape the daughters of Fortress.

The Bannisters were the only white family in the village. John refused to let that depress him. He told himself he was able to live alone with books, his Bible and his God; he was here in Fortress to do God's work. Still, during those early weeks, he looked out anxiously for Lillian Watt. Once, he saw her at a distance in Fortress's sparse, dilapidated market, but by the time he made his way over, she had climbed into a buggy and was gone. He feared she would return to Ireland and he would never see her again.

Letters arrived from Bruce; he was having a different experience. Cave Valley was more prosperous than Fortress and he had a lively congregation. There were three white families in the area, including a wealthy widower, still running a sugar cane plantation. Bruce travelled often to St. Ann's Bay and described a delightful coastal town set in a calm bay. John felt jealous. He replied, embellishing his life in Fortress. He described it as he wished it to be: he and the magistrate were friends, he was walking out with Lillian Watt, his school was under construction, his church was packed on Sundays, each week brought new baptisms, the villagers bowed their heads to him and smiled as he went on his way, he arbitrated in their disputes and prayed with them when their children fell ill.

But when he finished the letter, he folded it and put it in his Bible. He would not post it. He would use it as a plan, a guide, for the life he was constructing. He dashed off a single page to Bruce, writing lightly of the realities of his posting and assuring his brother he was well.

It was Cuba who provided the key to his eventual entrance into the lives of the people of Fortress. John sought his advice about the building of the school – he had received permission from the Baptist Mission for the undertaking, and even the promise of a teacher sent from Kingston. The farrier shook his head when John asked for his help with the construction.

"Dat field not good," Cuba said. He was pounding horseshoes on his anvil and a chestnut mare from one of the nearby plantations was tethered to a post nearby.

"Why not?"

"Mas Devon use it and Mas Georgie. Your horse eat it down and Mas Devon can't get fi cut grass to feed him goat. Him have to walk long-long way fi cut grass now."

Prudence had told him this. He felt both annoyance and shame. He had vowed to deal with the villagers on their own terms and already he was behaving like a planter. "But it's important the school is nearby or else no one will come."

Cuba hung one of the shoes on a nail in the wall and started on another. "Build di school next to di church. Nobody vex then."

"The land beside the church slopes; won't it be hard to build there?"

"Wi build di schoolroom on…" Cuba struggled for the right word. "Legs. Like dis." He demonstrated with pieces of waste wood.

"On stilts, you mean."

"Stilts? Eeh-he. Stilts."

John felt excited. It could work; assuming the person building the house had rudimentary woodworking skills. "Could you build it, Cuba?"

The farrier straightened and stretched his back. His face was shiny in the heat of the forge. The third horseshoe joined the others on the nail. This man could build Hadrian's Wall, John thought.

"Could build it, yes. Need two more man."

"How much? How long?"

"Well, depend how long it tek fi find wood. Not too much big tree leave 'round Fortress. If you buy wood in Falmouth, cost more, but time more short. What kinda roof you want? Thatch or tin?"

"Tin," John said, reckless. This was going to be a fine school.

"You want wall an window an door? Dat cost plenty more."

John had not considered a building could exist without walls,

165

windows and doors. Of course it could; this was the tropics. School would have to be suspended in the rain anyway; the pounding on the roof would drown out any teacher's voice.

"You tell me what's best."

Cuba pounded the fourth horseshoe. He did not speak for many minutes and John wondered if the conversation was over. The farrier picked up all four horseshoes and measured them against each other. John saw they were almost identical. Cuba walked over to the horse and spoke to her softly.

"Cuba? What sort of school should I build?"

"One room," the farrier said, picking up the horse's foreleg and fitting a shoe to the hoof. His head was bent over his work and John struggled to hear him. "About dis size. One back wall, facing di sunrise. Keep off di morning sun, but let in di breeze. Wooden floor. Railing 'round di outside; fi stop pickney fallin' over. Dem can use you outhouse." He began to file the horse's hoof and the shavings fell on his bare feet.

"Excellent. When can you start? What will it cost?"

"Five pound, if wi find di wood and tin. Another two fi di labour. I pay di odda man-dem. You decide."

"When can you start? How long will it take?"

"Start when you give two pound. Don't know how long. Depend on rain, odda work. It finish when it finish."

"Will you come with me to Falmouth to buy materials?"

"Dat anodda ten shilling; but could save you money." Cuba fitted the first shoe and began to drive the nails in, twisting each off as it appeared through the mare's hoof. John wondered who had trained the farrier to know just where to drive the nails.

"Can we go tomorrow?" he asked.

"Mi ready a daybreak." Cuba walked around the mare to start on the other foreleg.

Within a week, construction started on the school. Cuba had hired two of the Fortress men and the foundations were marked with string. The Reverend was disturbed by the heathen practice of pouring rum and the blood of a goat into the foundations, but judged it best not to object. He would deal with these old practices in time. The poles for the stilts were sunk and packed with stones, carried by hand from old walls that crisscrossed the land. John watched the men pack the stones, working stripped to the waist in the sun, raising their implements high and then bringing them down with steady, accurate blows. Sometimes the stones crumbled and even though the holes appeared full at first, after the men had pounded at them, there was a full foot of space at the top of each hole. More stones were fetched and the process repeated. While the men pounded, Cuba lined up the stilts with string, to make sure they were straight. The men did not speak as they worked and John heard few instructions from Cuba.

After a short time, John found himself unable to stand in the sun beside them. He could not imagine being able to wield the hammers, hour after hour. He felt ashamed of his slack muscles and white skin that burned easily. He would be useless in a cane piece or on a building site. He hovered near the men, in the shade provided by a scraggly shrub the villagers called macca bush. He could not quite bring himself to retreat to one of the rocking chairs on his verandah, to watch the work in comfort from a distance.

The work on the school started at dawn and stopped at eleven. Then the men ate bulla cakes and boiled yam and drank many bottles of ginger beer. They drew hard on their sweet smelling cigarettes and the smoke made John feel slightly ill. They rested under a nearby tree, their powerful bodies motionless; their eyes closed, their skins twitching when flies landed. They did not stir until nearly three o'clock, when the sun had passed its height, and then without words, they stood up, bits of grass and earth sticking to their backs and resumed work. John covertly studied their backs for signs of beatings, but these men were young; their backs were unmarked.

The villagers of Fortress turned out to watch the building, men, women and children. They brought food for the labourers and sometimes the women asked John for waste pieces of wood. The children had to be restrained from climbing the stilts and they ran around playing hide-and-seek and ring games. John tried to teach them to chant:

"*Make and mend and teach,*
Let honest work be done,
Let honest work be thine;

Do things within thy reach.
Reward, a hidden mine
Is lying at thy feet,
And tasks begun today
In God's own perfect way,
Shall bud and fruit complete."

Soon steps were built and John walked onto the newly-constructed floor of his schoolhouse. He tested the strength of the planks and looked out over the land. The schoolhouse faced away from the village and because it was raised, the breeze was light and sweet. It was an offering to God, a wooden plate lifted high, as yet empty of souls. He, John, would fill it, once the roof was finished.

On the day they began building the roof, Lillian Watt visited the site. She came in her buggy, driven by a male servant John had not seen before. He saw her slim figure and red hair visible under the sun top. He dashed inside his house to splash water on his face and comb his hair. He had not thought of Lillian much during the building of the school, but now he was in a fever to see her again – and to see her beside his achievement. He was waiting for her when the buggy pulled up and held out his hand. She took it and met his eyes; then lowered her lashes. Nurse Duncan, but he shook the thought away. "Miss Watt," he said.

"Pastor Macaulay, everyone's talking about your school, so I came to have a look." Her clothes were new and fashionable, her feet clad in leather boots with small heels and laces. He imagined undoing the laces. Her dress swished as she passed him.

"This is it." He pointed. The men pounded nails into the roof, sitting astride beams, balancing easily, spare nails in their mouths.

"No walls," she said, and the sun fell on her face, revealing its tiny hairs and the freckles that spattered her nose and cheeks.

"It's the tropics," he said.

"May I go up?"

"Aye, certainly. Be careful, though. Let me take your hand."

She offered him her elbow and they climbed the short flight of stairs to the school house.

"Oh my. What a view!"

"Beautiful, isn't it?" He held up his hand and the men stopped nailing. It fell quiet and the soft, afternoon breeze swirled around the people, the black men waiting to resume their work, the children paused in their games, the daughters of slaves staring at the white woman's elaborate clothes.

"Do you have a teacher?" Lillian asked.

"The Baptist Union in Kingston said one would be assigned once the school was finished. I will begin Sunday school in the meantime."

"Hmm."

"Why do you ask?"

"Well, Pastor, I wondered… no, it's silly of me."

"What is it? Please speak frankly."

"I am a schoolteacher. I taught in a primary school."

"Did you really, Miss Watt?"

"I did. I would so like to help with your school. My time here is almost up, but I would like to stay, and I need some occupation."

"Have you discussed this with your uncle?"

"I have. He's not in favour, naturally." She lowered her voice. "He doesn't believe in education for the Negroes."

"How will you stay then?"

She shrugged and he saw determination in her steady gaze. "I will find a cottage. I will teach in your school, until your replacement teacher arrives. Then – who knows?"

"I'm not sure it's safe for a young woman to stay alone in Fortress. The pay for a teacher will be small. And I don't know of any dwelling remotely suitable."

"I have few needs," Miss Watt said. "And I've seen a place I like: an old stone cottage on the East Road. They say it was a tavern for travellers in the old days. It just needs some repair."

John revised his opinion of her financial status. "Do you know your Bible?"

"I do. But I had planned to leave the religious instruction to you." She smiled at him and the space between them narrowed. "I will teach the pickneys their letters and numbers. You will take care of their souls."

She had obviously given this some thought. He became aware that work remained suspended. "Come, Miss Watt," he said. "Have tea with me. We'll talk about this further. We should let the men get on with their work."

"Of course. I'd be delighted to have tea with you." She linked her arm in his as they walked down the schoolhouse steps.

"Continue with the work, Cuba," John said, as they left.

The hammering began again. The children chased each other and the mothers watched; it was a golden afternoon. Pastor John and Lillian Watt settled into the rockers on the missionary's verandah – he thanked God he had purchased two chairs – and, together, watched the sun disappear behind the hills.

The roof of the school was almost finished, when, one day, the men did not appear. John had become used to being woken by the sounds of their work, and on this particular morning, he slept unusually late. The rooster had been silent and no sounds of construction had disturbed his sleep. He woke slowly, feeling a languid satisfaction. His courtship of Lillian was going well and soon he would ask for her hand in marriage. His dreams were coming true: he had found a woman to share his life, even here, in this tiny village. The hand of God was resting lightly on his shoulder; prayers of gratitude constantly filled his thoughts.

Lillian was still staying with her uncle, who had refused to countenance her living in the village. "Inviting rape and murder," he had said. Lillian had acquiesced, and each evening she and John rode out together. She was an inexpert horsewoman, so their rides were slow and filled with conversation. He learned she had become engaged to the publican recklessly, without her father's approval. He had been violent, and then killed in a fight. She had longed to travel, and when her father suggested a visit to the Indies, she had not hesitated.

John swung his legs over the bed, first checking his shoes. Rubbing his eyes, he went onto the verandah and looked at the school. There it was, the wood unweathered, the steps inviting, the railing secure. The roof was three-quarters finished. Where were the men? It would soon be the rainy season and he was anxious to have the roof completed before then.

"'Morning, Pastor," Irene said behind him.

"'Morning. What happened to the work crew?"

Irene shrugged. "Breakfast ready soon."

"Breakfast?" He was sick of the unvarying diet of cassava and salt fish. The Bannisters had shared a shipment of salt fish with him, exhorting him to keep it locked away from Irene or any other resident of Fortress. There'd been a few days relief from monotony when Irene had killed one of the hens, and they'd had a tough, but flavourful chicken stew. He realized how little he had considered the food situation in Fortress during the building of the school and his courtship of Lillian. He felt guilty, but told himself that he was putting things in place that would ease the villagers' burdens. He ate quickly, still wearing his nightshirt. He had become so used to Irene's hovering ubiquity that he longer observed the conventions for being in the presence of a woman.

He washed, dressed and walked down to the crossroads. Cuba must be ill. Although they had exchanged few words unrelated to the construction of the school, he regarded Cuba as an ally. He rode to the farrier's shop and was surprised to find the front door open for business.

"Cuba? Are you there?" Belatedly he added, "Is someone ill?"

Cuba came out through a narrow door at the back. John wondered fleetingly about his and Ella's living quarters – most of the dwelling was given over to the forge. Cuba wore only rough trousers and was wiping his hands on a rag. "Yes, Pastor?" he said.

"Why is no one working on the school?"

"Di man-dem get anodda work. About a week."

"But why? Why didn't they finish the school first? Irene tells me it will soon be the rainy season. Surely we had an agreement?" He was angry at Cuba's acceptance at the men's defection, then realized he did not know the names of the two men who had helped build the school. They were Fortress men; that was all.

"Dem soon come back. Di school soon finish."

"But when? You should have made sure they finished one job before starting another one."

"Soon."

They faced each other. "This is not right," John said. Cuba did not reply. He took in Cuba's physical presence: his powerful torso, his nappy hair, the touch of grey in the stubble on his face, his eyes sunk deep in his face, the whites faded to yellow, his fingers short and swollen, the skin around his neck loose.

"Can you not do some work yourself?"

"Hard. Hard to do a roof alone. Need a man on di ground."

"Could you not find another man to help?"

"All di man-dem gone."

So he was not counted as a man of Fortress! But what was there to stop him being the man on the ground? He tried to visualize it; he would dress in rough clothes, although not stripped to the waist, as his uncovered skin would blister and burn in less than half an hour. The weakness of his body would be exposed for all to see. The Bannisters would conclude he had gone native if not mad. Perhaps Lillian Watt would then refuse to have anything to do with him.

"I'll help you."

"Eeh?"

"You said you need a man on the ground. I'll be the man."

"You, Pastor?"

"Och, how hard can it be? The roof is nearly finished. I'll be the man on the ground. Come. Let's start right now."

Cuba's rigid stance softened. John thought he might smile, but his face remained sombre. "Tomorrow den, Pastor. Too late now. Sun high. Tomorrow at cock crow."

"Tomorrow, then."

The next morning, as a dusky grey light washed the land, Cuba knocked on the door. John was already awake, clad in his oldest clothes. He had not eaten or drunk his tea. They walked through the wet grass to the school, faintly backlit by the dawn. The moon hung pale in the sky and John felt apprehensive. What did he know about building a roof?

"How long to finish?" he whispered to Cuba. Perhaps the roof could be completed before the village woke. To his eye, there was not much left to do. Cuba made no response.

The remaining sheets of tin were stored inside the half-finished building. Cuba moved them himself, slinging several sheets onto his head at a time with a single sweep of his arms. He leaned them against one of the upright poles. He gathered a cloth bag of nails and secured his tools in another bag around his waist. He swung his legs onto the roof and settled himself on one of the

172

rafters. "Pass dat piece dere." He pointed to a long plank. John took a deep breath and hefted a heavy length of wood he had seen handed around the building site as if it were a mere handful of grass. He struggled, but managed to get the wood up to Cuba who fitted it into place with one hand.

The people of Fortress woke to the sight of Cuba astride the roof, and Pastor John, dirty and evidently flagging, on the ground, using his ebbing strength to slide wood and tin up to the farrier. The villagers stared and conferred with each other and before the arc of the sun could be seen over the hills, they had joined the work. The women took the lengths of wood from John, handed him bulla cake and a mug of cocoa tea and he collapsed, feeling dizzy on the grass. The work went faster and the gap in the roof was closed.

"Tired, Pastor?" He looked up and saw Icilda, flanked as she always was by her children.

"Very, Icilda," he said, reaching for her name.

"School soon finish." She looked up at Cuba. John followed her gaze and they watched him, the sun outlining his powerful shoulders, his arms raised to drive the nails perfectly into the wood. "Want some more cocoa tea?" John did not have the heart to say that he could not face any more of the bitter, hot drink, that his stomach heaved, that perhaps he had a touch of sunstroke, that his hands were blistered and would probably get infected, that all he wanted was to go inside and lie in his darkened room with a cool cloth on his brow.

"Aye, that would be nice, Icilda."

He composed a telegram to his brother. He was getting married and he wanted Bruce to conduct the ceremony. It was December and his life in Fortress had taken a pleasing shape. He was carrying out regular baptisms, sometimes at Ulster Spring, sometimes in the Martha Brae; his church was filling up on Sundays, although he had to concede his congregation consisted mostly of women. He judged the school a success. The children came at least three days each week, their faces washed, their eyes wary. Lillian led the lessons, mainly using chanting and repetition as her teaching style. They had not managed to procure books, slates or chalk.

The other labourers had not been happy to find the school

completed without them and rancorous negotiations ensued. In the end, John had paid full price for the job they had left undone. In truth, he feared this band of men: their scowls, their drunkenness, the sounds of contempt they made which Irene called "kiss teeth", their voices always raised in some contention, their aura of physical strength.

He had asked Bannister for Lillian's hand in marriage and he had agreed. John had written to his father and asked if he could have his mother's wedding ring to give to his bride. There had been no reply. Cuba made him a ring of copper, melted from an old jug, fashioned in an intricately entwined plait, faintly green. Lillian appeared entranced; they planned the wedding early in January. The Bannisters had wanted the wedding to take place in Falmouth, where people of substance could be invited, but John was adamant he would be married in his own church. He wanted to set an example to his congregation, all of whom lived in sin without benefit of the marriage sacrament. To his sermons on the importance of marriage, the people of Fortress seemed deaf. Even those in stable partnerships did not respond to his exhortations.

He handed the telegram to Leonie, the postmistress.

"'Morning, Pastor," she greeted him. She was an enthusiastic member of the church; she sat in the very front and punctuated the service with lusty "Praise hims!" and "Amens!" It was she who had taught him how to engage the villagers in the service.

"And what did the Lord ask of Abraham?" he would ask.

"To sacrifice him son," the congregation would chant.

"What persuaded Abraham put the knife to his son's throat?"

"Faith inna di Lawd! Praise be to God," they responded.

Leonie's daughters, Charmaine and Faith, regularly attended school. Her son, Silbert, unfortunately, preferred to roam the bush with a slingshot, bringing down birds too small to eat.

"'Morning, Leonie."

"What you have for wi dis Sunday, Pastor?" Leonie was always anxious to tell everyone the contents of his sermons in advance.

"Wait and see, Leonie, wait and see. I still haven't seen Silbert in school. When are you going to send him?"

"Lawd, Pastor. Dat boy. Him bad; him bad so 'til. Him is a

cross to bear fi true. Him don't listen to one word. Mi try wid him, but him won't go school. What you have dere?"

"A telegram for my brother. He's in Cave Valley."

"Him a minister too?"

"Yes. I want him to come and conduct the wedding ceremony for myself and Miss Watt."

"When di weddin'?"

"January."

Leonie took the telegram, stamped it with the vigorous authority of the civil servant and he paid. He bade her good day and walked out into what he had come to call the square. The food shortage had begun to ease. Crops planted by the villagers were being reaped and the small market was full of women, some buying, others displaying earthy yams and ripe bananas and mounds of gungo peas. The villagers greeted him as they hurried about their business. Fortress was a happier place; he was sure of it. He thanked the Lord for His many blessings.

Zachary slept through a night and half a day. There were no longer any luxuries in Bell Cottage – no framed water colour paintings, no mosquito net, no commode. But the bed was comfortable and even though he sweated in the heat, he woke refreshed. He had missed shell-blow. He did not know what day it was. He called for Anna and food was brought, still limited, but more appetizing than anything he had eaten in weeks. She brought a basin with water and he washed. The looking glass in his bedroom had gone and he shaved with difficulty. He could feel his hair was long and untended. He directed Anna to wash it for him; he bent forward over the basin and she scrubbed his scalp with slices of prickly *toona*. "Thank ye," he said afterwards and the words came strangely to his tongue.

When he walked outside, he knew it was Sunday. The plantation dreamed in the sun. Miranda was back; he could resume his old pattern, take a ride to the river and bathe. But it was too hot and too late and he was tired of being astride. He missed the silhouette of the cedar tree against the sky. He saw the trunk had been removed and the tinge of green it sprouted had gone.

He walked down the hill to the hot house and went inside, steeling himself for the anguish those walls always held. He saw Victoria standing at one of the windows, staring out. She was dressed in a loose shift. She must be healing then. He called her name and she whirled, ready to fight or flee.

"Victoria, thank ye for finding my horse."

"Dem tek wi food," she spat. "*You* tek wi food. *Wi* food. Di food wi grow."

"I was not here," he said. "But surely the food was shared?"

"*Share?* Buckra massa tek what him want. We get what lef'. T'ree pickney die. One fi mi own."

"The boy I saw you with?"

"Nah. Di gal. Di gal wid green eye." He had never seen her with a girl child.

"You have to stop fighting, Victoria. They'll kill ye with beatings."

"Mi name Madu."

"What?"

"Madu. Dat di name mi madda gi' mi. On mi name day. Is mi name."

He felt helpless. He feared her spirit. "Where were you going wi my horse?" he asked. She did not answer and turned her back on him.

The stores from Paradise arrived intact. The yacca table found pride of place in Mrs. Monmouth's dressing room; Amy and her daughter were absorbed into the estate. Zachary saw her in the fields but she looked at him without acknowledgment. Paul was right; no gratitude. Yet what had he saved her from? Yes, she slept with her daughter at night, but still they laboured in a white man's field and another day of separation could come at any time. Perhaps he had bought them some time. Time might count for something. When the girl became a woman, she might remember the feel of her mother's arms and her stories, even if they had been long separated.

November brought welcome afternoon thunderstorms; they banished the enervating heat and work slowed. By December, the evidence of the hurricane was fading: the trees were clothed again with small, bright green leaves, the undergrowth fought for light, vegetables swelled on their stems. The temperature fell and the light was soft and clear. It would soon be Christmas.

Zachary turned to his books, the pages sticking together in the humidity, and to pen and paper to dissect his feelings. He wrote to every member of his family without restraint, describing life on Bonnie Valley, the tribulations of the slaves, the old man holding his dead daughter at Paradise, Victoria's flashing eyes. He ran out of paper and spent some of his savings to purchase more. He addressed all the letters to his mother, but when he wrote, he spoke to each one in turn: his father, his mother, his sisters, his brothers. He did not send any of the letters.

He wrote to Trevor Manning and asked for news from London. Manning replied that he was in Kingston and would send him newspapers. The hurricane had missed Kingston entirely. He invited Zachary to visit.

After the hurricane and the trip to Paradise, Zachary began to fantasize about owning Bonnie Valley; he would apply the many useful methods of management Charles Monmouth had shown him, but his workers would be paid; they would not be slaves. They would sing in the fields and their songs would be of praise, not rebellion. *"While heard from dale to dale, walking the breeze, resounds the blended voice of happy labour, love and social glee…"* Perhaps there were no dales in the tropics, but surely there could be happy labour. When he rode out on Sundays, he planned it all in his mind: *there* would be a village for the workers, a proper village, with a market, a post office and a tavern for travellers. There would be travellers; people would come from all over the world to see the community he had built. *There* would be the grounds for the workers; they would no longer have to walk long distances to tend and reap their crops. The gibbet and the stocks would be destroyed, cowskin whips banned and Dr. Whitby would deal only with fevers, injuries and childbirth. His fantasies made him smile as he rode with Miranda ever responsive to his heels and hands, Martha ranging the bush, returning when he whistled. His mongrel had never been found after the hurricane.

December brought nights cold enough for blankets and fires. The slaves lit bonfires and roasted yam and the rules regarding drums were relaxed. At night, Zachary heard the drumming and the songs of the slaves and he thought there was no stranger place in the world. Here was an island adrift in the Caribbean sea, populated by black men and women who beat drums and sang of their lost homeland, gathered around an open fire, while white men and women planned Christmas rituals from lands of snow and pine trees. A wreath of holly had been hung on the huge front door of the Great House. Could a bundle of holly have been sent all the way from England, slightly brown at the edges, but intact? What kind of world would give birth to such a decoration?

One night, unable to sleep, Zachary crept down to the slaves' fire and stood in the shadows, watching. He saw their black faces, slick from the heat of the fire, he watched them laugh and listened to their chants. They laboured and lived in conditions he witnessed but could not imagine, and yet here they sat, men, women and children, exultant. He had always felt blacks to be different from white people, wanting different things, fit for different, lesser occupations, but watching the scene by the fire, he felt himself to be the weaker version of humanity. He left without being noticed.

Christmas brought days off from work for the slaves and riotous celebrations. He avoided the parties at the Great House as much as was possible without giving offence. Enjoying the cool, clear nights, he walked the plantation paths in the dark. The fireflies flashed their tiny lights on the fences and dew shone on the grass.

Charlotte's visits had never resumed after his return from Paradise. He had been relieved. He had watched her for several months afterwards, looking fearfully for signs of pregnancy. He shuddered at the risks they had taken and remained mystified at her motives. On the night of the 1786 New Year's Eve celebrations, he went to bed early and lay staring into the darkness. He heard the scratching sounds Charlotte used to make on his window. He lay still and did not respond. When he heard the sounds of footsteps retreating down the path from Bell Cottage, he got up and looked through the shutters. In the moonlight, he saw it was not Charlotte but Sarah.

In January, his thoughts turned to leaving Bonnie Valley, to going home. He had not made a fortune, but he had savings, surely enough to buy his passage back to Scotland. He had no idea what he would do with his future. Yet he did not want to leave Bonnie Valley, its misty hills and rippling fields, the cold green river, the strange blue pools welling from the earth, the verdant, bursting forests, the flashing birds. He had grown to love his solitude, his adulthood. But he had come to hate his days in the fields and the boiling house, the feelings crawling under his white skin of guilt, fear and shame.

The mathematical side of his brain led him to start keeping records. His unsent letters, containing long descriptions of plantation life, stopped and he began compiling lists of Bonnie Valley's assets, the yields of its fields, the number of hogsheads of sugar that left the plantation, the quantities of vegetables reaped, the amount and type of animals, their births and deaths. He made lists of the slaves, their names, their brands, their ages – as far as could be determined; their relationships, sisters and brothers, children, grandmothers. To do this he had to speak to them, to ask questions, to frame sentences that were not orders or threats. He practised on Anna. She had been born on a plantation in St. Ann's, named for her birthplace, and had known her mother until she was sold on her fourteenth birthday to Bonnie Valley. She claimed not to remember her mother's name, but Zachary did not believe her. He knew she feared what he might do with the information.

He found only one slave who said he had been born in Africa. He was a man past forty, small and wiry, his back only lightly scarred. He had learned the art of survival, how to negotiate the white man's rules. He smiled at Zachary and answered questions readily, although Zachary struggled to interpret his thick Creole speech. His name was Matthew.

"What's your African name?" Zachary asked, remembering Victoria's vehement claiming of her name.

"No African name," Matthew said. "Mi a Christian."

"Ye must have had an African name if ye were born in Africa."

"No African name. Mi a Christian." He grinned like a lunatic.

"Who baptized ye?"

"One preacher in Barrett Town," Matthew said. So there *were* missionaries preaching to the slaves.

"What are you doing, you piece of black dung?" Zachary heard Thompson's voice behind them. "Get back to work! I'm surprised at you, Mr. Macaulay, encouraging laziness."

"My apologies, Mr. Thompson. It'll no happen again." Zachary found himself ducking his head, as he had seen so many slaves do.

It was the day of the wedding and John sat on his verandah, waiting for his brother. Christmas had come and gone; he and Lillian had eaten their Christmas dinner with the Bannisters and the people of Fortress had enjoyed their own celebrations. He had told and retold the story of Jesus' birth in a manger among the animals and the virgin status of his mother. The people of Fortress loved the part where the star appeared in the east, and often, when John sat on his verandah after supper, he saw the villagers staring in to the heavens, looking for a star of uncommon brightness. He smiled when he saw this.

He had not seen Lillian for a week. She had decided that they should spend this time before their wedding apart. All around him, he saw the preparations: the trimming of shrubbery, the cutting of the grass around the church, the whitewashing of buildings and the clearing of rubbish from the roads and paths. The village of Fortress would be on show. Friends of the Bannisters from Falmouth had been invited, but it was not known how many would attend. There were few places for white people to stay in Fortress, though there was a roadside tavern about two hours' ride away on the road to the coast where John hoped the people from Falmouth might lodge. He didn't care whether they attended or not, but wanted Lillian and the Bannisters to be happy. He had tried to explain why he wanted the people of Fortress to attend his wedding; it was for the saving of their souls, but he knew the Bannisters were offended. He wondered if they would come.

He thought about his father and his mother. He wished his mother could be at his wedding, but he knew she would be looking down from heaven and he felt sure she approved of Lillian. He had asked for her blessing many times while on his knees in prayer, and was sometimes tempted to take the wavering of the candle flame or the stirring of the curtains in his bedroom as a sign of her assent. But now he wished for her physical presence.

"'Mornin', Pastor," Irene said.

"'Morning."

"A di big day, eeh?"

"Aye, indeed. Are you coming to the wedding, Irene?"

"Mebbe. Some mint tea?"

"Don't change the subject, Irene. I want you to come. You're risking hell and damnation outside the love of Jesus. Can't you see that?"

"Tea soon come. Not much breakfast fi you today; plenty-plenty food fi later."

He sighed. Irene was resistant to the Christian message. Perhaps, though, when she saw all the women of Fortress walking past her, on their way to church, she would change her mind. He was sure this wedding was the most significant thing to happen in Fortress in living memory.

He heard the sound of hoof beats coming from the square; a horse coming at speed. He stood and looked down the road. A horse and rider was racing up to his house; it had to be his brother Bruce, unable to resist the feel of the wind on his face on a morning such as this one. Bruce brought his horse to a skidding stop and vaulted from the saddle. He threw the tethering rein over the fence and strode through the gate where John had run down to meet him. They embraced and John smelled horses, leather and a faint whiff of rum.

"Let me look at you," he said, holding Bruce at arm's length. Bruce's skin was weathered and he had new freckles on his face. He had gained weight and his belly strained at his clothes. He met John's eyes then looked away and John felt the ghost of something unsaid. He caught the whiff of rum again.

"Come in, my brother. I was just about to have breakfast. You must be hungry. How have you arrived so early?"

"Slept at the tavern last night. It's not far and I woke early, so I came to find you."

"Where are your things?"

"I left them at the tavern."

"Why? Aren't you staying here with me? I hoped we could spend some time together. You're here for more than a day or two, surely?"

Again Bruce looked away. "I can stay about a week. I thought it best to stay at the tavern; you and your new wife will need privacy."

This was plausible, but John did not believe it. The only other bedroom in his house was small and it was true, he and Lillian would have preferred to be alone on their wedding night, but he felt there was something Bruce was holding back.

"Bellevue is only an hour away."

"An hour at a flat gallop," John said, dryly. "You haven't changed."

"But it looks like you have. You look happy, my brother. I'm glad to see it." Bruce smiled and John felt these words genuine. There *was* something Bruce wanted to tell him; it would emerge in time. Perhaps Bruce had regarded John as unmarriageable and was surprised he had managed to find a bride in Fortress.

"Did you not bring robes?" John hoped his brother did not intend to conduct the wedding in jodhpurs.

'I brought a few things in my saddlebags. But I knew I could borrow whatever I needed from you. So what about that breakfast you promised me?"

"It's coming. Irene!" John called to the kitchen. "My brother is here. You'll have to set another place. Do you want to wash up?"

"Aye. Do you have a man to see to my horse?"

"No, but I could send to the village for one of the boys."

"Well, let's eat. The horse can wait. And then you can show me around. What time is the wedding?"

"Four. We have time." John showed Bruce into his bedroom and left him to wash. He instructed Irene to bring two more cups of mint tea, while she prepared more food. "Eggs," he told her. "We should have eggs this morning."

John sat on the verandah and waited to hear what his brother had not yet said.

After they had eaten, John walked him around the village. They left Bruce's horse with Cuba to be rubbed down, stabled and fed. They inspected the school and the church, which had an army of women working on it, directed, John was surprised to see, by Mrs. Bannister.

"Mr Macaulay, I know this is your church, but this morning you should not be here. It's bad luck," she said as they approached.

"May I present my brother, Bruce Macaulay, Mrs. Bannister? He will perform the wedding ceremony."

"A pleasure," Mrs. Bannister said. "Where are you based?"

"Cave Valley in St. Ann's. The pleasure is mine."

"We journeyed to the Indies together," John added. "We haven't seen each other for many months."

"A double celebration then."

"Indeed. The church is looking beautiful, Mrs. Bannister."

"And it is not yet finished. You gentlemen must be getting on."

They took their leave and John found himself at a loss. Even on foot, Fortress could be seen in less than an hour. It was not yet ten o'clock, breakfast had been eaten, and he did not know what to do with Bruce. Their close shipboard relationship seemed to have vanished. His brother felt like a guest who had to be entertained.

"Do you have friends in Cave Valley?" he asked.

"Many." Bruce sounded guarded.

"And women?"

"Aye, brother. In fact, I, too, am betrothed."

"Och, that's wonderful. Why did you not tell me?"

"I am telling you now. You will meet her, I hope."

"When I visit. But tell me about her. What's she like?"

"You will see. Today is for you and your bride."

"Have you ever heard from father?" John asked.

"Once. He wrote just after I arrived. Not recently, though. Have you?"

"Never."

Bruce shrugged. "Don't let it bother you. He has his own demons."

They returned to their seats on the verandah. "It's a beautiful view, isn't it?" Bruce said, gesturing.

"Aye, it is. What's your own house like?"

"Very similar. On a slight hill. I have a view of the Cave River, though. Cave Valley is bigger than Fortress – maybe eight hundred souls. Closer to the coast too. Inclined to flood. Hotter. More mosquitoes. Probably more fever. Here has a pleasant climate."

"How have you found your ministry?"

Bruce shrugged. "It progresses well. There was a missionary

there before me, so there was already a congregation. This is your first wedding, but I've performed a few. I've found the people receptive to the Scriptures. Their lives are hard and they're glad to know rest and ease awaits them after death, if they are saved and repent of their sins."

"Do men come to your services?"

"Some. More women. Sometimes the women force the men to come."

"Who are your friends? Are there white families in Cave Valley?"

Bruce regarded him oddly. "A few. I don't see much of them."

"You don't? There are only the Bannisters here, and I don't much like them."

"You want white people to socialize with?"

"Well. You sometimes want sophisticated company."

"Do you?" It was not a question. "You do realize there are now more black Baptist pastors than us whites?"

John felt chastised and irritated. He was the older brother, after all. He wanted to ask about Bruce's fiancée but the subject seemed closed. But then they had never discussed their father and Nurse Duncan, not even during the long, empty hours aboard ship. "Perhaps you would like a rest?" he said.

"A rest? I'm not tired. Don't let me disturb you, though. I'll look through your books and be happy here for a while. Perhaps I'll do some exploring later."

"The sun is up and you might get lost. Remember the wedding is at four o'clock."

"You haven't changed, my brother. Always the worrier. I'll be fine. Being here has taught me to enjoy my own company. And I assure you, I don't get lost."

"Will you pray with me later? I mean, before the service." John regretted the needy tone of his voice.

"Aye, of course." Bruce smiled and John saw his baby brother flickering behind this strange man's eyes.

At quarter to four, the brothers walked to the church. Bruce was handsome and remote in his robes and John breathed more easily. The afternoon was bright and the church glowed in the sun. John realized the church had become what he had once imagined. Inside, the pews, glistening with polish, were decorated with small clutches of wildflowers, though already slightly wilted in the heat. Large copper pots were filled with palm leaves. Many of the villagers were already gathered, dressed in unfamiliar sometimes ill-matched assortments of clothes. Apart from Mrs. Bannister, there were no white faces in the church, but the people of Fortress had come in force to his wedding. He was bringing social change; he was a leader. Feeling pride and anticipation, he nodded to Prudence, Leonie and Cuba and took his place at the altar. He wondered if Lillian would have bridesmaids.

He heard the beat of a drum and turned to face the entrance. His bride stood on the arm of Henry Bannister, framed in the door, a veil obscuring her face. For a second, John wondered if he might be tricked into marrying a strange woman; then he saw the skin of the woman's neck was pale and freckled. Of course it was Lillian. The drum beat again in a muffled, echoing rhythm. It seemed wrong, heathen, and he wished for the familiar sounds of the wedding march played on the harmonium. There were no bridesmaids. Lillian held a bouquet of orchids, picked in the forest. She stood beside him and Bannister retreated. John knew it was the first time he had set foot inside the church.

"Dearly Beloved, we are gathered here together in the sight of God..." Bruce began. John let the words he longed to say himself carry him into the wedding ceremony. Afterwards, all he would remember was the slow, resounding beat of the drum, the moment when he lifted Lillian's veil and her face was revealed, and the slick feel of sweat under his clothes.

The people spilled out into the churchyard and greeted the new couple. There were tables set up with food and the villagers ate their fill. John felt blessed, but he longed for the celebrations to be over. He wanted to be alone with his bride. He admired the way Lillian moved among the people of Fortress, greeting them by name, asking after the children she had come to know through her teaching. Her dress of ivory satin dragged in the grass and he could see it was becoming soiled along the hem. One of Icilda's girls reached out to touch the fabric and Lillian turned and smiled at her. She handed her bouquet of orchids to the girl. John looked around for his brother, but did not see him in the crowds.

"You eat?" Irene asked, offering him a full plate. He had not seen her in the church and he did not know if she had attended the service.

"No, Irene. I'm not hungry, but thanks."

"You mus' eat. You need you strength tonight." She laughed and hit him lightly on the arm. He tried but failed not to be offended at her familiar manner and the ribald implications.

"I must find my brother."

"Mi keep a plate fi you. If you wait too long, not one drop a food leave."

Irene's mouth and fingers were greasy. John considered telling her to use her napkin, but decided against it. He wished Lillian would join him, would slip her gloved hand into his, would walk at his side. There was a crowd around her and she looked to him like a pale flame trying to take hold in a mound of dark, splintered wood. He shook off his thoughts and resumed his search for Bruce.

He went back to his verandah. He could see the crowd better from there. Bruce really was missing; his horse had gone. Had he had gone to purchase rum? There had been no alcohol at the wedding and Prudence's bar was closed. She and her children were all present at the ceremony. He sat in one of the rocking chairs facing the village.

Soon he saw a couple walking towards him, small figures at first, indistinct in the waning afternoon heat. He squinted and shaded his eyes. Yes, it was his brother, he could see that from the set of his shoulders and his walk. The woman was small, almost child-sized, dressed in something bright and loose and long. She wore a headscarf wrapped around so many times that her head seemed too large for her body. As the two figures came closer, John saw with disbelief the woman was black and his brother held her hand. As they came closer, he began to notice details. His brother was flushed and swayed as he walked. He *had* been drinking then. His clothes were dusty. He did not look ahead but appeared deep in conversation with the woman. He held one of her hands and John fancied he was pulling her along. Perhaps the woman was his servant and had refused to carry out some task and

Bruce was reproving her. The child-woman was so thin she seemed swamped by her clothes; she even appeared to have no arms. As she came closer, he caught the glint of the whites of her eyes in a black face that absorbed all the light; he took in the details of her face, high cheekbones and rounded lips, a wide, unlined brow. Small as she was, her shoulders were wide and square, her arms – which he could now see below the short sleeves of her loose garment – were thin but he saw muscles flex under her skin. She walked with the erect, effortless quality he had seen in most of the Fortress women. She was probably older than she looked. John saw his brother whisper something to her and he saw her chest rise as she took a breath. Bruce stepped slightly in front of her, but did not relinquish her hand. "Brother," he said. "Why are you here? Why are you not with your guests?"

"I was looking for you."

"I went to the village. There is someone I want you to meet." Bruce turned and faced the woman, urging her forward. "This is Sissy. My betrothed. Sissy, my brother, John."

Surely this woman, this Negress, would not call him John? What did Bruce mean, his betrothed? He must have misheard. "Sissy," he said, bowing his head. He did not hold out his hand.

"Pastor," she replied and looked down.

"This is my brother, John," Bruce said. "John. Say it." His words were slurred.

The woman looked at Bruce; John saw the appeal in her eyes. Perhaps she at least knew her place. "Please, Bruce," she whispered and leaned into him.

"Alright," he said. "It will come. This is my Sissy, my wife to be. I want you to welcome her to your wedding day."

"Can we talk? Can we talk alone? Irene will take Sissy to the kitchen."

"You sanctimonious bastard! The kitchen? How dare you?" Bruce took a step towards John, staggered and almost fell.

"Be reasonable, Bruce. Why didn't you tell me this before? Why spring it on me now? What will people…"

"What will people say? What *people*? Those bigoted upstarts the Bannisters? Your new *wife*? The people of Fortress won't care. What matters is what *you* think, what you say, what you…"

188

"Bruce," the woman said, softly. Although she had not said much, she sounded as if she had been educated.

Bruce shook off her hand. "No." It wasn't clear what he meant. "This," he said, taking a step towards John, "*this* is why I am not staying in your house. This is why I – we – are at the tavern."

John wanted to tell his brother that he was welcome at his house, he and anyone he chose to accompany him, but he found himself fighting a rage that surged behind his teeth, threatening to spew into Bruce's too-close face. How could you? What would our mother think? Sleep with the woman if you must, and beg the Lord's forgiveness afterwards. I know how lonely it is, how urgently the flesh clamours, but to *marry* a Negro woman? It was unthinkable. "Go then," he said. "Go back to Cave Valley. You have married us, you've done your fraternal duty." As soon as he'd said the words, he wished them unsaid, but still his anger raged. He hated his brother for the darkness he had cast into his wedding celebration. "Go!" he said again. "Take your things." He turned on his heel and walked back to the wedding.

Irene approached him again with a plate of congealing food. "I told you no!" he snarled; he had never spoken to her so harshly. He pushed his way through the crowds, people laughing with full bellies and the gift of an afternoon of ease, and pulled his wife away.

1787
Bonnie Valley Plantation

In May, Zachary noticed Victoria in the fields, working alongside Amy from Paradise. Her clothes were loose, but he saw the curve of her belly. She was just beginning another pregnancy. He did not know how many children she had; she had refused to answer any questions when he tried to add her to his lists. He could not bring himself to threaten her with punishment. He was sure the baby's father was Paul Monmouth.

In June, he was given time off to visit Trevor Manning in Kingston, accompanying Charles Monmouth on some business he had to conduct. The journey took five days; first through the hills and then along the north coast of the island. Just past the fishing village of Salem, Zachary saw a black man standing waist-deep in the sea, casting a net. He drew rein and watched. The man gathered the net and threw it in a perfect arc, his arms shining in the sun. The net landed on the sea and gradually sank. Then the man slowly hauled it in and as it came up, the water boiled with fish. The fisherman selected the largest ones and slipped them in a bag across his shoulders, then sank the net again, and stood watching the smaller fish escape. Zachary imagined him on the coast of Africa, casting into the surf of a continent an ocean away, with the same skill he now displayed. He must be a free man. Zachary wondered how he had come by his freedom.

They stayed in a tavern called The Morgan on the waterfront. Kingston and its streets were crowded with white people in extravagant dress, luxurious carriages, slaves in attendance. Zachary felt excited. It felt good to be in a city again.

Trevor Manning had written that he ate dinner in the Royal Hotel every night. Zachary washed and changed his shirt. His breeches were stained, but he had only the one pair. He cleaned his boots with spit. He walked out into the warm, noisy evening, wondering if he would recognize Manning; it seemed so long ago and their acquaintance had been brief.

He asked directions to the Royal Hotel – an easy walk down a dusty street to a two-storey wooden structure right behind the sea wall. He walked up the steps and found himself in a gloomy reception room. "Your dining room?" he asked a white man behind the counter.

"Ter the left," he said, in a strong Cockney accent. Zachary smiled. In Kingston, the shadow of slavery seemed less dense, less threatening.

The dining room was large and open on one side. Tables were set out on a wooden verandah where white men and women sat, the women fanning themselves lazily, the men smoking or looking out to sea. Boats of many different sizes were moored in front of the hotel. He saw Trevor Manning sitting by himself at the table closest to the sea. He was reading. He looked no older though his hair was longer. Zachary walked over to him.

"Young Macaulay!" Manning said, rising. "My God! You've become a man! Bonnie Valley has been to your liking, then." He held out his hand and Zachary took it, feeling awkward. He hardly knew this man. He had written to him because he knew no one else in Jamaica, because he had crossed the sea with him, because he had shown a wary boy kindness. He did not know why Manning had written to him.

"Mr. Manning." Zachary allowed himself to smile.

"Trevor, please. Come. Sit. Have you eaten?"

"No. We've just arrived."

"You must be tired then. Let's order quickly. Boy!"

Zachary asked for fresh fish, remembering the man he had seen on the coast casting his net. At Bonnie Valley, fish was always salted, but surely here, on the edge of the sea, the fish would be fresh.

"I'll join you in that," Manning said. "With some rum, then?" Zachary nodded.

"Tell me about Bonnie Valley," said Manning. Zachary thought of his lists. He could describe Bonnie Valley in numbers: seven hundred and eleven slaves, four hundred and ninety men, two hundred and sixteen women, thirty-five children – more or less. The children were always dying or being born – numbers were constantly in flux. Six hundred hogsheads of sugar annually. Eight white people. Thirty of the children were mulattoes. Forty cows, seventeen mules, nine horses, twenty-five pigs, five donkeys, fifty-two chickens, two bullocks, three peacocks. There had been four – but one had been eaten in the lean months after the hurricane. Zachary said: "It is like its name – a bonnie valley."

Manning raised his eyebrows. "And you've been working as their book-keeper?"

"Aye."

"How do you get on with the Monmouths?"

"Well enough. I dinna see much o' them. Nothing of Mrs. Monmouth. Charlotte – the eldest daughter – seems tae take an active part in the plantation. Paul too. We – Paul and I – dinna like each other much. My horse beat his in a race on my first day."

Manning laughed. "No, Paul wouldn't enjoy that."

"D'ye know them well then?"

"Not especially. They're like most planter families. The ones that are here, that is. Most aren't."

"I know. I went tae Paradise Plantation in the south."

"Aah. The infamous Mr. Maguire."

"How d' ye know him?"

"What did you think of Paradise? Up for sale, isn't it?"

"Aye. That was why we went. It was after the hurricane and we needed supplies and slaves. I hated it."

"You hated it?"

"Aye. I couldna hae stayed there."

"Yet you stayed at Bonnie Valley."

"Aye. But they are different. At least…"

"How are they different? There was something pointed in the question, as if Manning wanted precise details.

"Paradise is a place o' pestilence, low lying, prone to flooding, infested wi' fever. The slaves are tortured. It was…" His voice trailed off. He could not articulate his feelings; he no longer believed the thought he had been about to express. Certainly there were geographical differences between the two plantations: Bonnie Valley's elevation, the surrounding hills, the forests, but that was not what he wanted to describe. He knew that Victoria, owned by Charles Monmouth, did not face her life with any greater optimism than Amy had, when she had been Douglas Maguire's property. And Amy? Were her circumstances different now? Zachary saw Manning watching him closely and then his eyes shifted. "Aah. Here's our food."

The waiter brought large wooden plates with two whole fish laid diagonally across each of them. The fish had faintly red skin, cloudy eyes and thick white flesh. They did not speak again until the meal had been consumed. The light had faded and the sky was growing orange. Men shouted from the bar behind them; Zachary could not tell whether it was in mirth or anger. He pushed his plate away, suddenly overcome. He felt on the edge of the world. He remembered those old maps with the words, "Here be dragons", in unexplored seas; the ancient fear that ships could simply sail off the edge of the earth and plunge into some unimaginable, watery hell.

"And are you still a reader of Horace?" Manning asked.

"Aye, Sir. I still find much good sense and comfort in him."

"You know Horace was the son of a freed slave?"

"Aye, Mister Manning, that I do, and that he kept slaves himself on his farm."

"Do you think any son of a slave here in Jamaica could become a great poet like Horace?"

"I dinna ken about that."

"More rum?" Manning asked.

"No, thank ye. I must leave ye. I'm tired frae the journey."

"How long will you be in Kingston then?"

"I dinna ken yet. A few days, surely."

"Well, we have time to talk. What are your plans?"

"I have no particular plans. My employer is here on business, but he disnae seem tae need me. I just thought I would see Kingston."

"You could see Port Royal, or what's left of it."

"Port Royal?"

"The so-called wickedest city in the world. Sunk in an earthquake in 1692."

"How can I see it then?"

"Some of it remains. A fort. A church. A hospital. Some other buildings, half in, half out of the earth."

"I'll dae that."

"Will you let me pay for dinner?"

"Are ye a rich man?"

"I'll answer that if you will answer a question for me."

"I will try."

"Then I am a rich man's son. I myself have only inherited wealth. I do not work on a plantation. I lied to you. I'm a writer. I'm writing about slavery for the abolitionists back in London."

"Is that why ye befriended me? So I would give ye information?" Zachary stood, angry.

"I befriended you because I saw a young lad lost on a pier in Montego Bay. You wrote to me, remember?" Zachary did not answer.

"Sit, young Zachary. I'll not detain you long. But I entreat you not to leave in anger."

"I will pay for my ain supper, Sir."

"Whatever makes you comfortable. But you promised me an answer to a question."

"I promised ye nothing."

"Nevertheless. Why did you ask me to send you newspapers from London?"

"What is so noteworthy about that? I wanted news of home."

"You had been at Bonnie Valley many months without wanting news of home. You wanted newspapers after you went to Paradise. What happened there?"

Zachary sighed. "I saw a slave release his dead daughter from the stocks and lay his head on her forehead. I met Maguire."

"It repulsed you, then?"

"It repulses me, aye. It confuses me too. They say the slaves cannot survive without the plantations, that they live in trees in Africa, that they are savages and their conditions are improved in slavery."

"Do you believe that?"

"I dinna ken. But Bonnie Valley *was* – is different from Paradise." As he said the words, Zachary was not sure he believed them.

Manning stood. He held out his hand again. Zachary hesitated; he felt tricked. Manning had always been vague about his occupation. So he was a writer for the abolitionists; the people who would see the demise of slavery and thus the plantations. Yet he himself had longed to be free of it; he had kept lists of all that he saw. Why? So that he could bear witness? He shook Manning's hand. His anger eased and he wanted to talk more, but words eluded him.

"Please, Mr. Macaulay. Let me buy your meal. I can afford it and you will not be indebted in any way. You may walk away from this table and never contact me again, or I you. But I am at your service, should you want to know more about the abolitionist movement."

"Have ye been to Africa?" Zachary asked. "Have ye seen how the blacks lived there? Have ye been on a slave ship?"

"No."

"Then how can ye decide?"

"I decide because black men are men. However humble their circumstances, however different their customs, they deserve control of their lives. It should not be taken away from them by other men."

"Do ye believe they have souls?"

"I am not a religious man. I leave that to others in the movement." Manning touched Zachary's shoulder. It was the touch of a father to a son. "Go to your hotel. Sleep. I'll be here in the morning if you want to speak more. If not, I wish you well in all your endeavours. I mean you no harm, young Macaulay. I told you that the first time we met."

Zachary wanted to talk to this man; to release the thoughts that had burdened him for months. He wanted to tell him about Charlotte's night visits, the sexual dreams he had of Victoria, the rides through the forest, the view from the verandah of Bell Cottage. He thought Manning would hear him without judgment and the turmoil of his feelings would be eased.

"Aye," he answered. "Ye did. I thank ye, Sir. Thank ye for dinner."

"My pleasure. I hope we will talk."

"Perhaps," Zachary said. He thought talk might take him over that abyss at the edge of the earth. He imagined the sea pouring off a jagged edge, carrying everything in its path.

1887
Fortress, Trelawny Parish

"It's here," John said, opening the mail. He sat with Lillian at a small table on the verandah, drinking tea, awaiting breakfast. Lillian had commissioned Cuba to make the table; she thought it gloomy inside the house and wished to eat outside in daylight hours, when the mosquitoes were not too bad. John did not like eating on the verandah. He thought the villagers walking by would envy the food on their table, but he accepted Lillian's lead on domestic matters.

"What's here?" she said, distracted with her own letters.

"My name change. Your name change. The deed poll."

Lillian said nothing. She had not agreed with John's decision to change the spelling of his surname to emphasize his estrangement from his brother. She had not been especially concerned by the woman Bruce had brought to their wedding. She had heard that people in the Indies often took up with native women. Of course, he should not have brought the woman to the wedding; that was clear, but Lillian did not feel there was any need for an overt rift. The brothers could just drift apart, letters could be sent at longer and longer intervals, and that would be that. They were in the Indies, after all.

John stared at the papers that proclaimed him now to be John Arthur McCaulay and his wife Lillian Dawn Watt McCaulay. It was a year after their wedding; he had now been more than two years in Fortress. Across the table from him, his wife sat with one arm around her swelling belly. It was true her ankles were not fine and he worried about her lustiness in bed – surely her enthusiasm was unladylike – but other aspects of his fantasy were in place. Lillian brought him a hot drink while he worked on his sermons at night, she taught in the school, although there was now a full time teacher sent by the Baptist Mission in Kingston. He smiled at his wife. "Are you well, my love?"

"I am. I'm glad the nausea is over. Do you have baptisms today?"

"Only one. A four-year-old from The Rock along the coast." His first baptism at Ulster Spring was almost a year ago now. It had been pouring with rain and he had hesitated on insisting that Leonie enter the river, which was swollen and muddy. He and the Fortress postmistress stood on the river bank, a handful of people watching, and he could barely hear himself speak above the sound of the water. As he was deliberating on the wisdom of getting into the tumbling torrent, his feet slipped from under him and he crashed full length into the water. Leonie howled with laughter and leapt in beside him and quickly, before they could be swept away, John's first baptism was performed. Others followed on sunny days, with the banks of Ulster Spring lined with singing, swaying villagers. He often wondered if they were simply enjoying the drama.

Although John now knew everyone in Fortress and people no longer averted their eyes when they saw him, he also knew he had changed their lives very little. Oh, some of them came to church because he had learned the art of whipping up his congregation, because drumming and singing were part of his services, and because his emphasis on the pleasures of the hereafter struck a chord with people whose experience of the here and now was so hard. But he had not conducted a single wedding ceremony; the people of Fortress were resolute in their unsanctified relationships. Children came to school intermittently and the men who patronized Prudence's rum shop still drank and fought and passed out in the streets. People in Fortress, especially the children, became ill all the time – fevers, dysentery, lockjaw and strange, wasting illnesses, not to mention accidents – and death was commonplace. He had presided over nine funerals this year alone – from a population of no more than fifty people. He had known some of them: Devon, the man who used to cut the field where Friday was turned out; Jacob, Cuba's cousin. Three babies had died: Icilda's sixth child, Ella's first and the fourth child of a woman, Bethel, who lived in Hampden. The villagers asked why his prayers had not worked and John was left to stammer about the will of God. He knew Fortress badly needed a doctor; he had written several times to the mission asking for help in this regard, but no doctor had yet been found.

He often considered the awful consequences of either himself or Lillian becoming ill. They were lucky to have so far only experienced the occasional fever and head cold. He was deeply worried about his wife's pregnancy, much as he looked forward to having children, and prayed long for her safety. They discussed the possibility of her returning to Scotland to have the child, but Lillian was calm about the birth and adamant her place was with her husband. She had found a local woman in Falmouth who claimed to be a midwife and had arranged that the woman would come and stay in Fortress when her time was near. He worried about this too – a Negress delivering his child. Lillian had laughed at his fears; the woman was quite light skinned and presentable, she assured him, and if it was one thing the natives could do, surely that was birthing babies!

It was September, near the end of the hurricane season. There had been no hurricanes this year and the villagers' crops had been reaped and bellies were full. Fields were being prepared for planting when the rains came in October, and life in Fortress did not seem so precarious. John felt that whilst he was no longer so naively idealistic about Jamaica, he still loved the look of the land, the feel of it, the sounds of the bush, the force of the rain, the warmth of the sun, the brilliance of the island's colours. He rode occasionally to the coast and regarded the sea with pleasure too, but he no longer considered living on the coast. No, this small town in the hills, this was his place.

Of course the people were noisy, undisciplined, violent, governed by superstition. They thought *duppies* lived in the roots of the cotton trees, that the blood of an animal should be sprinkled in the foundations of a house and that owls brought death. They tied a lime leaf to their foreheads to cure headaches and boiled a foul-tasting brew called cerasee tea as a cure-all. They were also noisy, joyful and tough; they eked out food just as easily from stony hillsides as from the fertile valley bottoms; above all, they survived – and some thrived. Although the children of Fortress came to school, John knew their parents were not all that interested in education; he was essentially providing a child-care service. The adults of Fortress had simple priorities: food, land and autonomy. They wanted to put down roots; they buried their relatives beside their houses; no matter how much they ate they were never satisfied, and they hated to be told what to do.

"Sweetheart? Did you hear me?" Lillian said. "You seem far away."

"Och, I'm sorry, my love. I was just thinking. Wishing we had a doctor in Fortress."

"Are you worrying about me again? Women have babies. It's what we do."

"I know. It's just that…"

"Just that nothing. I'll be fine. We'll be fine."

John smiled at his wife. Her pale skin had reddened and coarsened, her eyes were often reddish and runny. Still, he admired the strength of her character and the optimism of her spirit. He thanked God for bringing him to Fortress, for the fight that had taken away her former fiancée, for the Bannisters who had introduced them. He was sure it was all part of God's plan, going back as far as the affair with Nurse Duncan, his father's lifelong disapproval, his mother's death. His life had flowed along a twisted, rocky course and here he was at a calm, spreading pool.

"Our new names might take a little getting used to," he said.

"At least they sound the same," she answered.

The luminous days of December came and went and the new year dawned. Lillian's time was near. The midwife, Carol, was staying with Prudence in the village. The spare room at the McCaulay house had been transformed into a nursery; Cuba had built a cradle and Lillian had sewn curtains. John had bought his wife a cane-seated rocking chair from another sale in Falmouth and they had kept the thin cot in the room for the baby's wet nurse and later for a nanny. Lillian had begun interviewing young women from Fortress and nearby Hampden; she rather liked Icilda's eldest daughter, Annalisa, and thought she would offer her the position of nanny, once the baby was weaned.

The couple waited through January. Afterwards, John thought of it as his last happy time. The days were short and cool, the light was translucent and food was abundant. The celebrations of Christmas lingered, people went about their days greeting each other and the shelves in Prudence's shop were full.

On the last day of January, Lillian's waters broke and John was banished from the house. He saddled Friday and rode out into the countryside. He cantered along the familiar paths to his favourite view from the top of one of the hills in the area. Mostly, these hills were thickly forested and it was impossible to get to the top, but this one hill had been cleared at some time in the past, and there was a path that wound its way around it in a narrow, rock-strewn spiral. He dismounted and tethered Friday to the blackened stump of a cotton tree – perhaps struck by lightning, perhaps the hill had been cleared by fire – and gazed out over the landscape. He sat on a large rock and wondered if his wife was crying out. He preferred not to think about childbirth – *I will greatly multiply thy sorrow and thy conception; in sorrow thou shall bring forth children* – and was glad he did not have to witness Lillian with her legs spread or hear her as she laboured. He prayed and watched the sun make its journey from a distant white circle high in a pale sky, to a glowing orange orb balancing on the horizon. Six hours had passed since Lillian had moaned with her first pains. It would soon be dark. He untied Friday, mounted and retraced his steps for home.

His daughter, Sybil, was six months old and just being weaned, when Ella woke him at dawn and told him that Cuba was missing. He had left a week earlier to shoe a horse at a plantation some days' ride away and he had not returned. She knew some harm had come to him.

"How do you know?" he said, feeling annoyed at the early interruption to his morning. "Perhaps there were more horses to be shod than he imagined. Perhaps he decided to stay at the plantation for a few more days. I'm sure Cuba is fine."

Ella shook her head. "Cuba don' like dem kinda place."

"How did he get there?"

"White man sen' a buggy for him."

"Didn't they have their own farrier? Or someone closer?"

Ella didn't answer this question. "Irene is here?"

"I don't think she has come yet. I haven't heard her anyway."

"She here. She sleep in your kitchen most nights."

"Irene sleeps in our kitchen?" Lillian asked, joining her husband. John realized it was entirely possible; he had never asked where Irene lived, not in nearly three years, and apart from the very early days of his arrival in Fortress, each morning he had found her in the kitchen when he woke and left her there at night when he went to bed.

"John. Look in the kitchen. See if Irene is there."

"Why do you want Irene?"

"Irene my sister," Ella said.

"Irene is your sister?" He had lived with Irene; she had fed him, washed his clothes, cleaned his house and dealt with his excrement, and he had no idea she was Ella's sister. The colour of their skins was quite different: Ella nearly as black as Cuba, Irene the grey-brown colour of the cedar tree.

"John!" Lillian spoke sharply. "Go and find Irene. Wherever she is."

He turned and went through the short passageway into the kitchen. It was as Ella had said. Irene lay on a pile of woven mats and lengths of cloth on the floor, her mouth slightly open, her hair in plaits. He saw she was an elderly woman, far older than he had thought. He called her name and she sat up immediately, her manner guilty.

"What, Pastor?" she said.

"It's your sister. Ella. She's at the door. She says Cuba is missing."

BOOK THREE

FERMENT

1987
Kingston

"You going to get patties?" Leigh asked Danny. She had left the Libbeys and was renting a small apartment at the side of a house in Mona. She felt settled in. Her job held no surprises. She had not yet returned to see her father or been to Portland. Her life was in Kingston now.

"Yep. You want one?"

"Which place you going?"

"Di one 'pon the corner."

"Joey's?"

"Eeh-hee. What you want?"

"You can bring a chicken patty for me?"

"Sure. You want drinks?"

"No. Is okay. Brought lemonade with me." Leigh handed Danny some money, buzzed him out and followed him to the door. She was stiff from sitting all morning. "You know what?" she said as they stood at the front door. "Why you don't let me go for the patties? I could use a walk."

"Follow me, den."

"Let me ask Delilah to fill in." She went back inside, found Delilah reading the newspapers at her desk, and asked her to watch the front door while she went with Danny to get lunch. "You want anything?"

"Danny getting it for me."

They strolled down East Street. It was not yet noon, but already the afternoon rain threatened. Leigh had heard there was a tropical depression east of Jamaica, but no one seemed particularly worried. "I hate to see the garbage in the sea after the rain," she said, kicking at a juice box at the side of the road.

"Why? Rain clean up everything and the sea tek it away."

"It just dirty up the sea."

At the intersection of East and Beeston Streets, waiting for the traffic lights to change, they saw Jelly, the coconut vendor, pushing his cart quickly along Beeston Street. When he saw them, he stopped. He seemed afraid and angry, looking behind him, gesticulating, but he spoke so quickly, Leigh could not understand half of what he said. She heard the words "Babylon" and "raid" and gathered he was complaining about a police raid nearby.

Danny patted him on his shoulder. "Be cool, bred'ren. No mek sense you get youself kill. Just tek youself offa di street. Go a you yaad." As the traffic light changed and they prepared to continue south towards the patty shop, a police jeep screeched around the corner and headed straight towards them. It stopped on the other side of the road and three policemen jumped out, all holding long guns.

"See him there," the driver shouted. "Him! The jellyman. Arrest him bumboclaat!"

Jelly abandoned his cart and began to run. Danny dropped to the ground, pulling Leigh with him. They crouched behind the cart. "What you doing?" she asked. She felt confused by the events, but not frightened. It was broad daylight in the middle of the capital. They were on their way to buy patties.

"Stay down!" Danny whispered. She looked at him and back at Jelly, who was fifty yards away, his torn shirt flapping, his arms pumping, running as if he were a young man. She saw two policemen shoulder their guns and point them at Jelly, saw a lick of fire from the gun held by the tallest policeman, his stance expert, heard the crack and echo of a gunshot, and saw the coconut man fall into the gutter. He fell as if an axe had cut off his legs at the knees and he did not move again. Leigh saw blood seeping through his torn T-shirt, welling from his body.

Then Danny was pulling her away and they were running down one of the lanes that ran at right-angles to East Street. "Run!" Danny said. "If dem catch us, we dead too." He ran, fleet and surefooted and she struggled to keep up. They kept changing direction and dodging around corners. The buildings were a blur, especially when it began to rain, first in big drops, then in a deluge. "Good," Danny panted. "Them nah find us in di rain." Leigh's chest constricted and her breath came in gasps.

"I can't go much more," she said, trying to wrench her hand away, but Danny's grip was unshakeable.

"You going run 'til I say you stop."

Eventually they slowed their flight in an area that looked as if it had been bombed. The buildings had no windows or doors, the open lots were overgrown with bush and strewn with garbage, the streets ran with muddy water and there were no people outside. A man leapt out of an alley and confronted them.

"Shit!" Danny pushed Leigh behind him. "Guinep! Me coulda kill you!"

Guinep gave a high-pitched cackle. "Come!" he said, disappearing into the alley. They followed and he pushed open a metal door into an abandoned office building. The sound of the rain on the roof was deafening. Leigh bent over and fought to catch her breath. She smelled rotting food, human waste and something dead and her stomach turned. She vomited on the cracked, filthy floor.

Afterwards, she thought she would faint. She shivered in her wet clothes and looked for somewhere to sit, but the pitted floors were too foul. Danny stood in the doorway, looking out. Guinep was gone. She pushed past him and stood in the rain, turning her face to the sky, trying to cleanse her mouth and her heart. The rain made her feel better and she decided she'd rather sit outside in the mud than in that stinking building. She slid down behind a shrub by a crumbling concrete wall, leaning against the wall, her face still upturned. Surely no one would see her there? As her body eased its clamouring for oxygen, her mind said: You just saw an old man murdered by the police.

The rain lasted through the afternoon. Leigh stayed where she was, in the meagre shelter of the shrub, listening to the popping sound the rain made on its fleshy leaves. Danny stood guard in the doorway of the abandoned building. She did not ask him to explain what she had seen, where they were, or what they would do when the rain stopped. Perhaps Jelly was indeed a dangerous criminal; if not, why had he run? Perhaps he was not dead. Maybe he had just tripped, fallen and knocked himself out. The policemen would have taken him to hospital, he'd be getting some stitches and, in a week, he'd be back on the streets with his cart, proud of his scar. Except she kept seeing the lick of flame from the end of the policeman's gun, and Jelly's headlong fall. Truth was, she'd witnessed that staple of the front pages: a police killing.

When it began to get dark, Leigh's fear returned. "Shouldn't we leave now?"

"No," Danny said. "Come inside. Bad smell nah kill you. We stay here tonight."

Leigh shook her head. "Them see you?" Danny asked.

"Who?" Leigh felt stupid.

"The police! Babylon! Them see you?"

"I don't know."

"Maybe them don't see you. But you so white… and you was just standing there…"

Leigh did not understand what he was getting at. "They killed him. Why didn't they arrest him? Why did they shoot him like that, in the back? Him do anything bad, Danny?"

"Old Jelly don't hurt nobody, just smoke him little herb, play little domino, drink him whites on a Friday night."

"Why the police shoot after him like that?"

"Happen all the time."

"You think him dead?"

"Him dead. Hear me nuh, Leigh. We stay here tonight. Tomorrow, me take you to your place. You forget this ever happen. When you go to work, you only hear 'bout it. You tell Miss Delilah and Father Gabriel that you get sick and go home and when you get home, the phone don't work, then the rain come, and that's why you never call them. You don't know *nutt'n* 'bout any police shooting, you hear me?"

"But… I'm a witness to a murder! I need to make a report."

Danny threw back his head and laughed. "Who you going report it to? The police? Inside a week, you dead too."

"So that's just it; the man is dead? *Murdered*?"

Danny kissed his teeth. "So it go. Nutt'n you can do. Nutt'n me can do 'cept survive. Come. We go inside and wait for dark."

"No. I can't go inside. Stay with me here, behind the bush."

"It muddy and you cold. Is better inside."

"No." She slid back behind the bush. The rain started again. Danny shook his head, but came and sat down beside her in the mud. Finally, he put his arms around her and she felt the warmth of his body and the comfort of his muscles. She relaxed against him.

"What's the name of this plant?"

"Duppy cho cho."

"Why it call that?"

"It have fruit just like a cho cho, but if you break it open, it full of feather that float away on the breeze."

A fruit that held feathers instead of flesh, like policemen uniformed to protect and serve who were really killers. In the shadow of the duppy cho cho, she bowed her head in the rain and the night closed in.

The minibus left Half Way Tree at seven. Leigh arrived early, hoping for a good seat. The driver put her in the front seat beside him. Another time, she might have objected, insisted on sitting in the back with everyone else. Now, she accepted the front seat with gratitude. A boy shouted "White gal!" at her from the side of the road. She had become sick of it. The boy approached the window and asked her for money. She shook her head.

She watched neatly dressed people arriving for work, wiping sweat from their faces, vendors setting up stalls, scabby dogs foraging in garbage, 'ductas giving their aggressive sales talk to get people onto their buses, a policeman slapping his thigh with a baton, a homeless man urinating into a concrete planter, the plant long dead. She watched the policeman, smart in his uniform, the red seam along his trousers making his legs seem long. He sauntered down the road, his cap hiding his eyes. Not so long ago, she would have walked up to him and asked directions, but now she regarded him with aversion. He could be looking for her – a nameless white woman, who worked at a homeless shelter on East Street. A white woman, who was a "person of interest" in a crime. A white woman, who could easily be found with a quantity of ganja in her possession, and then suffer some unfortunate accident in a prison cell. She'd read a newspaper story about a man who the police had taken into custody for drunkenness. The next day, his body was found floating spreadeagled in the sea. Since Jelly's murder, a knot of fear lived under her breastbone. Sometimes she felt the fear heavy in her groin, like arousal, and wondered if that was why men were willing to go to war.

Her few possessions were at her feet in a backpack. She had quit her job, given up her apartment and was moving again. Her father was taking her in. It sounded like a script from a soap opera. She would stay at Edinburgh through most of the tourist season, until the following Easter. She had no idea what she would do then.

The policeman peered into the minibus. She tried not to look uncomfortable, met his eyes, smiled and nodded slightly, and then leaned down and extracted a book from her backpack. She opened it at random and pretended to read. She saw the driver and the policeman talk and an envelope changed hands.

Eventually, the bus filled and lurched away from the sidewalk. The driver cranked up the radio. Leigh put away her book, opened the window and stuck her face as far outside as was possible. The breeze made her eyes water.

She thought of Danny, of their furtive journey through the flooded streets of Kingston to her apartment after a night under the duppy cho cho, of the moment on her doorstep when she had to decide whether or not to ask him in, of the way he filled the space in her rooms and made her think she had never occupied them alone. She closed her eyes. It had been so long since she had taken anyone into her body, and she remembered the relief of it, the seductiveness of his youth and eagerness, and her own willingness to welcome him. In the end, it had been uncomplicated, two people who had been frightened together and wanted to remind themselves they were still alive. He fell asleep after and she got up to wash away their body fluids and the mud that still clung to her. She climbed into the small bed beside him and her body was heavy and slightly sore. She fell asleep instantly and it was not until the next morning, that she thought of condoms and the potential ramifications of Danny's presence in her bed.

Well, that had been that. It was Danny who said she had to leave Kingston. He maintained the police would find her, she was too conspicuous, too unlikely to keep silent. She could not pull the people at Kingston Refuge into a conspiracy to protect her. No, she should go into work and tell Father Gabriel that she was returning to the States, make up some story about a sick relative. He would not be surprised. Many volunteers discovered sick relatives, some soon after they arrived. Then, if she would not leave Jamaica, which was the best option, she should go to her father in the country and keep out of the way until the case of the coconut vendor, killed, according to the newspapers, in a shootout with the police, was forgotten. That same morning the radio brought news of eleven killed and several hundred made homeless, many in Kingston, by the previous day's storms. But despite the floods, the racket of traffic starting up, the diesel fumes and smoke wafting in through her open window – and the danger, she felt sorry that he was willing to see her vanish from his life, even if the reason was to save it. She leaned back in her seat, closed her eyes and tried to empty her mind of Danny and Jelly, Guinep and the other street people. Perhaps the interior would be simpler.

The minibus arrived in the crescent-shaped Falmouth town centre. Leigh shouldered her backpack and left the bus. The place was jammed with cars and vendors and the sun beat down. She felt lost. Her father was to meet her in front of the bank and drive her to Edinburgh. She hoped he would be alone. She crossed the street and a taxi driver blared his horn and flung his arm at her. She stood under an awning at the bank, fished out her sunglasses and looked around. The streets were full of people and for a while, she felt reassured: surely no one could find her among such throngs. But she knew she would never be inconspicuous, never have the comfort of anonymity as a river of black people flowed around her, parting to let her stand alone.

She heard a horn blowing insistently and stepped back farther under the shadow of the awning. Then she heard her name called and saw her father leaning out of a battered jeep. He was double-parked and she saw a policeman approaching him. She hung back, not wanting to have any interaction with the police, no matter how routine. She watched her father catch sight of the policeman in his rear-view mirror, lift his hand in greeting and talk to him, the policeman leaning on the car window, before walking away.

"Leigh!" her father called again. "Come on!" She went to the jeep and threw her knapsack onto the back seat.

"That's all you have?"

"That's it."

"You travel light."

"Always have," she said. And she was sick of it.

"Dem find Cuba," Irene told John and Lillian as she served dinner. Her voice shook. It was three weeks later and the island lay baked and still under a white August sky. Ulster Spring was low and muddy.

"Who found him?" Lillian asked.

"The constabulary."

"The constabulary?" John said. "Why were they looking for Cuba?"

"Dem say him kill somebody. At a plantation, where him did go to work."

"Lord, have mercy!" Lillian said. "John, you will have to say prayers for his soul."

"I find it hard to believe Cuba could kill anyone," John said. He saw gratitude in Irene's eyes and realized how rarely their eyes met. Cuba, his partner in the building of the school, Cuba whose strength he had only seen employed in some useful task, Cuba, whose eyes were always lowered and full of sadness. What could have happened at the plantation? Surely a case of mistaken identity. But what did he really know about Cuba? He had not known Irene slept on his kitchen floor.

"Do you know anything else, Irene?"

"Mi hear sey somebody stealin' from di plantation; punkin one week, yam di next, couple a goat-dem, egg, chicken. Dem a think Cuba do it."

John tried to recall Cuba's face, but all he could see was the form of his body, bent over his work in the forge. Lillian reached across and helped herself to some mashed green banana. "You should go and speak to Henry Bannister, John. He probably knows all about it."

"Probably." John knew it was best not to disagree with Lillian, but he had no intention of speaking to Bannister. He tried not to feel annoyed with Irene for bringing this unwelcome news. He did not want to have to deal with it. He remembered watching one of

Icilda's sons – Sam, was it? – finding an ants' nest in the churchyard after services on Sunday. The boy found a stick and pushed it into the nest, and then sat back on his heels to watch the ants swarming out. This business would stir an ants' nest in the village.

"Aren't you eating?" Lillian asked.

"I'm not hungry." Was the person Cuba was supposed to have murdered white or black? Man or woman? He had to know more.

He left Lillian and walked into the village. The endless dust of summer was settling. Fortress needed rain: for the people, the crops, the animals. He walked through the darkening roads until he came to Cuba's forge.

He walked up to the door, ran his hand over its rough surface and pushed it slightly. It gave a little and then held. Perhaps he could kick it in. Don't be a fool, he told himself. What do you want to go in there for? What will you see? Old tack, cracked and covered with dust. Cuba's tools. Rats and spiders, probably scorpions or even a snake. But I could see where they lived. You're losing your mind. No, his thoughts came back. I never knew how they lived. I want to understand. I want to know why he killed. If he killed. He pushed harder at the door again, but it resisted. In the darkness, he could not see what was holding it. Probably a lock. Irene. She'll have a key. Tomorrow I'll ask her for it and go inside. He had to know what had happened to Cuba. Once he understood, he would visit him in gaol in Falmouth, offer prayers for his soul, even stand with him at the gallows. There was no question he would be hanged if the victim was white. A Negro could not kill a white person and be punished merely with prison. *The least we can do for Jesus is precious in his sight.* He would pray for Cuba's soul. He continued to walk, prowling the streets of Fortress, until he was sure Lillian was asleep.

He was waiting in the morning when Irene let herself into the McCaulay house. She was no longer sleeping in the kitchen. He did not know where she lodged; he had merely decreed it was unseemly for her to sleep on his floor.

Irene asked no questions when he requested the key for the forge. She took it out of her bag and handed it to him. Even in the dim light of early morning, he saw she had lost weight. He wondered if she was now paying rent. He saw a bunch of bananas on a plate. They had been picked too soon and had not ripened properly. That was how it was in Fortress: either drought cracked the land and shrivelled crops, or storms delayed the ships, made food fall off the trees and rot in the soil. Whichever way, people went hungry. He broke off two bananas and left with them.

He found no surprises in Cuba's forge. It was as he had imagined, dusty, abandoned, except for insects. Pieces of leather hung on the walls, the anvil stood in the centre of the room and ash lay on the ground; the rough table that usually held Cuba's knives, his rasp, and a box of horseshoe nails was bare. There was no sign of horseshoes or of Cuba's other tools. Then he saw a door at the back of the room and opened it.

The door led to a room as small as a prison cell. It was tacked onto the main structure, made of a hodgepodge of materials – thatch, tin, mud and wattle and discarded wood. The floor was dirt. There was a pile of rags and woven mats in one corner. He touched one of the mats with his foot and it fell apart. There was nothing recognizable as a piece of furniture, although there were lengths of wood stacked against one wall. Perhaps Cuba had planned to make a bed. There were a few items of clothing hanging on a nail. A tin bucket sat in one corner with a piece of crocus bag spread over it. There were gaps between the walls and the thatched roof and sunshine speckled the opposite wall. The room smelled of food gone bad, of human sweat, of insect droppings. He held his breath and spread out the mats and rags and lay down on them. He stared at the thatch above him. It was the first time he had been inside a Fortress house. Here two adults had lived. He felt wrenched with helplessness and confusion. His mind rang with the same phrase: *there must be something…* He could not form the end of the sentence.

He packed his gear into saddlebags. He would ride to the plantation where Cuba had gone to shoe a horse. He would find out not just what had happened, but why. He had never ridden so deep into the forest, never slept outside. He really had no idea what to take with him, but filled the pewter canteen that had some connection to this

214

land, that had journeyed from the island and back again with him, though he knew it would hold far too limited a supply of water. Irene put together field rations for him, tied in a faded cloth. He had directions to the plantation from Magistrate Bannister – who had asked no questions as to the reason for the journey. When he saddled Friday, he included an extra thick saddle blanket, which he thought he could use to lie on at night. It would be sodden with horse sweat, but better than nothing. He borrowed a flat-ended cane machete from Prudence and fashioned a strap to hold it to his saddle. He tried to eat an extra large breakfast before leaving, but was too tense.

It was just past nine in the morning and already hot. He had hoped to leave earlier, but the preparations had taken longer than anticipated. Each time he thought he was ready, he thought of something else. Irene had given him one of her headscarves and he had fastened it around his neck, not wanting to hurt her feelings. "What's this for?" he asked.

"All kinda ting," she said. "Wet it and put it unda you hat – will keep you head cool. Rest it over your face a nighttime – keep off di mosquito-dem. Dip it inna di wild pine up inna tree-dem an' you find water."

"Thanks, Irene. I'm grateful. Look after Mrs. McCaulay and Miss Sybil for me. I will be back in a week; maybe ten days."

Irene nodded. "Ride good, Pastor."

He stood in the doorway and looked at his wife. She sat on the verandah floor on a white blanket, playing with Sybil. She did not look at him as he approached. He touched her shoulder and she looked up, unsmiling.

"I know you don't understand this journey, but I'll soon be back," he said.

She shrugged. "I don't know what's happened to you, John. If you want to see Cuba, go to Falmouth. See him in gaol. Speak to the Magistrate. Why ride for days to this plantation? I'm sure the family will have left after such a tragedy."

He knew she spoke sense, always spoke sense. He thought of his brother, now married to a black woman, probably with children of mixed blood, claiming a new place on the island. He, the missionary, the one who was supposed to have the answers,

215

lived in a state of confusion and uncertainty. He touched Lillian's cheek, ruffled Sybil's wispy hair and walked down the steps and into the street, where Friday waited, tethered to the fence. He swung into the saddle, settled himself, checked his pockets and saddlebags once more and then he rode through the streets of Fortress into the countryside, the canteen bumping at his side.

Leigh moved into a small suite of rooms at Edinburgh Plantation, above a storage shed where the tractor and tour jitney were parked. There was a tiny bathroom and a living room, with an overstuffed sofa, a desk and chair. The bedroom was small, holding only a single bed and a night table. The rudimentary kitchen downstairs was used by the workers for midmorning tea and snacks.

The single window in the bedroom looked out to the east. Her first morning, she lay in bed and watched the sun rise over the distant hills. It was sublime. She left the shutters wide open each night, let down the mosquito net around her bed, and looked forward to the next morning when the sky would lighten first to grey, then to amethyst, and finally explode in bursts of pink and orange. Then a blade of sunlight would slice into her room. She went to bed early, lulled easily into sleep, the country night silent, except for an occasional barking dog and the creaking of whistling frogs.

Her father and stepmother lived in a stone cottage close to the Great House; it had been one of three overseers' cottages in slavery days; two were in ruins. She ate with them each night, usually soup with thick slices of hard dough bread. She treated her stepmother with wary politeness and Sarita did her best to keep a faltering dinner conversation alive. She was obviously ill, sometimes resting her elbows on the table and bowing her head, as if the drinking of soup was a trial. It was impossible to think of her as the bimbo who had snatched her father away.

Robert McCaulay watched TV after dinner; a large satellite dish was hidden from the eyes of tourists behind the cottage. Leigh hated this intrusion and never stayed to see what was on. She excused herself after dinner and walked the paths and roads of the old plantation. Sometimes the land was moonlit; other nights were so dark she had to walk with her arms outstretched in front of her; still others were washed in the pale glow of a sky crowded with stars. She thought of Kingston on her walks; the crowds and the cacophonies of daily life, and remembered Portland's rain from her childhood, the singing of the whistling frogs, the sounds of the sea. In coming to Edinburgh, sometimes it felt as if she had left the island without knowing. She thought of her mother taking her away from Portland, and of Danny. Her fingers curled at her sides as she remembered the tight kernels of his hair and the muscles in his back. She fantasized about setting up house with him, a young man who would adore her character, while she worshipped his body. She knew what her father would say if he learned she was sleeping with a black man. Well, she wasn't any more.

When she felt tired, she retraced her steps, climbed to her small bedroom, flung wide the window, crawled under the sheets and let down her net.

"It's good you got out of that hellhole. Kingston is not fit for beasts," her father said when Leigh told him about the murder she had witnessed. She let the comment pass. He had the grace, though, to ask little about her life before returning to Jamaica.

Her duties were easy. She took the tour bookings on a two-way radio in the office, supervised the meals, made sure the jitney worked and everyone's costumes were clean. She had refused to wear a costume herself, much to her father's annoyance. She met the tourists wearing khaki trousers and a plain white shirt and no one complained. Unexpectedly, she found she liked meeting the tourists. As mere visitors, she could feel superior to them. She was lean and fit from all her walking; she watched the overweight, sweating tourists come off their buses indulgently; she loved the moment when one of them would ask, "You *live* here?", and then await the responses of envy and incredulity.

There had been tours almost every day in December. She had not yet started to look through her mother's things. The need for a birth certificate to claim her inheritance had never been urgent, and now it seemed even less so since she spent hardly any of the money she earned. Sometimes, she felt she would stay at Edinburgh for ever, waking with the sun, eating eggs still warm from the coop, dressing in her tour-guide clothes, strolling up to the office in the Great House, greeting the workers, meeting the tour buses, joining the tourists for lunch by the river, waving to them as they left, drinking a cup of tea on the verandah of the Great House (she had added this feature, remembering the English quartet on her tour), reading for a few hours, eating an early dinner with her father and stepmother, and then walking around the plantation in the dark.

To the concern of the Edinburgh's workers, one of her favourite walks was to the graves under the grove of cedar trees in Palisade Paddock. She went there so often she had worn a track through the grass. She had visited the graves in daylight and tried to read the worn inscriptions, but only a few letters could be read. She kept meaning to ask Grace about the plantation's past, but decided she preferred the mystery. Because of the dense shade under the cedar trees, the grass was patchy and not inclined to grow high, but she had borrowed a machete and blistered her hands clearing the area. Whenever she visited, she ran her hands over the stones, and picked up fallen leaves. She wanted to put a bench in the grove, so she could sit in comfort. She had seen the gravestones backlit by moonlight, a sharp study in black and silver, and seen them in the deepest shadow of the darkest nights. One night the graves had been lit by peenie-wallies, their lights flashing in unison, as if someone had decorated the marble stones with pepper lights for Christmas. It would be a good place to be laid to rest.

On an unusually grey Tuesday, a week before Christmas, the scheduled tour was cancelled. Usually, she knew in advance when she would have a day off, and made plans to go to Falmouth with Banjo to do some shopping. Now she had no plans. She would not put off going through her mother's effects any longer.

She changed into her oldest clothes and went in search of her father. She found him watching CNN and stood for a moment, reminded that the world continued. She had not seen a newspaper in more than a month; even on her rare trips to Falmouth, she had not bought a *Gleaner*.

"Dad," she said, "can I get the key to the storeroom? Today's tour cancelled, so I'm going to go through Mom's things."

"Why'd the tour cancel?"

"Not enough people signed up."

He made a face. There were those who said no one wanted to visit the old plantations; that people who travelled to Jamaica came for sun, sand, rum and sex, not a trip to the interior through run down villages, with a history lesson at the end.

"The rest of the week is fully booked."

Her father rummaged in a desk drawer and gave her a key with a label tied with a piece of string. "Here. You know where the storeroom is? Second right, beside the old tack room."

"You showed me."

"Wear a mask. That place hasn't ever been cleaned out. It's full of stuff no one's looked at in decades. Maybe centuries. Have you cancelled lunch?"

"Not yet. I'll do that now."

She went to the Great House kitchen, an echoing, outside room that had been joined to the main house via a covered walkway sometime in the past. The kitchen staff – Pauline, Alberta and Rose – were preparing for lunch, grating coconut, seasoning chicken, peeling pumpkin. The yelling tour driver – Dervol, wasn't it? – who had first bought her to Edinburgh was sitting at the kitchen table.

"'Morning," she said to him, deciding not to ask why he was there in the absence of tourists.

"Miss." He stood as if he was a student in a classroom and she a teacher. Now there was no trace of the clown she remembered.

"The tour cancelled," she told Pauline, the head cook.

"Umm-umm." She shook her head. "Chicken start season already."

"Can't you refreeze it?"

"Not good to do that. Dem tell us when wi get food handler permit not to put meat back inna di freezer."

"Well, you'd better have a cookout for everyone, then. I'm going to look through my mother's stuff in the storeroom."

"Dat place full a old tings," Pauline said. "Even things from slavery time."

"Oh, I doubt that," Leigh said. "A hundred and fifty years ago? Nothing would survive that long with rats and cockroaches."

"Some tings last one long-long time," Pauline murmured,

turning back to the chicken. Her bare hands were slick with soy sauce, onions and scotch bonnet pepper; Leigh hoped she would remember not to rub her eyes.

She got a headscarf from her room and went to the storeroom. The door was old, carved from a single piece of wood and hung deep in the stone walls. There was a large keyhole, but the key she had been given was for a modern padlock, secured by hasp and staple. She opened the door and peered inside. It was dark, but she could see dust motes floating in the daylight just in front of the open door. She felt around for a light switch, found one and turned it on; a single, unshaded light bulb shed a weak light. The roof was low, made by rough, wide planks of wood. The corners of the room were thick with cobwebs. The floor was stone, some parts crumbling and giving way to dirt. This room had to be very old.

There were large shapes at the back, draped in cloths. Furniture, probably. A box with books; she picked up one and it crumbled in her hand. There was a stack of framed pictures leaning against the wall. Old watercolours of flowers behind cracked glass, the colours faded. A sepia photograph of a family, formally posed in a shadowy room. On the back, written in ink: Jeremy, Kate, Belinda, Elizabeth, Rosemarie, baby Anne. She put it aside to look at more closely in the light. There were things hanging on the wall – what looked like the remnants of an old harness and a battered, tarnished canteen. She unhooked the canteen and wiped the dust off with her hand. Silver or pewter? The remains of a leather strap fell off at her touch. She looked around, irresolute. No need to take on all this; she should just find her mother's box.

As her eyes adjusted to the dim light, she spotted a plastic box with a clear top, April McCaulay written on the side in marker pen. She could take it outside, to her room, and go through it in comfort. She put the canteen down and tried to lift her mother's box; it was heavy and an awkward size. She hauled it out into the sunlight and called for Aston, the handyman whom she had seen in one of the stables.

"Yes, Ma'am!"

"Help me get this up to my room." She attempted to lift one side, but Aston took it from her and carried it easily up the stairs to her apartment. She dusted her hands and turned to lock the door, but saw the canteen where she had left it. It had a pleasing shape and she thought it might look nice on her wall. She turned it over and saw there was a date inscribed on the bottom: 1780. Really old. She took the canteen with her.

In her apartment, Leigh cleaned the dust from her mother's box and opened it. At first, she found nothing unexpected: albums stuffed with familiar photographs, her parent's wedding, Andrew's christening, faded photos of the family at play on beaches and rafting on the Rio Grande, climbing waterfalls, at birthday parties, sports days, school functions. She looked at a group photo of the school outing she remembered to Dunns River, trying to identify the faces. The names came back: Petula. Shauna Kay. Marlene. Patricia. And there were Carol and Felicity. There were no pictures of Zoe.

There were some black and white studio photographs of her mother, her hair coiffed, her lips dark and slightly parted, her cheekbones shadowed by professional lighting. Leigh looked for herself in her mother's face, but could see no resemblance. There were no letters or diary, no indication of who her mother had been. She fingered a pair of elbow-length, yellowing gloves her mother must have worn to her wedding. They were stiff with age.

There were some old black and white photographs, tied together with ribbon. She knew none of the people. She turned them over. Only a few were captioned: John, 1903. Lillian at Myrtle Bank. She wondered if these were her mother's relatives.

The last items in the box were four manila envelopes, secured together with a large paper clip. The first contained her birth certificate. The second had Andrew's name on the front, but was empty. The third envelope contained her mother's papers – birth certificate, marriage certificate and her death certificate.

She unfolded the birth certificate, which was yellowing and faded. The edges looked burned. April Joan Wycliffe. Date of birth February 24th, 1926. Place of birth Guildford, Surrey. *Surrey?* Her mother had not been born in Jamaica?

The last envelope contained a newspaper clipping. There were two stories, one incomplete, of a government mission to Washington DC, the other of the winners of a Four H competition. She turned the clipping over. "Elderly Woman Murdered after Road Mishap" read the headline. She was putting it aside when her eye caught her mother's name. "Citizens of a squatter settlement beat 60-year-old April McCaulay to death in the early morning hours of October 5th, 1986. According to eyewitnesses at a nearby church, Mrs. McCaulay was driving home after a party when her vehicle hit and overturned a pot of soup being prepared at a street dance. She failed to stop and some distance down the road, community members barred her way. She was dragged from her car and beaten. She died two days later at the University Hospital from internal injuries sustained in the beating. Chairman of the St. James Parish Council, Mr. Ansel Beckford, has called for a crackdown on street dances: 'The situation has long been out of control. It is time the police took forceful action.'

"While condemning the violence and expressing regret for Mrs. McCaulay's death, human rights activist Norma Miller insisted the police must use restraint in their investigations. 'We are far too willing to lay blame at the feet of an entire community,' she said. When asked if the loss of a pot of soup was worth anyone's life, Mrs. Miller said, 'That analysis of what happened is overly simplistic.' The police are appealing for witnesses to the attack to come forward.

"April McCaulay was a well known socialite in Portland during the 1960s. Funeral arrangements will be announced in the press."

Leigh stared at the clipping. Her mother had been beaten to death after overturning a *pot of soup?* Why had no one told her this? Had Andrew known? She thought back to their stilted phone conversation after she had received his letter; he had simply repeated the car accident story. Maybe no one had told him. But her father, he must have known. Her mother; beaten to death in the street. Had she been drinking, who had she been with so late at night, had anyone tried to intervene, who had taken her to the hospital, had anyone visited her there? The sound of shattering cosmetics was merely a tinkle in comparison to the clank of an overturned soup pot in the street.

The people had barred her mother's way. She could have

driven through them, letting them take their casualties, and gone straight to a police station. That was the conventional wisdom as to how to deal with a car accident in a bad area. Leigh wondered what she would have done, might yet have to do, in such circumstances. The people had barred her mother's way and killed her over spilled soup. They weren't killing *her*, she thought; they did not know her. They were killing the *idea* of her, her carelessness, her remoteness. As they might me. And here I am on a plantation. *Time for talk. Long past time.*

"Leigh? You have to speak to Banjo. He's been late with the jitney for the past four tours," Robert McCaulay said, as she came through the door to his office, holding the newspaper clipping.

"I n-need to talk to you," she said, her voice trembling. "Why didn't you tell me my mother was m-murdered?"

"What? Calm down, Leigh. Sit. I thought you knew. I thought Andrew would have told you. You didn't seem to want to talk about it, and I certainly didn't."

"Andrew didn't tell me. No one told me. Everyone said it was a car accident. Not that she was beaten to death in the street. I found this in the box." She held out the newspaper clipping.

"I'm sorry. Don't cry. It *was* awful… but…"

"I am *not* crying. And she wasn't born here… she was born in Surrey." She began to pace. "Surrey! And why did you leave us? Why did you leave *me*? What are you *doing* here, on a plantation? Don't you realize…?"

"Leigh. Please. Sit down. Let's talk…"

"*Now* you want to talk?"

"Yes. I…" The door opened and Pauline stood there. "Yes?" Robert McCaulay snapped.

"Sah. Banjo still not here and Tropic Tour say dem a fifteen minute away." It was the week between Christmas and New Year and Leigh knew they were booked solid. She had noticed Banjo's tardiness, but had not wanted to be the boss. Suddenly she was desperate to be out of her father's company.

"I'll go," she said to Pauline. "Where does he live?"

"Blessing," Pauline said. "Rose will go with you."

She was reckless in the jeep. Rose held on with both hands

and said "Mercy!" every time they hit a pothole. Blessing was the nearest village to Edinburgh, little more than a bar, grocery shop and a tiny church. Leigh had only ever driven through it. Rose directed her to the bar, which was open, though it was not yet eleven-thirty. She went inside and came out shaking her head. "Him must be at him yaad," she said. "Turn right over dere."

"Down that track?"

"Yes, Miss."

The jeep bounced down a grassy track. Cane grew on one side and brushed the vehicle as it went by. There were yam hills on the other side, the green vines trailing over sticks. Leigh wondered who was farming the land.

The track was getting worse. She wondered how she would turn around; she might have to reverse the entire way. "Are you sure you know where we're going?"

"Yes, Miss. Not far now."

The track came to the faintest of crossroads. "Turn left," Rose said. Leigh shook her head. If they didn't get back to the plantation soon, the tour would be there. She felt her anger ebbing. Then she saw a small concrete building with a slanted zinc roof, and then another. They looked like tool sheds.

"Bauxite house," Rose said.

"What?"

"Bauxite house. After dem move people offa bauxite land, dem mek dis kinda house fi dem. People who live here, dem come from St. Ann. But some a dem can't stand it and dem leave. Banjo buy Miss Cynthia house, after her son send for her. Stop over dere." Rose pointed to a small flat area. "You wait. Mi soon come."

"No, I'm coming with you."

They walked along the path, past three more of the tiny houses. Nothing seemed planned about the settlement; the dwellings seemed to have been simply cast on the ground, as if the builder had been throwing dice. One of the houses was fenced with sheets of zinc, reminding Leigh of Kingston, where everyone was anxious to deflect prying eyes.

"Last one a Banjo own."

They walked up to an unpainted wooden door and knocked.

The land around the tiny house had been cleared at one time, but was growing up again. Leigh saw a zinc outhouse at the back, partly hidden by a few banana plants.

"Banjo!" yelled Rose. "You in dere? Mi hear him, Miss." She tried the door handle and the door opened.

Banjo must be dead. He was not a young man; perhaps he had taken ill and died by himself, here, in this meagre dwelling. She did not know if he had family; in fact, since the day at Edinburgh Plantation when she'd been masquerading as a tourist, she had not spoken more than polite greetings to him.

The little house was dark inside and smelled of sweat and rum. The floors were stained a dark red and Leigh could just make out a cot and a tiny table, covered with a plastic cloth. Then she saw Banjo, lying on the bed, naked to the waist, his mouth open, snoring in painful gasps. He was drunk.

Rose shook his shoulder and his eyes opened briefly, but closed again. Leigh took in his thin chest, dotted with curly white hairs, his grimy fingernails, his ropy neck. His breath was foul. Leigh dredged for anger – this was a work morning and there was no other job for Banjo for miles – but she could not find it. Banjo was older than her father – much older – and he lived alone here on the edge of the forest in the kind of shed the Libbeys might have built to store their lawn mower. No wonder he was drunk.

"Will anyone look in on him?" she asked Rose, and felt like a fool.

"Yes, Miss. Miss Bertha, she live next door, she keep an eye on Banjo, cook him a meal now and den." Then Leigh remembered how high he piled his plate with leftover food, when the tour was over and the tourists had left. She had often heard Grace and Pauline teasing him about it. "Old man, you look like one mawga dawg, but you eat like you is a Doberman." Banjo never raised his head from his plate to respond to the taunts.

"Come," Leigh said to Rose. "Let's go. We have to hurry. Someone else will have to drive the tractor."

"Yes, Ma'am." They closed the door of Banjo's house behind them and got into the jeep. Leigh managed to turn the vehicle around and they drove back to Edinburgh.

★

"Turn off the TV, Dad," she told her father a few days after her first, interrupted, attempt to talk to him about her mother.

He aimed the remote at the TV. It clicked off. "Alright, Leigh. What is it you want to know?"

"My mother wasn't born here."

"No. She was born in England."

"Who were her parents? What brought her to Jamaica?"

"Her father was a diplomat – posted here when she was about three. She didn't really remember England, but I guess she had been brought up a certain way. She thought of herself as English."

"Where in England did she come from?"

"She was born in Surrey, but I think the family lived somewhere near Oxford."

"What happened to her parents?"

"They died in a car accident; run off the coast road in Portland. You must have known that. They drowned."

"God. Another car accident. How old was she?"

"Twenty. We'd just started to go out. That's why we got married. Young women didn't go out and get an apartment and a job back then." *The way you did* hovered unspoken.

"How come her parents stayed in Jamaica? Diplomats have postings for a few years, don't they?"

"They loved Jamaica. Her father got a consultancy with an import/export company and they stayed. I remember him well: good-looking, larger-than-life man. They had April young, you know; I think her mother was seventeen when she got pregnant. They died before they were forty."

"How come I never heard this before?"

"Your mother didn't like to talk about it."

"Why April?"

Her father shrugged. "Never asked. And she wasn't born in April, so…"

"The article about her death said she was a socialite."

"It was the time, Lee-Lah. White people were in the papers… at parties, whatever. She was a beauty, your mother."

"You still left her, though."

"A broken marriage is never about one person."

"That's convenient. You left us too."

"It broke my heart, Leigh. Your mother wasn't… I don't want to talk about it. She's dead and it was all a long time ago. We're here now. I'm glad we've reconnected."

"I don't think we have." She began to pace. "I'm working for you. That's it. And I'll be leaving soon. Tell me about my mother's death. No. Before that. Why did she come home?"

"A man. Steve-something. She met him in Florida and he was about to be posted to Jamaica. She came back with him."

As simple as that. No big mystery. My mother came home because of a man. "So tell me about her death. Her murder."

"What is there to tell? She'd moved to Montego Bay, she was going around with Steve; he worked for a donor agency. He liked Jamaica and he stayed."

"So you were in touch with her?"

"Yes, sometimes. We weren't friendly, I guess, but we spoke. Jamaica is small. We saw each other around and it would have been stupid not to…"

"Go on, she was dating an American…"

"More than dating. They lived together. He left Jamaica after her… accident."

"What happened?"

Her father looked at his hands. "They were out at some ball and had a fight. She'd been drinking; they'd both been drinking. Many people saw them. He left her at the ball – what was its name? Pineapple Ball, I think. Anyway, people saw her leave at about midnight, they said she wasn't that drunk, and they knew she hadn't far to go. She drove through a street dance and knocked over the soup and they killed her. Not the first time that kind of thing has happened; not the last either."

"Who took her to the hospital?"

"A priest. A guy working in the area. He stopped the beating and got into her car and took her to Cornwall Regional. But she died that night. Internal injuries."

"Did you go to her funeral?"

"No. It was in Kingston, and I couldn't leave Sarita."

"Why was it in Kingston?"

"I don't know, Leigh. She's buried at St. Andrew's Parish Church. You could talk to the priest there, I suppose."

"I went there. I went looking for Grammy's grave, but I couldn't find it. Too much goat shit."

"Well. It's hard to find money to maintain cemeteries these days. Her grave was probably close to Grammy's."

"How did you come by her stuff?"

"Steve called me. He said he had a box and would I come for it. When Sarita next went to the doctor in Montego Bay, I did. That's it, Lee-Lah. That's the whole story. It was a tragedy, and I'm sorry you had to find out they way you did, but I thought you knew. Jamaica is a violent place, as you've seen yourself. You should go back to the US. I'm glad to have seen you, glad to have spent these months with you, but this place is finished. It's too late for me, but not for you."

Leigh did not answer. Yes, Jamaica is a violent place. Always has been. Begat, born, abiding in violence. Perhaps her father was right; there would never be an end to it.

She had not been afraid to come home and, for many months, not afraid to walk Kingston's streets. The Libbeys used to marvel at this, but they put it down to her ignorance and recklessness. Perhaps they had been right.

Her father reached for the remote. "Wait," she said. "Tell me about your family."

"Lord, Leigh, too many questions."

"Tell me."

1787
Bonnie Valley Plantation

Two storms brushed the plantation in quick succession in September. There was damage, but not devastation. Victoria took the opportunity presented by the weather to try and escape and she was flogged again. Zachary stood in despair, watching Thompson lay into her flesh. She was suspended from a tree branch, and her belly was round and tight. He wondered if the child inside could feel his mother's agony. He wrote to Trevor Manning and asked for information about the abolition movement.

Then in the third week of October, during another unusually dry spell, as he was riding deep in the forest, a serpent crossed the path right in front of Miranda. She reared, lost her footing on the loose rocks and fell. Zachary flung himself wide of the thrashing mare, trying to avoid her hooves. He hit his head. Conscious but confused, he failed to reach Miranda's tethering rein. He heard her hooves pounding the uneven ground and the tearing away of bush as she galloped away. Loose stones rattled down the slope. He closed his eyes. More recently, he had become lax about marking his way, but he thought he knew the forest paths well, and Miranda would cut a swath that would be easy to follow. He would just rest for a while.

When he woke, the light was fading. He tried to stand and a bolt of pain drilled his ankle. He hooked his boot over a fallen branch and tried to ease it off. His vision darkened with the pain. The boot was stuck. He sat and waited until the faintness passed, reached for his knife and cut the boot from his leg. It was not easy to do and by the time he was finished, it was nearly dark. He ran his hands over his ankle and could feel the swelling under his skin. He would have to spend the night in the forest. He felt the brush of bats on his skin and saw their small, black shapes flying recklessly through the trees. He reached for Trevor Manning's canteen and found it, still around his shoulder. He had a little water and tomorrow, when it was light, he would fashion a crutch or a splint and he would walk home. It would be slow, but he would find his way. And he would be missed. If he was not present at shell-blow, a search would begin. Miranda would appear at Bonnie Valley riderless and they would look for him.

He propped himself against the trunk of a tree and drank some of the water. His ankle throbbed. He tried to wriggle his toes and they moved at his command. Not a serious injury then; his ankle was not broken. It was just a night in the forest. He closed his eyes and hoped for sleep.

He woke with the dawn. The air was still and the birds were quiet. His ankle was swollen and purple. He looked around for a stick to make a crutch, refusing to think about the difficulties of walking the steep, rocky paths on just one leg. He saw a shrub with a crook at about the right height and crawled over to it. He began to cut at it with his knife. It was young and green and he made little progress. His gloves tore and he took them off. His body ran with sweat and the pain in his ankle made him nauseous. He turned away to vomit, but there was nothing in his stomach.

He hacked at the shrub for an hour. His hands were blistered by the time he'd severed the stick he wanted. He shaved the branches off and fitted it under his arm. It was slightly too short. He heaved himself up and leant against a tree. He waited for his dizziness to subside. He took a step. The crutch held. The going would be very slow, but he thought he could make it through the forest. He wondered whether to follow the broken bush that marked Miranda's path, or look for his own old marks on the trees. Miranda might take him on a long route and he needed to get back to Bonnie Valley as quickly as possible. He looked around for knife marks, but there were none where he had fallen. He saw the path, but did not know which way to turn. These paths snaked up, around and down hills all the time and it was not easy to guess any path's eventual destination. He had to choose; he chose downhill. He began a limping, halting retreat.

A warm, gusty wind began to shake the tree tops. The birds were silent and his water was finished. Zachary's groin grew heavy with fear; could it be another hurricane? He remembered the stillness before the storm of the previous year and he remembered the

231

roaring sound. He heard thunder in the distance and it began to rain. At first, the trees sheltered him from the downpour, but as the wind rose, gaps opened in the forest canopy and he was pelted with fat, stinging raindrops. He looked around him, feeling his fear expand, searching for shelter. He saw nothing but trees and vines and shrubs and rocks. Perhaps this would only be a storm, like the recent ones. He knew that were he to be caught in the forest in a hurricane, he would die. Then he heard the roaring noise he remembered well and he wrapped his arms around the nearest tree and held on.

Although it was still daylight, he could see nothing. The trees groaned and swayed and cracked. Torn leaves hit his face. At least he would not die of thirst; he found himself laughing. The tree he clung on to danced like a live thing. Did wild animals survive hurricanes?

He clung on, waiting for the eye of the storm, but there was no break in the wind. His arms ached and his one good leg burned from bearing his weight. He was tempted to lie down, to give up, relinquish his body to the storm. He was thirsty and opened his mouth to the sky. He was hungry, but had no provisions. He had become careless, imagining the forest a friendly place.

Eventually the wind eased and the noises of branches breaking stopped. He did not know what time it was. He released the tree trunk and slid to the sodden earth, leant back and opened his mouth again. A man could live for weeks without food, but without water he would be dead in days. He thought of the plants high in the trees that held water. He would not be able to reach them on one leg.

He spent his second night in an unceasing, solid downpour. He tried to sleep, but it was like trying to sleep in the river. He thought about the blue pools of the risings; this was how they were filled. Then he remembered the caves and wondered if there he could find shelter.

The next day the rain continued. Zachary got to his feet and cast around for his rough crutch. It was gone. He was surrounded by fallen branches and leaves, though few trees had come down. He tried to put weight on his bad leg and cried out with the pain. He leant against a tree and wiped tears and rainwater from his face. Then he realized he could see a distinct path ahead through the undergrowth. This time he would go uphill.

He looked around for another suitable branch for a crutch, saw none, then remembered he had put the one he had carved at his feet by the big tree. He cleared the mud and laughed out loud when he found it. "Now I will make it out," he said aloud. He thought he heard a voice say, "Shh!" and his flesh crawled. The blacks thought the forest was full of spirits. He braced himself and began limping towards the path he could see.

One laborious step after another, Zachary climbed the path. His breath came harshly and he began to feel feverish. He recognized nothing, but he kept going up, questioning his decision with every step. It would be easier to simply sit and drown. He howled with laughter again. He would be the only man in history to drown in a forest.

The path crested a small hill and as it started down, Zachary suddenly knew where he was. A large cave was just ahead. He had climbed into it once or twice, but never stayed long enough to explore, because he feared Miranda would pull her rein and leave him in the cave. Now he would discover its nooks and crannies.

Panting, his head swimming, his throat burning, covered in mud and the slime of pulverized leaves, he eased himself over the rim of the cave, stopping to let his eyes adjust to the dark. There was a wide rocky ledge just below him and below that, a black void. He heard the sound of water charging through the cave. Then on the ledge below, staring up at him, a stick raised in her hand, he saw Victoria, with her lips drawn back in a snarl, her clothes soaked and muddy, her eyes white in the gloom. He let himself slide down the steep slope and crumpled, exhausted and beaten, at her feet.

"Dinna hit me," he said. He felt manic and laughed at his own words. He had heard dozens of versions of that plea, but the blows had fallen nonetheless. There was no reason to imagine mercy from Victoria. Perhaps another slave might have extended an arm and helped him, but not Victoria. She would kill him.

"Is you gone mad?" she whispered.

"Why are ye whispering?"

"*Duppy*. Dem mus' stay in sleep."

Zachary felt relief. She was a superstitious black woman; that was all. He sat up. "What are ye doing here?" he said. She did not answer. She walked past him to the rim of the cave and looked out. He leaned against the cave wall and waited. Victoria did not return. We're travellers caught in a storm, he told himself. We are sharing a refuge. When the rain is over, we will go our separate ways. He knew this was a fiction. Victoria had no right to be in the forest at all. She must have taken the opportunity to run again. If they caught her this time, they would flog her one final time then lock her in the gibbet.

As the hours passed, Zachary's hunger grew keener. The cave was dry enough where they sat, although he could hear dripping from the roof. He upturned the canteen over his mouth, but it was completely empty. Victoria remained on watch until the light was gone. Bats streamed from the cave on their night excursions. He covered his head. All he had to do was endure. Perhaps endurance was the only skill worth having. He had endured his father's moods, the loss of his family, endured the months at sea, the ride to Bonnie Valley, the hurricane, the lonely nights in Bell Cottage and the violence all around him. But he wanted a life in which such endurance was unnecessary; *a life which he made*. He heard Victoria leave the cave. Don't leave me, he thought, but could not say it. He heard her moving around just outside. He stretched out on the rocky shelf and let exhaustion do its work.

He awoke to the sounds of birds. His muscles hurt, but the throbbing in his ankle had lessened. He could hear Victoria's steady breathing and wondered at her calm. He felt creaky and old. He shivered. His head hurt, his throat still burned; he knew he was getting a fever.

He struggled to his feet and limped to the cave's opening. He still could put no weight on his ankle. He looked out. If I get sick here, I will die here. If she leaves me here, I will die.

He turned his back on the dawn and struggled to his place on the ledge. He saw the gleam of Victoria's eyes. She reached inside an Osnabruck bag on the ledge beside her. She took out a piece of dried fish and gnawed at it. He watched her. What happened next would decide his fate. If she shared her food with him, she would not leave him to die. She finished the fish and licked her fingers. Despite her pregnancy, she vaulted over the ledge of the cave in one lithe motion and disappeared into its depths. He heard loose rocks slide under her feet and he prayed she would not fall. Unless there was another way out of the cave, she would have to return and step over him to get out. Perhaps then he could persuade her to help him. He could trade his life for her freedom.

Victoria returned after only a few minutes. Her face was washed and her hair was tucked under her headscarf.

"Gi me," she said, holding out her hand.

"What?"

"Fi wata." He realized she wanted his canteen. Would she take it from him, hastening his demise?

"No." She made a sound of exasperation, leaned down and dragged it over his neck. Then she disappeared over the ledge again.

She returned with the canteen and handed it to him. "Thank ye." He felt hopeful. "Will ye help me?" He wanted the uncertainty over with. If he was going to die in the forest, he wanted to face it now.

"Help *you*?"

"Help me get back to Bonnie Valley."

She threw her head back and laughed without restraint. "Di massa want me fi help!" He began to laugh too and the cave echoed with their mirth.

She undid her headscarf and wiped her face. He saw her hair was woolly and very short. Despite the pain that flickered on and off all over his body, he felt aroused. She stood, hands akimbo, looking down at him.

"Where are ye going anyway? They'll catch ye and flog ye and kill ye this time."

"You no business where mi go."

"Ye think ye can find the Maroons, and that they will take ye in? Well, they willna. They will take ye back tae Thompson and he'll skin ye alive and then he'll gibbet ye and leave your bones for the crows."

"You lie, *Massa Zachary*. No black man send me back to Overseer Thompson."

"They will. It's in their treaty. Why dae ye think so few slaves manage tae run away without being caught? The Maroons bring them back. If ye help me, I swear, *I swear*, I will buy your freedom."

She squatted beside him and stared into his eyes. He saw her face at close quarters, the scar on her cheek, now fainter than it had been when he had first seen her in the fields, the brand marking her a slave, the straight eyebrows over deeply set eyes, the unusual gleam of the whites of her eyes that held not the faintest touch of yellow or of red, the small coils of hair in front of her ears, the curving cheeks that never lost their plumpness, no matter how thin she became. Rage and sorrow churned in her eyes. He wondered how old she was; whether she had left her family as a child or as a mother. He wanted to touch her, to reach out and hold her, she who held his life in her calloused hands. He wanted to hold her like a lover or a weeping child, to bring her his strength and comfort; to draw strength and comfort from her, to assert his dominance and to relinquish his soul and his body to her forever. He waited.

Finally she stood and stretched. He saw the swell of her belly; her pregnancy was advanced. "Rain soon stop," she said. "Time fi go. Drink first."

He drank and then she held out her hand and he grasped it. She pulled him easily to his feet. "Na worry, Massa Zachary, you not far from home."

She helped him out of the cave and steadied him while he leaned on the crutch. "You cut him too short," she complained. "White man sure a useless." He held his head down, hiding his eyes from her. He was ashamed of all he had been to her, all he was. She was going to help him get home. She draped his arm over her shoulders and together, they began a slow progress out of the forest.

Victoria did not hesitate as she half led, half carried him through the forest. Wide paths had been cleared by the storm and it was easy to see the way ahead, but Zachary had no idea which way to walk. They could not see the sun and there was no landmark he recognized. He bit back his questions: shouldn't we be bearing more west? He did not know which way west was.

She did not let him rest and never slowed their halting pace through the forest. His breathing became laboured; hers remained steady and even. He felt her strong, swollen body all along his side; she smelled of mud and sweat and ashes.

The rain held off for a time, but then it came in gusty squalls. He began to shiver and his skin felt tight, as if it had been stretched over his bones, as if it would split, spilling bones and viscera to the earth. His soaked and filthy clothes chafed him. He longed to be naked; submerged in the river. He closed his eyes and thought: endure.

Then she stopped. "Dere. See di ride through di South Field? Wait dere. Dem soon come, looking fi di animal-dem." He saw the flattened cane fields spreading to the edges of the valley, the river overflowing its banks. This land was impossible: hurricanes, heat and brutality, and now the fever wracking his bones. She released her hold around his waist and took his arm, limp as sodden rope, from around her neck. She nodded and turned to leave him.

"Wait!" he said. "I telt ye, I will buy your freedom. Dinna risk the forest and the Maroons. Come back wi me and I will tell them what happened. Please."

"You caan' buy me freedom," she said. "Not fi you to buy." She left him then and in seconds he could not see her, nor hear her passing. He had not told her he was grateful.

Zachary lay with eyes slit against the sun. He heard the sounds of hoof beats. He tried to call out, but his voice merely croaked like a frog. He tried to wave, but his arm fell back. The fever crushed his head. Then a shadow fell over him and he looked up. It was Hannibal mounted on a mule, in defiance of normal rules, looking, as Victoria had predicted, for escaped animals. "Massa, me did think you drown!" he said. And then Zachary felt muscular arms gather him up, limp as a fainting girl. Hannibal lowered him face first over the mule's withers, and they began the long walk home.

1888
Bonnie Valley Plantation

John rode through Bonnie Valley's stone pillars and drew rein. The road forked; one branch led to farm buildings, the other up the hill to the Great House. He wanted to speak to someone in authority so he rode up to the tethering post near the front door of the Great House and dismounted. He knocked, stood back and waited.

He heard footsteps, the sound of bolts being pulled back and a key turning. The door opened a crack. "Massa?" a woman said.

"I am Pastor John McCaulay, from the village of Fortress," he said. "I heard about the tragedy here and came to offer prayers and counsel. Is anyone here?"

"Mi here."

"Yes, obviously. I meant any of the Monmouths."

"Massa Mark here, but him not inna di house."

"Where is he then?"

"Him somewhere, Massa." The door remained almost shut and his irritation grew. He was no Negro to be treated with suspicion.

"Please open the door so I can see you."

The door opened and he saw an elderly Negro woman with a hunched back. She regarded him steadily.

"Good afternoon." He felt the encounter should begin again. "As I said, I'm the Pastor…"

"From Fortress… You di preacher what buil' di school."

"How do you know that?"

The woman shrugged. "Evybody know."

"I'd like to speak to Massa Mark."

"Den just ride you horse an' look for him." The woman began to close the door.

"Wait!" John said. "What's your name?"

"Clarice."

"Were you born here?"

"Eeh-hee. What you want know for?"

"Please just answer my questions, Clarice."

"Me answer you."

"So you were you born a slave?"

"Eeh-hee. So *dem* sey." He heard the sarcasm. Her eyes were intelligent. She was like a lump of coal hiding heat and light inside a dull exterior, waiting for a match to ignite her flame.

"So you saw emancipation?"

"Mi see it. Mi a house slave before; after, mi a maid."

"But no one can sell you now."

"Dem going sell di plantation. Maybe nobody buy it and alla we here dead fi hungry. Maybe we haffi come a Fortress. What you going do wid us dere?" No answer was expected and the door closed another inch.

"Wait. Were you here when it happened?"

"When what happen?"

"You know. The murder. Cuba."

"Mi was here. Mi hear him bawl out from di gibbet…"

"The gibbet?"

"Inna di stableyard. Where dem lock him. Him go mad di second night."

"The *second* night? In a gibbet?"

"Two night and one day dem lef' him in dere. Inna di day dem throw cow shit at him and laugh."

"What do you mean; he went mad?"

"Him just go mad. Start bawl for him granny and him pickney and for some place call Tetegu. Him call 'pon Jesus and di Lord God Almighty. Him sey him see di forest down below him and di sea takin him home. Him say him fly on di wing of a John Crow, di one dat eat di dead, all the way back to Africa. Him think dem going keep him inna di gibbet 'til him dead and den lef' him to rot."

"Then what happened?"

"You find Massa Mark. Him tell you what you want fi know. Mi have work to do." The door closed firmly in his face.

John turned and looked over the valley. The afternoon was growing old and the heat was easing, but visibility was reduced by the haze. Although drought scorched the lawns and banks, the fields were lush. Perhaps they were irrigated. There seemed no-one around, and the canes stood green and still. John walked down the steps, untied Friday and mounted. His muscles ached and he longed for a bath and his bed and the sight of his wife's skirts as she left a room. He rode down the hill towards the farm buildings, into a cobbled courtyard flanked by low buildings on three sides. One row consisted of stables; they had half-doors painted dark green and at the sound of his approach, horses put their heads over the doors, their ears pricked. The doors to the other buildings were shut and he could not guess their purpose. There was no one around.

He dismounted and tethered Friday to a ring outside the end stable, and stood for a minute under the overhanging roof. He was glad to be out of the sun. Friday lowered his head and mouthed his bit, evidently thirsty. He reached for his canteen and shook it. Almost empty. He gazed over the stableyard and saw a trough at the open end. Then he saw the gibbet right beside it.

He had heard of gibbeting. It had been practised in Britain up to a couple of centuries ago. Criminals were locked in a man-shaped metal or leather case and left to die of starvation or exposure. Their dead bodies were then left on display as a deterrent for others. It was only fifty years since the practice of leaving hanged men to rot in a gibbet had been outlawed. He had read that there were places in England where a traveller entering a town could be met with a line of bone-filled gibbets.

His head swam and he went to the water trough, dipped the scarf Irene had given him into the scummy water and wiped his face and the back of his neck. He decided it best not to drink. He turned to the gibbet. It hung from a tall rectangular structure and the bottom was well out of his reach. It looked small, and he could not imagine Cuba fitting into it. He could not see the mechanism that would allow for a full-grown man to be hoisted to hang there all day in the hammer of the sun and chilled by the night's dew. What would such a man think? Would he watch the arc of the moon, dreading the dawn? Or would he hate the dark of night and long for the rising sun? Would he pray or curse? At what point would he lose his mind? How long would it take for someone to die of thirst and heatstroke? Could a man will himself to die when circumstances were beyond bearing? He squinted and tried to see the contraption clearly, looking for blood on the frame, but all he could see was rust. Why had they put the farrier in the gibbet? Who had done it?

"Can I help you?" a voice said from behind him.

John turned and saw a white man standing in one of the doorways. His eyes were bloodshot and his hand rested on a gun on his hip.

"Aye. Good afternoon. I'm sorry to intrude like this; I did go to the Great House but your maid directed me to... Are you Mark Monmouth?"

"Yes. And you are...?"

"John McCaulay. Pastor John McCaulay. I'm from the town of Fortress, two days' ride from here."

"What can I do for you?"

"Well, I heard what happened. I came to offer prayers and my sincere condolences. You see, I knew the man called Cuba."

"I suppose you have come to gawp, like the others."

"No. Well, I suppose it must seem that way. I wanted to... I don't know. Help. Understand."

Mark Monmouth spat on the ground. John was shocked and wondered if he might turn violent. "I'm sorry. I've disturbed you and invaded your privacy. I'll go. Would you be kind enough to allow me to water my horse? I've been riding all day and it's been many hours since I left the banks of the river."

"You've been riding for two days?"

"Yes."

"You look as if you're about to collapse. So you knew this Cuba?"

"I did. I do. He helped me build a school in Fortress. He was the farrier there. I'm sorry. I need to sit down."

"Come inside," Mark Monmouth said. "You can have some food and drink before you leave. I suppose it would be ill-mannered of me to send a man of the cloth out into the night in this godforsaken island."

"God does not forsake," John said. He did not want to pass out in front of this man. He followed Mark Monmouth into a small office and collapsed onto one of the chairs. He put his head between his knees. His skin was clammy and he began to tremble.

"You're ill as well as exhausted," said Monmouth. "You'd better stay the night, then. You wanted to see Bonnie Valley and hear what happened. Why not? It's lonely enough here for me,

241

with only niggers and ghosts for company. Stay the night, McCaulay, and I'll tell you about the animal you call Cuba."

"I thank you, sir. I'm grateful. A good night's sleep will restore me, I'm sure." John sat up and his stomach steadied. He was parched, ravenous and dirty. He would be content to spend the night on the floor in this stuffy room, in the shadow of the gibbet.

Monmouth walked to the door. "Lewis!" he shouted.

"Massa!"

"We have a visitor. Look here and see to his horse." He turned to John. "Can you walk up to the house?"

"I think so. I thank you for your graciousness."

"Hmm. It's the tradition of these places, is it not? White man to white man?"

"I suppose it is."

An hour later, John lay on clean sheets in a stone room with a low ceiling. An unsmiling maid had filled a bath for him with hot water and brought him towels. He had removed his filthy clothes and sunk gratefully into the water. It slopped over onto the floor. He wished it were possible to go to sleep in the water. He thought of the people he had baptized, telling them their sins were cleansed. Although he could feel his skin softening in the bath, he knew only his body was cradled by the water – his soul felt unwashed. He had always imagined his soul like a shadow-John, a shape in the outline of a man, but glowing, like the tropical dawns he had come to love, but perhaps his soul – his white man's soul – was formed in the shape of a gibbet.

He dressed, wishing he had clean clothes and walked outside and gazed over the valley, the farm buildings indistinct in the dusk. He could no longer see the gibbet, but he wondered if the screams of a man would be heard up here on the hill. He turned and saw there were lamps on in the Great House and he walked towards the light.

His host was sitting in a large armchair, going over a ledger. "Ah, Reverend," he said. "I trust you're somewhat revived. Dinner will soon be ready. Would you like to join me with a glass of rum while we wait?"

"I thank you, Mr. Monmouth, but think it unwise to drink on an empty stomach."

"Of course. Please sit."

John sat and watched Monmouth studying his ledger, smoking and, from time to time, drinking from the glass on a silver tray by his side. They were silent. Moths fluttered around the lamps on the walls.

"So what brought you to Jamaica?" Monmouth asked, closing one of the ledgers with a snap.

"Oh, the usual, I suppose. I come from a line of churchmen. My grandfather was born here. I grew up hearing stories of the islands. And you? Are you here to close up the plantation?"

"Close up? I'll sell it to anyone fool enough to buy it. My brother wouldn't listen to sense – he thought he could still make a go of it after the niggers were freed. We all knew he'd die here."

"It's a beautiful place."

"Can't see the point of beauty myself. Does beauty make money? Sell the blasted place and be done. It's cursed anyway."

"So tell me what happened."

"What is there to tell? Someone was stealing. We set a guard with some of the dogs and they caught him."

"Then what happened?"

"Well, the men didn't have anywhere to lock him up, couldn't find keys, I don't really know, but I gather there was a debate about flogging him. Then Cartwright – he's the overseer here – came up with the idea of putting him in the gibbet for the night. They thought the most he'd get were a few mosquito bites. They'd take him down in the morning and see about getting the police here. Ah, Clarice. Is dinner ready?"

"Yes, Massa. Dinner serve." John saw the woman who had refused to let him in earlier, dressed in the black and white uniform of a maid.

"Shall we go in?"

"Wait. Please finish your story."

"Not much else to say, really. Your man started bawling and no one could sleep, so Cartwright got up, got one of the others, and they took him down. When they let him out, he went berserk. Broke Cartwright's neck, took his machete, and the other man who

243

was there, Moses, ran screaming into the bush. He claims your man's eyes glowed with fire and he heard the sound of chains. Superstitious nonsense. Then he killed them all. Massacred everyone in the house. By the time I got here, it was cleaned up."

"He killed *them*? Who? How many?"

"Everyone sleeping in the house, including three niggers. My brother, his wife and four children. Even the baby. Cartwright. Ten people."

"Merciful Father. I had no idea. I heard of one murder."

"No, Pastor. An entire family, the overseer and three servants."

"Why not Clarice?"

"You'd have to ask him that."

"Clarice said Cuba was in the gibbet for two nights."

Monmouth stood. "Possibly. What does it matter?"

"Wait. One more thing. Why did the men here assume Cuba was a thief? My understanding is he came here to shoe a horse. That a buggy was sent to Fortess for him."

The two men stared at each other in silence. Eventually, Monmouth shrugged. "There's no one left to ask about that." He led John into the dining room.

John slept fitfully and rose at first light. The land was grey and silent and a soft breeze brushed his face. He walked down to the stableyard, where Friday stood saddled and ready.

He savoured the solitude of the early morning ride. He felt calm, as if he had come to a resolution, although he could not put his feelings in words. He listened to the sounds of the land awakening, the low coos of doves, the caws of parrots and, in the distance, the sound of water. To his left, he saw a large fenced field. There was a grove of trees at one end and he saw wooden crosses in their shade and a man sitting with his back to one of the trees. He dismounted and walked up to him.

The man sat with his head back, his eyes closed. He did not hear John's approach until he was quite close. He sprang to his feet and said, "Massa, you lost?"

"No. I've come to pay my respects to the Monmouths. Are these their graves?"

"Yes, Massa. Dem bury here. Marble stone don't come yet. But dis a where dem rest. Under di cedar tree. White folks don't bury near cotton tree. Dat a for di slave-dem and di children of slaves-dem."

There was something askew about the man. He was wringing his hands and his eyes slid from side to side.

"Are you Moses?"

"How you know dat?" He appeared terrified.

"I stayed at the Great House last night and Massa Mark told me the story of the murders."

"Mi Moses, yes. Mi see di man dat night, di second night, mi see all di duppy-dem of all di slave who ever live and die at Bonnie Valley. Him sey dem all come to him and tell him dem story and it come in like him feel dem pain. It too much for one man. Dem shoulda never put him in dat ting. Mi did know sumpn bad-bad go happen when him come out."

"So you ran away after he killed the overseer."

"Mi run, yes. And mi don't go back a Bonnie Valley neither. But mi come here sometime; is peaceful under di tree."

"I knew him. Cuba. I knew him."

"You was his frien'?"

"Yes," John said, although he knew this was not true.

"Mi give you…" He stopped. "You wait." He walked into the bush and John waited, his head bowed, his eyes closed, his mind empty of prayers. He heard Moses returning and lifted his head.

"Here." Moses held out a well-worn canvas bag.

John took it. "What is this?" he said, but he knew.

"Overseer tek it. From Cuba. Den him did t'row it inna di bush."

"Moses. Did you see Cuba arrive? Did he come in a buggy?"

The old man rolled his eyes. "You give it back to him," he said, shaking his head.

"I will." John hoisted Cuba's bag of tools over his shoulder.

Before he left he looked at the wooden crosses, which had only names and dates etched in the wood.

Jeremy Alexander Monmouth 1853-1888.
Kate Farnsworth Monmouth 1859-1888.

Belinda Catherine Monmouth 1881-1888.
Elizabeth Gloria Monmouth 1883-1888.
Rosemarie Arlene Monmouth 1885-1888.
Anne Morgan Monmouth 1886-1888.

Each raw mound of earth held a small urn with dead flowers. This was the weight of old crimes reverberating through generations. The sins of the fathers. The sins of his own countrymen. One day people would shake their heads at Bonnie Valley's gibbet and the brutality of men. Some would fear that it would never end. Perhaps violence could be tamped down, like a fire made ready for the night, but always there would be some glowing coal, some sudden wind, to set the flames shooting high again. John bowed his head and prayed for everlasting peace.

As he rode away, he realized he had left his canteen beside the stable door where Friday had been tied. It did not matter. He would follow the river all the way back to Fortress. He would see Magistrate Bannister and present his evidence that Cuba had merely gone to Bonnie Valley to shoe a horse, that he had been driven mad by his two nights in the gibbet, that what had happened afterwards could be understood, if not condoned. But why the women, he asked himself. Why the children, Cuba? Perhaps all he could do was change a death sentence to life imprisonment. Which was worse he did not know.

1987
Edinburgh Plantation

For many evenings, Leigh sat with her father unearthing her family's history. It was not surprising she was so ignorant: her parents had separated when she was young, then she was in boarding school, then in Kingston with her mother, then she was gone.

Her father knew little about her grandparents on her mother's side, but his family had been in Jamaica for generations. "My grandfather was a missionary," he said, with a strange irony. "I told you that. He's buried in Fortress."

"Where's that?"

"Little town on the edge of Cockpit Country. In the Baptist churchyard."

"Was he married?"

"Yes. Twice. First to Lillian and then to May Isabelle. They – John and May – died within a few months of each other."

"My mother's parents died together and your grandparents died together? How weird is that?"

"Well, John and May didn't exactly die together. He was off on a mission somewhere in Latin America. She became ill and died and he was sent for. On the way back to Jamaica, his ship foundered in a hurricane. 1905, I think."

"Looks like the sea got a lot of McCaulays."

"I suppose. Maybe you should stay away from boats."

"And cars." Maybe islands too. Or maybe just this island. "How did he manage to be buried in Fortress if he drowned at sea?"

"His wife was buried there. Go and look at the grave, you'll see what it says."

The complexity of this family history was bewildering. One of her ancestors was a Scottish missionary, another an English diplomat. Strands of her family had been in Jamaica since, oh, maybe the mid 1800s. Did this, finally, make her Jamaican? More pertinently, did her great grandfather's mission absolve her from her white skin's link with riches gained from slavery? She imagined a new discourse when tourists asked her where she was from:

"But you're not Jamaican, are you?"

"Fourth generation."

"Did you own slaves?"

"My great grandfather was a missionary."

"Oh."

This was unsatisfactory. She knew next to nothing about Baptist missionaries. She had an impression they had been involved in efforts to abolish the slave trade. She revised her lines:

"But you're not Jamaican, are you?"

"Fourth generation."

"Did you own slaves?"

"My great grandfather was a missionary. A *Baptist* missionary."

"Oh. They were against the slave trade, weren't they?"

"They were." She needed to know more about the Baptists. She resolved to visit her great grandfather's grave, as soon as she had a day off.

Fortress was a dilapidated small town a few miles from Ulster Spring. Leigh stopped at the postal agency and asked directions for the Baptist church. "Up on the hill," the postmistress said. "Next to the primary school."

"Can I leave my car here?"

The woman shrugged.

"Is it walking distance?"

"Depend on how far you can walk."

Leigh felt the woman's judgment. She wanted to say, my great grandfather was a Baptist missionary, but she merely thanked her, keeping sarcasm out of her voice.

She walked up the hill towards the church, easily visible from the crossroads in the centre of town. There was a cottage in great disrepair beside it. The church itself had been desecrated by a modern addition on one side. The gate to the churchyard stood open and she walked in. She peeked inside the church, but it was empty. She walked around the building. There was a small, modern office building at the back, but its door was locked and the louvre windows shut. She looked around for a graveyard, but saw no sign of one. The land fell away on one side and she could see the green aluminium roof of a primary school below. She heard the sound of a lawnmower and walked in that direction.

The lower slope came into view and she saw the graveyard, fenced with chain link. A man was mowing the grass between the graves. She walked towards him and stopped at the fence. She tried calling out, but he did not hear her over the noise of the mower. She walked into the fenced area and began to look at the gravestones. The graves were modern, nothing older than the 1960s.

The man caught sight of her and turned off the mower. She saw his stooped back and wondered if all Jamaica's manual labour was being done by its old people.

"Yes, Miss?"

"I'm looking for my great grandfather's grave. But these graves seem too recent. Is there an old graveyard anywhere?"

"Where you come in."

"I didn't see any graves up by the church."

"Yes, Miss. Dem is dere. Inna di car park."

"Okay. Thanks." She began to retrace her steps and she heard the old man's footsteps behind her.

"Mi come with you."

"Thanks, but I don't want to bother you."

"Is awright." He took a large handkerchief from his pocket and wiped his face. He smelled of cut grass and turned earth. They walked together to a flat area near the gate into the churchyard.

"See. Dere. Di old grave-dem." He pointed at the ground and Leigh realized the spaces between the gravestones had been paved to make a car park. Had her great grandfather's grave been covered over. She felt anxious; surely she would not lose this mark of her history just as she had found it?

There were only eight graves. Some were cracked and the inscriptions hard to read. Her great grandfather's grave was the fourth she looked at. It was in perfect condition, except for a chipped corner. There was a pattern of maple leaves at the top. The inscription read:

In Memory of
MAY ISABELLE
Beloved wife of
REV. John McCAULAY
Died 9ᵗʰ April 1904
Aged 28 years
Also
REV. John. McCAULAY
Drowned at sea
June 1905

She squatted and ran her fingers over the letters. John, drowned at sea. May Isabelle, died aged 28 years. There had been a year between the deaths. How would he have been contacted and how long would it have taken? Surely not a year? Despite his wife's death and the existence of four children, John had taken a year to start his journey home. Why? She was frustrated by how little she knew. There was a first wife as well. She stood. As soon as the tourist season was over, she would return to Kingston and haunt the libraries and newspaper archives, until she found out more about her family. She turned to the gardener, who stood a little way off watching her. "Here," she said, taking ten dollars from her pocket. "Look after this one for me. Trim the grass around it." And, she wanted to add, keep cars off it.

"Tanks Miss. I will."

"I'm leaving at the end of April," Leigh told her father. "It's too far away from the world. I'm over thirty, Dad. I'll never find anyone to be with here." This was an argument he would understand.

"What am I going to do about the tours? Sarita can't manage…"

"Well, Dad, you might have to consider giving up this particular business. Sarita isn't getting any better. It might be best if you were nearer to medical services. Or you could simply hire someone to replace me. I'll do some interviews in Kingston, if you like."

"End of April – that's in six weeks! Stay until the summer; hardly anyone comes in the summer. We run only one tour a week."

"What do the workers do then?"

"The workers?"

"Banjo and Grace and Pauline and Rose and…"

"I don't know. What has that got to do with anything?"

"Dad, I'll stay until the end of May. Not a day more. And I need a week off soon. I want to go to Kingston."

"A week off! I can't manage without you for a week. Why are you going to Kingston?"

"Research. I want to find out more about the missionary, John. I want to look through old copies of the *Gleaner*, maybe visit a Baptist church. I want to look for Nanny Ros. And Zoe. And see my new friends. Just take a break."

Her father made a sound of disgust she remembered from her childhood. He was being inconvenienced. Well, too bad. "You'll manage. Grace and Pauline are more than capable of dealing with the tours. I'll let you know when I'm going beforehand."

"What about the murder? It could still be dangerous to go back."

"It's been months. I can't believe the police would still be looking for me. But I'll ask at the shelter what they think before I go." She would call Danny. She wanted to hear his voice. She was suddenly afraid that he might have left Kingston Refuge; she had not spoken to him since just before Christmas.

1787
Bonnie Valley Plantation

He had been tried and found guilty. He was a witch, a sorcerer. He was being burned at the stake and Victoria was watching, laughing. His flesh melted and fell away. He screamed without restraint and his screams became birds and soared above the forest.

He was locked in the gibbet; he was broken on the wheel. He saw a faint light and it drilled his eyes and exploded in his skull. His skull split in a line above his eyebrows and his hair peeled off. His screams became moans. They were not his moans.

A man – who was this man? – held his head and made him drink. Other hands sponged his limbs and he whimpered. He had not the strength to scream or moan.

The secret was to keep his eyes closed against the light. It was simple, after all. He heard his father's voice, "I am the way, the truth and the life; no man cometh unto the Father, but by me." Did he say "life" or "light?" He would have to tell his father that light was the enemy. He would never see his father again.

He heard a man's voice. "Mr. Macaulay, you must eat. Try. Your fever has broken. If you eat, you will live." He risked opening his eyes, but the light was still there, waiting, ready to pounce. He felt something hard against his bottom lip and tasted a thin gruel. It made him retch. His lips moved again and he heard someone – was it him? – say, "Leave me."

The heat woke him. He opened his eyes and recognized the hot house. He ran his hands over his naked body and was shocked to feel himself: all ribs and hipbones. He thought it was the middle of the day and he could hear the sounds of the plantation at work. He was covered with a linen cloth; the same kind Dr. Whitby threw over the slaves after they had been flogged. Had he been flogged then? He remembered nothing. What crime could he have committed to merit a flogging – he was a white man! Had Thompson not realized who he was? He tried to lift his head, but it was too much. He fell back and watched the lizards in the roof. He counted the blinking of his eyelids. The day went on and on.

When the light began to dim, the hot house door opened and he heard footsteps.

"You're awake," Charlotte Monmouth said.

"Aye," he croaked.

"You had us worried for a while."

"Why was I flogged? Is my mother here?"

"You weren't flogged, Mr. Macaulay. What an idea. You were caught in the forest and there was a storm, luckily for you, not a very strong one. You were found in the South Field near death. That was almost two weeks ago. You've been fighting a fever ever since."

"In the forest?" He could not grasp what she was saying.

"We assume that's what happened. You don't remember? You went riding; Miranda came back riderless, the storm hit, and three days later, Hannibal found you in the South Field. He thought you'd drowned."

"I thought I dreamed it."

"Rest," Charlotte said. "I'll bring you some food and drink. You must eat to get your strength back."

"How bad was the damage?" he said, trying to sound like someone in his proper senses.

"The storm?" she said. "Not as bad as last year. We had more food stored and the Great House roof held. Eight slaves died and we lost some animals." She smiled. "You were not here to count. Rest," she said again, and laid her hand on his brow. Her palm was soft and he thought of his mother and his sister. Then he remembered Victoria's calloused skin and firm grip, and he remembered the fall from his horse and the cave and the halting walk through the forest. Had she been recaptured? He could not ask.

1887
Falmouth, Trelawny Parish

John stood outside Henry Bannister's office, carrying Cuba's tools. He had been away from home for nearly a week. He hitched Friday to an iron ring and went inside.

The light in the Magistrate's offices was dim, but the thick walls made the interior cool. Sunlight streamed through a window off to his left, but the light threw only shadows. He rubbed his eyes and longed for cool water.

"May I help you?"

John saw a young man, dressed formally in white shirt and cravat. A clerk, he assumed. "I would like to see the Magistrate."

"Do you have an appointment?" The young man's voice registered his disdain for John's appearance.

"No. But I am his neighbour in Fortress, the Baptist minister there." He stopped, embarrassed, as if he had told a lie.

"Aah. Your name, Sir? I will see if the Magistrate is in."

"Pastor John McCaulay, at your service."

"Wait here, Sir." The young man glanced at two wooden chairs and seemed to consider offering John a seat, thought better of it and disappeared through a door at the back of the small room. John swayed on his feet. He went over to the chairs. He would sit whether or not he had been invited.

He waited. The noise of the street was muted. He looked at the bag of tools between his legs. Would Henry Bannister take this as evidence that Cuba had merely been to the plantation for work, had been falsely accused and imprisoned, that there were reasons for his actions? But were there any mitigating circumstances for multiple murders? Depends who commits the murders, he thought. He doubted anything could be done for Cuba, but he wanted to try. He wanted to understand what had driven him to wield a blade against a baby in a cradle. He knew that he might be suspected of the kind of impulse that had led people to attend public executions through the ages. He tried to pray but he stumbled over the words. He pictured the graves under the cedar tree, Cuba's room at his forge, Ella standing on his doorstep and Irene lying on his kitchen floor. He remembered handing up roof timbers to Cuba straddling the apex. He closed his eyes.

"Pastor?"

John jumped. He must have dozed for a moment. The supercilious young man stood in front of him. "The Magistrate will see you. He asked me to tell you he does not have more than about ten minutes."

"That is all I will need. I thank you."

"Go up the stairs. You will see the Magistrate's door as you enter the landing."

"Thank you."

He climbed the stairs which gave onto a narrow landing with tall shutters, all open. He could see through them to the streets below, see the merchants in their buggies, the finely dressed women, the Negroes walking in the dust. The door to Henry Bannister's office was ajar and he went in.

The Magistrate sat behind a mahogany desk. He did not get up. "Mr McCaulay," he said, and John saw his eyebrows rise.

"I apologize for my attire. I have been riding for days, sleeping in the forest."

"Indeed? How can I help you?"

"The farrier, Cuba. Has he been hanged yet?"

"No. The hangman is on his way from Kingston. We used to have our own, in the old days, but now…"

"He's in the gaol, then?"

"Naturally. What's this about, McCaulay?

"I *know* this man. Cuba. We built the Fortress school together. Ella – his common-law wife – is my maid's sister. She came to me for help, said Cuba had gone to a plantation to shoe a horse and had not returned. I went there. I spoke to one of the Monmouths. I was given this – Cuba's tools. It's true that he must have gone there for work. Someone thought he was stealing and put him in the gibbet. For two nights. I think he lost his mind and that's why he… did what he did."

The Magistrate snorted. "Who gave you the bag?"

"A man who worked there. He told me how Cuba was put in the gibbet and how he called out on the second night, all night."

255

"A nigger, then."

"Yes. But the tools speak for themselves. Cuba must have…"

"A bag of tools says nothing," Bannister interrupted. "A bag of tools is not *evidence*. The tools could have belonged to anyone."

"Maybe Ella could identify…"

"Mr McCaulay. Even if what you say is true, what does it matter? It is not in doubt that this murderous animal killed ten people. That is the end of it. Now, if there is nothing further…"

"May I see him? I would like to pray with him."

"*Pray with him?* I told you your church would do no good. These people are savages, fit only for labour, kept in line only with the lash. In the old days he would have been flogged and broken on the treadmill already."

"Even so. It is my mission to offer comfort and pray with the condemned."

"I can write you a note. You can take it to the officer and perhaps he will let you in. That is all I can do."

"I'm grateful, Sir."

The Magistrate dipped his pen and scribbled on a sheet of paper. "You should go home, McCaulay. It seems to me you do not have the temperament for the tropics. Wait. Take that bag with you. I have no use for it."

The gaol was some way out of town, a simple brick building with bars on the small windows. It faced the street, but behind it, the coastline stretched east and west. The waves curled gently onto the beach and John smelled salt and escape. He went inside.

A ragged man with no teeth in his head and a bottle of rum in his hand directed him to the two cells at the back. There John saw Cuba, curled in sleep, his face swollen and bruised. He was naked, except for a pair of rough trousers and his feet were bare. He breathed deeply and John thought he looked peaceful and comfortable, as if he slept in a bed made with the finest linens.

"Cuba," he whispered. The farrier did not move. "Cuba," he called again, more loudly.

"Poke him wid a stick," said a voice from the second cell. "Him nah talk to nobaddy. Dem say him fool-fool. You know what him do? Chop up plenty-plenty white people." The voice laughed.

"Cuba!" Cuba did not respond. John walked over to the other cell. The occupant was a skinny black boy, no more than fifteen. "You say he does not speak?"

"Him nah talk. Dem ask him and ask him and ask him and him just look at dem. But mi hear him a nighttime. Him talk and him say him is going home."

"Why are you in here?"

"Dem sey mi steal a goat, but mi no do it. Magistrate put mi here for six month, sey mi mus' tink about mi evil ways." He laughed again. "You have any food, Massa? Food in here *awful*."

"I'm sorry. I've been travelling. I have no food." He turned and saw that Cuba still slept in the corner of his cell. Perhaps it was as well. He no longer knew what questions he might ask and in any event, he feared the answers. "Father, in Thy gracious keeping leave we now Thy servants sleeping," he said, and the blessing sounded inane, like a nursery rhyme. He hoped that Cuba would never wake. He left the gaol and went out into the street.

John walked behind the prison and was soon on a small beach, strewn with the detritus of the sea: driftwood, mouldering seaweed, a fallen coconut tree, a broken wooden crate. The sky flamed and the sea met the land with no discernable movement. He thought he could walk upon it, so still it looked, so solid. The sunset colours bled into the sea and he felt dizzy, as if the sky and the sea had changed places. He yearned again for immersion, the immersion that leads to salvation. He wondered if he still believed in salvation. He looked around and finding himself still alone, he undressed behind a bush. His skin crawled with exposure and he waited, making sure no one watched him. Then he walked, naked, into the warm, welcoming sea, and there he felt God's returning presence.

When the water lapped at his neck, he floated, his face turned to the sky, his ears crackling with underwater sounds. The salt water held him. There were no answers; he would never know the reasons. He thought then of his own wife and child and he felt a distant affection for them, for a life he had somehow already left, and he thought of his brother, who had already left him for the best of reasons. He would find Bruce and beg his pardon. He floated, buoyed up, cleansed, where the island shelf fell away into the depths of the sea.

1787
Bonnie Valley Plantation

The day came, after he had resumed his duties as book keeper, after, with Trevor Manning's help, he had booked his passage to Scotland, after he had given his notice to Charles Monmouth and was simply waiting out his days; the day came when he heard a commotion in the yard and saw three black men, strangely dressed, who between them held Victoria, so hugely pregnant it seemed that her child might at any second fight its way out of her stomach, straight out, through her stretched and agonized skin. He could see exhaustion and despair in the way she held her head low and the way her bare feet trailed in the dirt, no longer fighting to keep herself upright. The men stopped in front of Thompson and released her arms. She stood, swaying. They said words Zachary did not understand and Thompson nodded.

"You one stupid bitch," he said. She lifted her head and met Zachary's eyes and he saw she was resigned.

He did not stay to see her flogging. Monmouth had decreed no night in the stocks was necessary: she was simply to be flogged and gibbeted the next day. Her spirit, the overseer told her, would never return to her homeland.

Zachary went back to Bell Cottage and packed his notes, his clothes and his money. His ship was still two weeks away but he could not stay at Bonnie Valley another day. He would ride to Montego Bay at dawn and hope to find lodgings he could afford.

That night he lay sleepless. Victoria would be in the hot house, getting a meaningless show of medical care, awaiting a slow execution. He wondered what it would be like to be locked in the gibbet, swinging high off the ground, how it would be to know the certain but prolonged end. Could he help her escape again? She had been flogged to insensibility, he was sure, but she was indomitable. Could he throw her across Miranda's withers, as Hannibal had done with him, and could they both journey out of this damned and gorgeous valley? He threw his legs over the side of the bed and dressed. Then he left the door of Bell Cottage ajar and walked out into a clear night, a waning moon low in the sky, the peenie wallies winking on the fences of Bonnie Valley.

He found Victoria in labour. She was naked, her back a bloody pulp, and she squatted at the end of the bed, holding on, straining and grunting, until the veins stood out on her forehead.

"What can I dae?"

"Catch di baby," she gasped. "Him coming now."

"How dae ye ken it is a boy?"

"Mi know." He saw the muscles bunched in her arms and she bared her teeth and threw back her head. "Catch di baby!"

He knelt before the straining, labouring woman, embarrassed and afraid of this intimacy; he saw the bulge of a black head from between her legs and a sudden issuing of blood. He held the baby's head and it slithered out, rubbery and slick with fluid and blood. He saw it was indeed a boy, fair skinned, with straight wisps of hair plastered to his skull. Paul's child then. Or the child of any other white man passing through Bonnie Valley.

"Hold him up. Slap him." Victoria slumped to the floor in a spreading pool of blood.

"What? Let me call Dr. Whitby."

"Do it!" she snapped and her voice was strong. He slapped the baby's back and he cried. "Give him," Victoria said. He looked around for something to clean the baby with. "Give him to me," she said again. Zachary handed her the baby. He saw the cord still pulsed at his belly, disappearing into Victoria's body. She took the baby and held him to her breast. He sucked for a short time and then turned his head away and seemed to sleep. "Find some string," she said, holding the baby close.

Zachary found Dr. Whitby's stores and a length of cord. He took it to her. "Tie it 'round di cord; close, close to him belly."

"Let me get Dr. Whitby."

"Do it now," she said, her voice weaker. She was still bleeding.

He grasped the cord. It was slippery and hard to hold. He persevered. "There," he said. "It's done." The baby still slept. Victoria bent her head and bit the cord and the baby was free.

"Ye are bleeding."

"Yes." She leaned against the bed, holding her child; he could see her resolve unravel.

"Please, Victoria, let me call Dr. Whitby."

"Mi name Madu. White man doctor caan' help. Mi wi' die an' mi is ready." She closed her eyes and seemed to sleep.

Zachary sat on one of the beds and watched them. He saw Victoria still bled in a slow, spreading tide. Whatever she had said, he would go and get the doctor. The sky was lightening outside. He stood. Immediately, Victoria opened her eyes.

"Find something to clean di baby."

"Victoria…"

"Mi name Madu."

He found some clean cloths and she wiped her baby boy. She offered him her breast again and he sucked. Zachary saw her grief. "Mi name Madu," she repeated. "Dis boy name Addae. It mean di sun. Mi think. Mi forget." She closed her eyes again.

"How many children dae ye have, Vic…?"

"Five baby mi bear. T'ree girl, two boy. All die, 'cept Kwame and now dis boy. T'ree mi bury by di cotton tree." Her skin was the colour of ash.

"I'm so sorry." He regretted the words. Useless, meaningless, inadequate words. She did not reply. The child still slept.

"Who's child is Addae?" He stumbled over the unfamiliar name. She did not answer. The dawn light crept into the room and explored the corners. A rat scampered. He heard the sounds of the plantation awakening. Soon it would be shell-blow. He wanted to take her hand, but feared his gesture would be rebuffed. He wanted someone else to come into the hot house, Dr. Whitby, preferably, with his expertise and matter-of-fact manner. No one came.

When a shaft of sunlight fell across her face, Victoria opened her eyes. Zachary saw her tears had stopped.

"You know Faith?" she said. "Small woman. Wuk in di kitchen garden?" He shook his head. There were too many of them to know, never ending waves of black people, fathers and daughters, sons and mothers. It had been better to regard them as an army of ants, existing only in the collective, but as he sat beside the dying woman, he was no longer able to.

"You find her. She have baby girl last week an' she die. She still have milk. She give it to di big pickney, to give dem strength."

"I will."

"An' Kwame. Ask Faith to look out for Kwame."

"I will."

"Tell her…"

"Yes? Tell her what?"

"Tell her mi sorry." Her voice faded.

He shook her shoulder and she did not respond. "Victoria," he said, urgent. "Ma-du!" He stumbled over the new name.

"And do not bury di navel string of my son on dis place. Tek him to Africa. Or burn him. If you bury him here, mi will curse you seed."

"I will."

"Say mi name again," she whispered.

"Madu…"

"Madu." He saw her eyes had clouded over like the eyes of a fish, dead on a plate. The baby murmured and moved his tiny lips, wanting to suckle. Zachary reached over and eased him from Madu's arms and held him to his chest. The baby bloodied his shirt.

Later that day, Zachary stood at the new mound of earth under the cotton tree and tried to pray. He had buried her himself because he could not bear the thought of her body being discarded in the forest. He knew there would be a reckoning when Thompson looked for her to lock her in the gibbet. As she had requested, he had thrown the leavings of birth and death into Bonnie Valley's fires. Take it to Africa, she had said. Impossible. It was hard to tell how many people had been buried under the cotton tree; only a few places were marked with rudimentary wooden carvings but there were many mounds of earth in all different sizes. There were no names.

He watched Faith in the kitchen garden. She carried Madu's child in a sling and Kwame walked behind her, as he had walked behind his mother. Sometimes he saw the baby's arms wave, pale against Faith's skin. Paul's son, he was sure. A white child. An almost white child. A black child. An African child; an English child. An island child. A child of a continent. A child born in slavery, with skin white enough to set him free.

He would tell Charles Monmouth the boy was his own blood and ask to buy him. He had a little money still saved after paying his fare. He would take him back to Scotland and his sister would raise him. He would be named Arthur and no one would know his true origins. The boy would not have to explain an African name, would never hear stories of his mother or meet his brother, but he would also never work without choice and a lash would never carve his back into submission. Zachary was not sure his mother would approve of this bargain, but it was the best he could do.

1988
Kingston

Leigh returned to Kingston with her backpack, her birth certificate and a bag of yams and green bananas. She had contacted the Libbeys, who were happy to have her stay with them. Danny also felt she could return, as one of the policemen who shot Jelly had been killed in a drive-by shooting. He was not sure about the others, but thought the pressure was off. Everyone would be glad to see her, he said. Father Gabriel especially. What about you, she wanted to ask, but didn't.

Banjo drove her to Falmouth. They had never mentioned her visit to his house and Leigh did not know if he remembered it. He still came late to work at least once a week. She could find no conversation as they drove; she knew the basics: he had been born near Edinburgh and worked on the plantation all his life, that he had two children, both in America, that he lived alone, that he drank too much, that he was thin and old and hungry and lived in a shack at the edge of the forest. She wondered at the gulf between them. Was it race and class, experience, history or education – or was it her own feelings of discomfort, even of shame? What are you ashamed of, she asked herself. That I sleep in a bed? Always have. That simply being born with white skin has given me an edge, a jumpstart. That I've never gone to bed hungry one day in my life. That this old man is working harder than I've ever had to. That I can't speak to him as an equal, no, as someone my senior, someone deserving of my respect. Oh, shut the fuck up. Middle class guilt. So boring and predictable.

"Banjo, what you know about Edinburgh Plantation?"

"What you mean, Miss?"

"My name is Leigh. Please call me Leigh."

"Yes, M-m… Leigh."

"I mean about the history of the place. You been here long-long time. What you know about it?"

"Nutt'n to know. Is a sugar plantation. A big one. Some piece-dem sold off back inna di forties, so is not as big as before."

"Who were the original owners?

"White people."

"I know. What them name?"

"Me no 'member. Mon-sumpn. Dem bury in Palisade Paddock; why you no look at di gravestone-dem?"

"They're kind of hard to read."

"Look inna di storeroom. Plenty tings in dere from slavery day. Mi father show mi a old book one time with list upon list a slave-dem – like di credit book Miss Bertha keep for her shop."

"Really? I saw a box of books, but they were in bad condition."

Banjo did not answer.

"I guess I'll have a look when I get back."

They did not speak again until they approached Falmouth. Then, as he looked for a place to let her off, Banjo said, "Dem was all chop up."

"Who was chopped up?"

"Di owner-dem. Alla dem. Dem all bury under di cedar tree."

"Who chopped them up?"

"Dunno. A man. Story say dem try fi put him in di gibbet and him go crazy. So mi hear. Dem say di man come from a line of warrior-dem. Dem say di man grandfather fight for freedom, burn cane piece, get hang in Falmouth square."

"Good Lord."

"You look inna di storeroom when you come back, Miss Leigh. Maybe you find di story a dis place in dere. Edinburgh a new name. Not always call Edinburgh. Old name was bad luck so it got change, round about 1953, when di plantation sell."

"What it was called before?"

"Bonnie Valley. Bonnie Valley Plantation."

1789
At sea

Zachary stood at the weather rail of a merchantman, the *Trinity*. He watched the island recede. It was late afternoon, the sea was rough and the light bouncing off the waves hurt his eyes. The blinding tropical light. Perhaps nothing could be hidden in the end. When he got back to England, he would tell others what he had seen in Jamaica, show them his account of slavery in lists. Maybe he would even travel on a slave ship, to see for himself. He had bought Faith's freedom and she and the boy were safely in his cabin. Kwame was left behind, a slave on Bonnie Valley Plantation. The brothers would never know each other. This brother, the baby Arthur, would never see his mother's grave.

A burst of cold spray drenched him and he turned to face west. He would wait on deck until sunset.

"Welcome back!" Phyllis Libbey embraced her. "How was country?"

"Country was good," she said. "Brought you some food."

"Thank you, my dear. These days the yam from Coronation market is old. Glad to get this. Beryl! Miss Leigh bring us some food!" Mrs. Libbey held out her hand for the bag.

"Not all of it is for you; need to take some to the shelter in the morning. I'll take it in the kitchen and show Beryl."

"You go right ahead. I don't know why that woman can't come when I call her. These days I tell you, helpers don't know when they have it good." She shook her head. "You know where your room is. Make yourself at home."

It was evening and Leigh was tired and hot. Despite her wish to leave the plantation at the end of the tourist season, she had stayed until mid-August. She had never managed to take a week off. Her father kept finding excuses why this week it was impossible for her to leave. She had placated him by leaving most of her things in her room.

"You *will* be back, then?" he said.

"Yes, Dad. But not forever."

She had taken a taxi from Falmouth, but the driver had stopped in almost every town on the way for one reason or another: to go to the bathroom, to buy food, to hail up a friend. He had talked non-stop and she had given up either trying to quiet him or to respond to his chatter. She had simply stared through the car window and watched the road unwind.

She went into the kitchen of the Vineyard Town house. Beryl was nowhere in sight. She divided up the yams and cut the green bananas into hands. She put the food for the folks at the shelter back into the bag and went to her room. She wanted to sprawl, sweaty and dusty, on the bedspread and go straight to sleep, but forced herself to undress, take a shower and put on clean clothes. It would soon be time for supper. She was not particularly hungry, as she had eaten along the way, but she knew the Libbeys would want to hear her news.

Two hours later, she stretched out on the bed with relief. Kingston clamoured outside and she felt the loss of the evening silence at Edinburgh... Bonnie Valley, whatever it was called. Bonnie Valley was a better name; why name a rural valley after a city? The Scots had put their stamp on the land, along with the Spanish, the Irish, the Welsh, the Germans and the English. The imprint of the Tainos was only faintly recorded in language and shards of pottery. She strained to hear sounds of nature, but not even the whistling frogs chirped – too dry, she thought. She stared at the square of night sky through the top of the sash window; it was not the indigo of the country, but iron grey, with the stars faded into each other, forming swathes of paler grey. Here in Kingston, when the bush rustled, she startled and got up, standing on the chair to stare through the window into the night. Here, a rustle in the shrubbery might not just be a lizard or a rat.

She planned her first week back. She would go and see the lawyer, take him her birth certificate. She would go to the National Library on East Street. Suddenly, she longed to see Andrew, to talk to him, to ask him what he knew about their family's past. Missionaries and diplomats and entrepreneurs and famous beauties: privileged people, even normal people, but folks who had never wielded a whip, who had even tried to do good deeds. She imagined John at his pulpit, white skin and light eyes, his voice soaring over a congregation of black people with lowered faces. What would have taken him to Jamaica? Chance? Religious fervour? She doubted she would ever know for sure. Not unless he had left a diary and it was in the National Library. She smiled at the fantasy, finding a journal with crumbling pages and faint writing, setting out in detail her great grandfather's life.

She would go to the shelter too, see Father Gabriel, Delilah and Danny. She did not want to examine her feelings about Danny. Yes, she wanted to see him, but that was stupid, wasn't it? Best to let what happened stay in the past. So, she would visit with them all, talk to whoever had replaced her, and then she would walk down the street and do her research. She would be scholarly and dispassionate. She would probably have to spend several days there. Each day, she would take her lunch to the waterfront and eat it looking at Kingston Harbour, imagining the ships coming in to ports along the coast, bringing all the people who came, in canoes and ships of the line, slavers and merchantmen, banana boats and finally, the people who came in cruise ships and required entertainment. She settled her pillow and willed herself to sleep.

She pressed the buzzer at Kingston Refuge. She heard the click as the locking mechanism released and she went inside.

"Yes?" a young white woman asked from behind her desk. "Can I help you?" Peace Corps, Leigh thought.

"'Morning. I'm Leigh McCaulay. I used to work here. Is Father around?"

"Hi," the woman said, getting up and extending her hand. "I'm Madison. From Utah. I'm volunteering here."

"I see that. Utah, huh? You're a long way from home." And why did you come here? Did you tire of winters and sharp, icy mountains and long for warmth and greenery? Or did Washington choose for you?

The woman laughed. "I guess. I'm an Army brat, though, so I've moved around a lot. You know where to find Father?"

"Sure do." Leigh noticed her speech had relapsed into Americanisms.

"Leigh! I thought I heard your voice. Welcome back. We missed you, though Madison here has done a great job since you left." It was Delilah, dressed in kente cloth, and an elaborate head wrap. Leigh embraced her.

"Good to be back, Della. Brought you guys some food. Where is everybody?"

"Around. Well, Danny not here today, but Father in his office, and … Who else you did know?"

So Danny was avoiding her and Delilah had already forgotten the shape and inhabitants of their days. "I'll go and see Father."

"You do that. Then come see me and we catch up."

The visit to the shelter was disappointing. Father had been distracted, Danny missing, and Delilah pestered by the telephone. Leigh saw that as soon as she had left, others had filled her space. There was no point hanging around. She made an appointment with the lawyer for three that afternoon, and then she left, with promises to return when Danny was there. She walked towards the Library. Might as well find out what was required to do research there; perhaps there would be a fee, or an appointment needed, or a written list submitted.

In East Street sewage still greased the gutters, garbage littered the ground and a goat licked at the inside of a condensed milk tin, its tongue delicately avoiding the sharp edges. Jamaican goats were survivors; they had traffic sense, were rarely run over in the streets and ate anything that was available. Perhaps that was all a Jamaican needed: adaptability, watchfulness and a rootedness in the present. At Beeston Street, she looked right to where Jelly had fallen. Jelly had made no mark

She passed the Institute of Jamaica, with its brick walls and white columns. There was a banner on the façade of the building advertising an exhibition: *The Legacy of Slavery in Jamaica*. The banner included a picture of the kind of shackles she realised she'd seen in the storeroom at Edinburgh. She glanced at her watch. She had time; she would go and see the exhibition. She went inside and a security guard directed her to the exhibition rooms.

She found herself alone, in a series of small rooms, painted white, with sentences from old books inscribed on the walls in red, words describing torment, repulsive words. There were mixed-media pieces made up of faded photographs of white women, decked with jewels, and cartoonish images of black people, with red lips and outsize biceps or buttocks, depending on their sex. A plaque under these pieces explained that the women would often sew fireflies or peenie wallies, as the slaves called them, into the necklines of their dresses. There were items of the period on display: a pewter jug given to the Baptist church, reminding her of the pewter canteen she had found in the storeroom and left in her bedroom, hanging on the wall. She stared at a small branding iron, looking more like something that might curl hair than an implement for burning human flesh. She saw a china platter with the crest of a plantation on it, the ivory background scored with a network of fine cracks. There were expensively framed drawings of romantic landscapes, populated by white women holding parasols, clutching the arms of white men wearing top hats and tails. She saw corroded shackles, here like an old key to an unknown lock found in the turned earth of a freshly dug garden.

The exhibition drew a link between the artifacts of slavery and their place in modern life, how these remnants of brutality had been sanitized and made respectable, even sought after. Solid clay jars of perfect shape, used to import olive oil to the plantations, now resided in the best houses, flanking entrances. The coppers, where sugar was boiled and splashed out and burned the slaves, had been turned into lily ponds. Felicity Mitchell's family had owned such a pond, and Leigh remembered she had found it beautiful: the uneven skin of the copper, green showing through, the lilies blooming on the surface of the water.

She left the main exhibition hall and walked through an open door into another small, white-painted room. One wall was lined with cubicles, like a mail room, and in each slot there was a African head, exquisitely carved out of wood: men and women, with different expressions and features, each one singular. Behind the heads there was a mirror, reflecting the heads endlessly and the face of the onlooker. Leigh met her own eyes and could not bear the sight of her face, not in this context, not with the description of the amount of space allotted for each slave on the Middle Passage inscribed on the white walls. She left the room quickly.

She found herself then in a squalid room, smelling of paint, looking like a modern workman's quarters, like Banjo's house. There were ragged clothes on the ground, white rum on a table; the room was hot and oppressive; on the wall there was enraged graffiti: *we must enslave every white person, humiliate their men, rape their women, take their land*. She felt faint and looked around for somewhere to sit. She saw a female security guard seated in front of a flight of stairs.

"Tough huh?" Leigh said to the guard, trying to enlist her in some kind of sisterhood. The guard said nothing. She walked over and sat on the stairs and lowered her head.

271

"Miss? You alright?"

"Yes. Thanks. Just felt faint for a minute. Haven't had lunch."

So what did it all mean for her, a white woman born here, sitting in an exhibition hall in Kingston, recently arrived from running a tourist attraction on a sugarcane plantation, her mother having been beaten to death in the street? What should be done with the clay jars, Georgian architecture, sugar coppers, bone china, and shackles? Should relics of pre-emancipation Jamaica belong only in museums under a huge banner: "Lest we forget?" Should the gorgeous Great Houses and their history be razed to give way to some new West Indian truth? And what might that look like, she wondered, thinking of the unrendered concrete buildings of Kingston, caged with bars, without proportion or grace, but solid, present and unmistakably what Jamaicans wanted?

Were those who were living a comfortable middle-class life, whoever they were and whatever they were part of, to be held responsible for this great historical crime? Were they all either the conquered or the conquerors? Could she be responsible for blood shed in the land where she was born, long before she had been born? Were you responsible for crimes you had not committed, but crimes that had brought you benefit nonetheless? How many generations would it take for the obscenities of the past to lose their effect on the present? Might they never be lost? How long before those who still cut cane in Jamaica's fields, or squatted in the West Kingston ghettoes would live comfortable lives? Were the poor always to be with you? She got up.

"You see di gibbet?" the guard asked.

"No. What's that?"

"Di gibbet. What dey used to do to di slaves. It upstairs. Mi can show you."

No, Leigh thought. *No more.* But she nodded and the guard led her up the stairs.

They walked through a room full of glowing, handcrafted furniture explained by discreet plaques: the wood was yacca, a kind of wood she had never heard of before her visit to Edinburgh. She thought of the craftsmen who had made it, slaves, whose skill and patience was carved in every detail. Yes, they were symbols of cruelty and oppression but also of survival and grace. She would not destroy them.

She passed through another room of rich oil paintings with elaborate frames, to a series of wrought-iron panels which forced viewers into lines like those in immigration halls. She felt stupid, threading her way alone through the empty queue. At the end she saw a small metal contraption, not especially human shaped, although she could see the head and the legs and the iron piece that would go between the legs.

"Dem put di rebels in dere," the guard said, standing too close. "Dem save di gibbet for di bad-bad slaves. Dem hang dem high and leave dem to die. "

The gibbet was another form of crucifixion, she thought, and wondered what made us so cruel, so afraid of each other. Seeing it left her bone-weary. The plaque said it had been found in Half Way Tree in 1965 and the bones had been those of a woman. She looked at her watch and was surprised to find it was nearly time for her appointment with the lawyer. As she negotiated the corridors of the museum, she saw another exhibit: *A Tribute to the Abolition Movement.* There were photographs and short biographies of William Wilberforce, Thomas Clarkson, Granville Sharpe and Zachary Macaulay. She stopped. She read all the biographies, leaving Zachary Macaulay's for last. The son of a Scottish Minister, he had come to Jamaica as a 16-year-old lad, sent away in disgrace for some unknown transgression, and he had spent only a few years in Jamaica as a bookkeeper on an unnamed sugar plantation. He had committed "cruelties" the biography said, and was at first inured to the crimes against humanity he had witnessed, but for unstated reasons had come to be repulsed by slavery. He returned to Britain and became a member of the Society for the Abolition of the Slave Trade. In 1794, when he was only 26, he became the Governor of Sierra Leone. A year later he travelled on a slave ship in the hold, to experience for himself what the Middle Passage had been like for millions of enslaved Africans. When he returned to Britain, he began writing about the practice of slavery as he had witnessed it. He was a skilled statistician and used the data he had collected while in Jamaica to develop his arguments against slavery, at a time when there were many conflicting accounts of what actually happened on the sugar plantations in the Americas. He was a founding member of the Society for the Mitigation and Gradual Abolition of Slavery, later named the Anti Slavery Society. He was the editor of the *Anti Slavery Reporter* and died in 1838. There was a photograph of plaque commemorating his life and work in Westminster Abbey and under the engraving on the plaque of a kneeling slave the words: "Am I not a man and a brother?"

There was a black and white photograph of the bust in Westminster Abbey and a reproduction of a small painting of Zachary Macaulay. He had deeply set eyes – she could not see their colour – and a sensitive mouth. He looked like any other man of his time, formally dressed in cravat and jacket.

What had taken him to Sierra Leone and how had he become its governor? Why had so few people, so few *white* people, taken a stand against genocide? How did those few find the courage to oppose the might of the economic powers of their day? Did their friends warn of their recklessness, the physical risk, the certainty of failure? Did their wives counsel caution? Did their children ask why they were so rarely home? Leigh wondered where she could find out more about Zachary Macaulay. Maybe they were related and her Jamaican provenance would include an abolitionist.

There was another framed poster beside the bust and photo-graph. It contained the words of the inscription in Westminster Abbey. She read:

"In grateful remembrance of Zachary Macaulay, who, during a pro-tracted life, with an intense but quiet perseverance which no success could relax, no reverse could subdue, no toil, privation, or reproach could daunt, devoted his time, talents, fortune, and all the energies of his mind and body to the service of the most injured and helpless of mankind: and who partook for more than forty successive years, in the counsels and in the labours which guided and blest by God first rescued the British Empire from the guilt of the slave trade; and finally conferred freedom on eight hundred thousand slaves; This tablet is erected by those who drew wisdom from his mind, and a lesson from his life, and who now humbly rejoice in the assurance, that through the Divine Redeemer, the foundation of all his hopes, he shares in the happiness of those who rest from their labours, and whose works do follow them. He was born at Inverary, N.B. [North Britain] on the 2 May 1768: and died in London on the 13 May 1838."

She touched the glass with her palm. *At least they did not forget you*, she thought. And then – *but they forgot the ones you fought for*. They forgot the individuals, the ones who died on the way from their villages to the coast, the ones who were thrown alive overboard, who died of starvation and disease in the holds of ships, the ones who were worked to death, flogged, maimed, burned, tortured, gibbeted. The ones who constructed the Great Houses and made the lustrous furniture. They became merely the slaves. Leigh covered her eyes and wept.

There was a banging on her bedroom door. "Who is it?" she said, sitting up, her heart racing.

"Is me, Phyllis. Time to get up. Quick. Hurricane a come!" She noted how Phyllis's over-correct English had slipped into Jamaican. A hurricane was coming? Presumably it was some days away – she'd heard nothing on the news – so why was Phyllis getting her out of bed with such urgency. "Soon come!" she replied through the door and began to pull on clothes.

She opened the door. Phyllis stood there fully dressed, a line of worry between her eyebrows. "We have to prepare. Conrad gone to hardware store for ply to batten down the window. I going shop. You can fill the water tanks?"

"Fill the water tanks?"

"Yes. Fill the two outside tanks; the hose on the pipe already. Then fill all the buckets in the kitchen. Then the bath." She articulated the words slowly, as if talking to a child.

"Why?"

Phyllis kissed her teeth in irritation. "Because after the hurricane, no water."

"Oh."

"Eat some eggs. Everything in the fridge going spoil. But fill up the tanks first."

"Okay," Leigh said, and she began to feel anxious. "What's the name of the hurricane?"

"Gilbert," Phyllis said, over her shoulder. "Hurricane Gilbert."

The day passed in frenzied preparations. Water pressure was low and only a trickle came out of the pipe in the garden. All day, she watched the slow rise of the water level in the tanks. The street was full of people, going and coming, carrying canned goods, kerosene, batteries and radios. There were sounds of hammering and drilling; the streets took on a carnival atmosphere. Regular bulletins were issued on the radio. Neighbours waved at her over the fence. "Hurricane not going hit," they assured her. "The Lord always turn them away at the last minute and send them some other place. Jamaica a blessed island." Leigh wondered at the sins committed in the places where the hurricanes hit.

Conrad came home with several sheets of plywood in the back of a pick-up he had borrowed. He set them up on a stone in the yard, took off his shirt, and began to saw them into lengths, his head bent, sweat dripping onto the wood.

"Come help me," he said to Leigh when he had finished sawing.

Leigh held the sheets of plywood while Conrad nailed them over the windows. "Now we have to take everything inside," he said. They picked up lawn furniture, buckets and garden implements and stowed them in the garage. Phyllis's potted plants were taken inside; the small living room became crammed with objects, the plants shedding mud and leaves on the floor.

"How long will the hurricane last?" she asked Conrad.

"Maybe a day. This one moving fast-fast."

"I need to call my father," she said. "Maybe he doesn't know about the hurricane."

"He will know," Conrad said. "In the old days, they used to hoist a flag on the post office."

It was mid-afternoon before preparations were completed. The weather was hot and still, and Leigh saw flocks of birds flying across the sky. She wondered what happened to them in a hurricane. She helped herself to lemonade from the fridge and tried to call her father. The phone rang without an answer. Her anxiety notched up a level.

At seven, she watched JBC TV news with the Libbeys. The lead story was the hurricane and there was a satellite image. She realized the hurricane was definitely going to hit the island. It was huge and taking direct aim. The weather forecaster thought the island would begin feeling the effects by early the next morning. Small craft were warned to return to port; this was followed by a list of hurricane tips. Representatives from government agencies spoke about the necessity to move from low-lying areas and lists of shelters were read out. Curfews were already in effect in some parts of Kingston, and the news report showed army vehicles, bristling with soldiers, patrolling the streets. The Prime Minister asked for calm and everyone's prayers, his facial tic working overtime. The Libbeys watched in silence.

"That hurricane going nyam us," Conrad said.

"What will be, will be," Phyllis countered. She patted Conrad's hand. "We going pray and the Lord will stand with us. He is our shepherd and our salvation."

"Mmm," Conrad said.

Leigh wanted a shower, but both baths were filled with water. She had been given a small bucket for washing. She excused herself and went to her bathroom. She scooped some water from the bath, and then realized the water supply had not yet been turned off. How bad could a hurricane be? It was 1988, not 1888. Houses were built of concrete and steel and roofs were properly secured. She thought about the Kingston Refuge and wondered if Father had opened his doors to the street people of downtown Kingston. She wondered where Danny was. She felt ashamed that she had not offered her help to the shelter.

Standing on the bathmat, she sponged her limbs and was grateful for the coolness of the water. She was surprised how little water it took to wash her body. The tiles were wet. She dried, dressed and went for the mop to dry the bathroom floor. All over the house, old towels and newspapers were blocking the cracks under doors and windows.

Phyllis made cocoa tea and they sat in front of the TV, dipping hard crackers into the sweet, hot chocolate. They watched news reporters tell stories of defiant folks who would not leave their homes, of harried school principals who really did not want their schools used as emergency shelters and of fishermen pulling their canoes up onto beaches. Leigh's eyelids were heavy and she dozed in her chair.

She was roused by a knock on the front door.

"Who that?" Conrad cried out.

"Is Danny. From the shelter. Leigh is there?"

Conrad looked at her. "You know a Danny?"

"Yes. He helps out there." She knew her manner was embarrassed, even as she felt a happy weakness at his presence on the doorstep.

"He a foreigner?" Conrad went on. "Peace Corps?"

"No. He's Jamaican." Leigh was irritated at the questioning. She got up to open the door.

"Wait," Conrad said. "Where he come from?"

"What you mean, where he come from? Jamaica. Kingston. Downtown. What does it matter?" Leigh said. She flung the door open. Danny stood there, drops of water glistening on his hair. It was blustery outside, but not yet raining hard.

"Danny? What happen?"

"Man tek over di shelter," he said. She saw he was almost crying, and even though the night was hot and still, he shivered.

"What you mean, man take over the shelter?"

"Man come. Them kick down di door. Them say me must leave or dem will kill me. Them want di place to stay inna di hurricane."

He was still standing on the doorstep and she told him to come in. Danny walked in and bowed his head to the Libbeys. "Conrad, Phyllis, this is my friend, Danny."

"Sir, Ma'am," he said.

Conrad grunted in response. No one offered him a seat or a drink.

"Sit, Danny," Leigh gestured to the chair she had been dozing in. "Tell me again what happened?"

Danny remained on his feet. "Nutt'n more to say. Downtown Kingston full a man roaming, trying to find place to stay. Them tek over di shelter and tell me to get out."

"Did you call Father?"

"Phone line cut."

"Well, you can stay here. In my room. Don't worry, Danny, you safe now."

"He can't stay here," Phyllis Libbey said, her voice tight. "Tell her, Conrad."

Conrad grunted again. "You don't know this man. Him could

chop us up tonight. Him can't stay here. Him must go to a shelter, like the government say on the TV."

Leigh stood. She dug money out of her pocket and put it on one of the side tables. "I'm paying you rent. My room is mine. Come, Danny. This way. You hungry? Thirsty?"

Danny shook his head and she took his hand and led him to her bedroom. They lay on the bed and Leigh turned her face into his neck, and remembered the night under the duppy cho cho, the feel of his chest against her back, solid and strong. She held him close and felt the trembling of his skin ease.

The hurricane had still not come by the morning of September 12th. Leigh wished she could see outside, but all the windows were covered by plywood. In the dark, airless room, she sitting at one end of her bed, Danny at the other, it was hard to catch her breath. She had not been able to reach her father. She still raged inside over the Libbeys's attempt to evict Danny.

At ten, rain rattled on the roof and they heard the wind rising. "Soon time to plug out the fridge," Leigh heard Conrad say from the living room.

"Fix us a cold drink then, Dads," Phyllis said. "Soon no ice leave between here and Miami."

"You want a cold drink, Danny?" Leigh said, desperate for something to do, wanting to confront the Libbeys with their heartlessness. Danny did not answer and Leigh opened the bedroom door. *She* wanted a cold drink. Assuming the roof stayed on, she thought, riding out a hurricane might require nothing more than patience. The kitchen was dark and when she opened the fridge, the light inside surprised her. She put her head inside as far as it would go, and let the cold air wash her cheeks. She took out the lemonade pitcher and poured the remaining contents into two glasses, adding as many ice cubes as would fit.

"After now, we don't open the fridge unless we have to," Conrad told her, taking out the plug. He stood with Phyllis in the kitchen doorway and his voice held contempt.

"You don't know what you are doing with that man," Phyllis added. "You could get us kill today."

Then Leigh heard the rising sound, like a machine, a train

perhaps, or a boiler overheating, a shrieking, raging sound that hit the house and made it shudder.

"Gilbert come," Conrad said. "Anyway, I glad it in the day. Hurricane much worse at night."

All day, the hurricane tore at the Libbeys's house. The wind really did howl as it pierced every crack, hole and flaw in the house. After the first hour, the towels at the base of the windows and doors were sodden and had to be changed. Leigh became bored and turned to face Danny. Finally, he met her eyes. She stripped off her T-shirt and jeans and Danny moved towards her. He kissed her and she touched the pink of his mouth with her tongue. He turned her on her back and entered her, with none of the urgency of their earlier encounter. As the hurricane raged outside, they made love, lazy and slow and safe, their skins slick in the heat, the bedroom door bolted against storms and judgment.

Afterwards, they lay apart.

"My mother was murdered," Leigh said.

"True? How?"

"She knocked over a pot of soup with her car. They beat her to death in the street."

"Umm-hmm. That was you mother?"

"Yes. You heard about it?"

"Them talk about it, yes. White woman beat to death – must talk 'bout." He stroked her hair. "You know my Walkman?"

"The one the Peace Corps volunteer gave you?"

"Eeh-he."

"What about it?"

"She did like me off, you know. Father Gabriel tell me is either di job or di girl. Man who work there before get a volunteer pregnant. Big problem. Me need di job."

She realized he was explaining his reticence over the months when they had spent time together. She wanted to ask if all women who worked at the shelter were off limits or just the white ones, but she remained quiet and let Danny speak.

"Why you come back to Jamaica?" he said, surprising her.

"Why? I was born here. It's home. Why you ask me that?"

"You could be any place. Have anything."

"Not anything. My mother took me away before I was ready to go. Then she died. I had to come back."

"You going stay?"

"I don't know. I don't know yet."

He pulled her to him and they held each other and the sound of the wind began to ease. "The eye coming. Soon. Tell me about foreign. About going on a plane."

"What you want know?"

"Everything."

"If I tell you, will you tell me?"

"Tell you what?"

"About here. About your life."

"My life." He shook his head. "Nutt'n to tell."

"Plenty to tell. Tell me the first thing you remember."

"Being dead for hungry. You?"

"The sound of the sea."

At about four, the noises of the storm started to come at longer intervals. "It going," Danny said. "Gilbert come and gone."

"Don't talk too soon," Leigh said, but by five, it was clear the worst was over. They left her bedroom and joined the Libbeys in the living room. Conrad turned the big radio up and they listened to reports of damage where reporters had been able to venture outside. The Yallahs River was in spate and the ford was impassable. Junction Road was blocked by landslides. A light aircraft had blown into a tree at Norman Manley Airport. Thousands were in shelters. "Time for some food," Conrad said, bent over the radio.

The two women went into the kitchen. "Bully beef is hurricane food," Phyllis said, opening a tin, as if nothing had happened between them. She directed Leigh to chop onions and scotch bonnet pepper and mixed the seasonings into the bully beef along with catsup and pickapeppa sauce, cut thick slices of hard dough bread and made a quick foray into the fridge for margarine and cool water. The wind came in gusts, but the rain was a steady deluge. The buckets set to catch leaks began to fill more quickly.

Years later, Leigh remembered little about the actual storm. It was the aftermath that remained vivid, the weeks without electricity, water or telephone services, the long lines at gas pumps, super-markets and hardware stores, the city clogged with traffic, the gangs of young men roaming the streets, carrying machetes and stolen television sets, the roofs covered with blue tarpaulins, the tense faces of insurance adjusters as they combed the wreckage of the city, carrying clipboards to mark their legitimate purpose. She remembered the smells and the noise – diesel generators and rotting garbage, and the smoke from a thousand fires, as the city tried to rid itself of fallen trees and shattered fences. They ate bully beef until Leigh thought she would rather starve to death than face another such meal. She could not reach her father and there was nothing to be done about it. The hurricane had tracked right through the centre of the island and laid it bare. Trees were down or leafless, rivers swollen and muddy, home satellite dishes lay like crumpled tinfoil on the ground, sheets of zinc were wrapped around utility poles. Each night, the main TV newscast was filled with stories of homeless, desperate people. Everything was broken, dirty and wrecked beyond repair.

Worried about her father, missing Danny, who had left after a second night in her bed, bored with the long, dark evenings, sick of sweet, warm drinks that failed to quench her thirst, Leigh ventured out to watch the slow recovery begin. The airports opened, foreign crews began to replace electricity poles, a brown trickle of water came through the pipes, Jamaican entrepreneurs imported refrigerated containers filled with ice and sold it at exorbitant prices. Jerk chicken men did a roaring trade on street corners. Every day, there were new reports of roads being cleared, schools reopening and electricity being restored to areas of the city. Leigh packed and repacked her backpack, with no idea what to do next. She wanted Danny, but she did not know where he was. She thought about their conversations during the storm: her stories of exile and freedom, his of deprivation and survival. "I want to meet your mother," she had told him. He had smiled, "And me want to meet your father." She wondered how that would go. While the storm raged outside, it was easy to pretend only their own wishes mattered. But it's not 1888, she told herself. In the aftermath of Hurricane Gilbert, she batted her choices back and forth: to stay in Jamaica, or to go. Where and how to live. Who to see. Who to love.

Then, six weeks later, while the phone at the Libbeys was still down, a letter arrived from her father. It was postmarked Montego Bay and the envelope was damp and the address smeared. He wrote that during the week before the hurricane, Sarita had begun to lose her sight and they had gone to the Cornwall Regional Hospital, where she had been admitted. They had ridden out the hurricane in the hospital and were now renting an apartment in Montego Bay. He believed Edinburgh had been badly hit, but had not managed to get there. He thought the roads were open, but was not sure. He doubted they would return there. He hoped Leigh had not been affected by the hurricane and asked her to get in touch.

"Come with me," Leigh said.

"Where?" Danny answered.

"To where my father was. Edinburgh Plantation."

Kingston Refuge had reopened. The invading men had trashed it, but a grant from the US Embassy had bought new desks and beds and repaired the bathroom fixtures. A foreign crew had cleaned shit from floors and painted the walls. Leigh was volunteering at the shelter, living on her savings.

"Why you going in there?" he said.

"I want to see it. Get my stuff. My father was not there when the hurricane hit. I have to…"

"Have to what?"

"Have to decide what to do."

Danny touched her cheek. "Father will give me time off."

The journey to Edinburgh-Bonnie Valley took almost seven hours by taxi. Spoon drove them; they sat in the back seat but when Leigh tried to hold Danny's hand, he shook his head. They rode in silence, staring out of the car windows. Leigh gasped when she saw the denuded hills, the roofless housing, the brown scars of landslides, the mud in the sea, the fires. But she also saw men and women in small, uneven fields, readying the land for planting, children in neat uniforms walking to school, a man with a chain-saw carving downed trees into usable lengths of wood, and small shops open for business, their roofs tacked on, broken glass from smashed soft drinks swept to one side. From the open doors of these small places, she heard the lively beat of a song which had taken over the airwaves: Lloyd Lovindeer's "Wild Gilbert."

> *Water come inna mi room*
> *Mi sweep some out with mi broom*
> *Di likkle dog laugh to see such fun*
> *An di dish run away with di spoon*
> *When mi look up in di air mi see zinc like dirt*
> *Whap, whap Wild Gilbert*
> *Mi save mi brief but mi lose mi shirt*
> *Whap, whap Wild Gilbert*

Jamaicans – *we* Jamaicans – she thought, we tek serious ting an mek joke.

Spoon drove through the stone pillars at the entrance to the plantation.

"Stop," Leigh ordered. She got out of the car and stood at the rise that marked the entrance to the estate, just where the gravel road began to fall on its way to the Great House. The weather was overcast, but she could see everything. The Great House was annihilated – only the oldest of the stone walls were left standing. The canepiece planted for the tourists was flat and she could see where the river had spread across the land in a muddy swirl. The only trees that stood were those that had survived earlier hurricanes – the trees with the roots pointing to the sky and their old trunks lying solid on the ground. "My God," she whispered. "It's gone."

"Place mash up good," Spoon said, leaning against the car, smoking a cigarette.

"Wait here," Leigh said to Spoon, and began to walk down the hill; Danny followed her.

It seemed entirely deserted. The stableyard was a heap of rubble, collapsed concrete and stone, a few mangled sheets of zinc, the remnants of furniture and farm equipment. She looked for the old storeroom, which she had never managed to go through properly but could not find it. She saw the frame for the gibbet still stood. The water trough was full of stagnant water and mosquito larvae. The apartment where she had lived was gone – all that was left was the concrete slab where the tractor and the jitney had been parked.

She walked up the hill to the Great House, which looked as if it had been bombed. She heard Danny's footsteps, but she did not turn around. The spaces where doors and windows had hung gaped. The furniture was broken up. She saw no beds or mattresses and wondered if people around had salvaged the wreckage. She walked onto the black and white marble floor, now covered with debris.

"Tek care," Danny said. "Something could fall."

"Fall from what? The sky?" She saw the staircase curving at one end of the marble floor, the old wood shining, and she imagined women descending the stairs in ball gowns, peenie wallies sewn into their dresses for decoration, a small sacrifice. She imagined those who had been detailed to catch the tiny, hopeful lights; they had probably been children. She saw herself in Portland's bush, at night, with a bottle in her hand, searching for peenie wallies. She looked up. The stairs from the great room at Edinburgh simply ended in mid air, the wide mahogany planks of the upper floor were missing. There was nothing left for anyone.

She was dry eyed. She thought she had loved this valley she had briefly lived in and perhaps she had, but gorgeous as it had been, she was glad the Great House was gone. Shepherding tourists through a sanitised version of history could not now be her future. She walked out onto the grass and retraced her steps down the driveway. She felt Danny join her, and in the shadow still cast by the ruins of the Great House, he drew her to his side.

As they passed the old stableyard, Leigh saw Banjo pushing a wheelbarrow, full of broken things.

"Banjo!" Leigh said. "You okay?" She broke into a run on her way to the old man. "Your house okay?"

"Praise di Lord. Roof come off, but mi find back di zinc and it nail back already. Edinburgh mash up bad-bad though. Your father not here."

"I know."

"What you doing here, Miss Leigh?"

"Banjo."

"Yes, Miss Leigh?"

"My name is Leigh. Not 'Miss Leigh.' Leigh. Say it."

Banjo shrugged. She knew the words that were in his head: crazy white people. Then he smiled and put down the wheelbarrow. "So what you doing here, *Leigh*?" he said and arched his back to ease the strain.

"I came to say good-bye."

Spoon drove them to a small guest house on the north coast, still without electricity and lit by kerosene lanterns. That night they walked on a littered beach, a low moon rising, the sky clear, the waves gentle. Lightning glowed on the horizon where the world fell away. She remembered how she had once seen herself, striding khaki clad, conquering the hills and the valleys, claiming the island she had once left. She no longer wanted to claim anything. Now she hoped the land would claim her, just as complex as the sea, with all its depths, dangers and cruelties. She would swim in it, sometimes on the surface, face turned to the sky, sometimes diving into the murk, but always trying to feel its rhythms, understand its past. All history is crime, she thought, and all of us are displaced but some displacements are worse than others. The island had risen from the sea and it had been alone for aeons, battered by storms and the hammer of the sun, and then finally, the people had come for all their different reasons. Centuries later, people stayed, even though the past lived large in every second of the present, in every tree, mountain, river and crumbling ruin, in a people noisy and unbroken, impossible to constrain or discipline, a people still holding on, churning a culture, singing and dancing as they walked and still, planting yams in the sun. Leigh knew that all the people who came, all of them, could walk along the seashore with those they loved, as she was doing, and they could decide, as she had decided, finally, to stay.

"Come with me to Portland." She put her arms around his waist, laid her cheek on his chest and he held her.

"What you going do there?"

"Buy a piece of land. Build a small house. Look for some people."

"Me, I don't know country."

"We in country now."   She lifted her face to his and he smiled."Just for a short while," she said. "Come with me for a little."

When I was a child, I heard the story of my four orphan ancestors. My paternal great grandfather, John McCaulay, was a Baptist missionary, twice married. His first wife, Lillian, died, leaving him with a daughter, Sybil. He married again and had three other children, Gerald (the only boy and my grandfather), Lilymay and Gladys. Following a buggy accident, which sent her into premature labour, his second wife, May Isabelle, also died. The child lived; she was the last McCaulay daughter and was "never quite right in the head". The Reverend John happened to be away at the time of the accident, carrying out his mission somewhere in South America, when he was sent for.

"How was he sent for?" I'd ask.

"However they sent for people in those days," my father would say.

This lack of detail was frustrating. I wanted to know how these people lived, what they thought, and most of all, how they came to be in Jamaica.

"Why did Reverend John come to Jamaica in the first place?" I'd ask.

"People came," would be my father's only answer.

"Where was he from?"

"Scotland," my father said. "Clan McCaulay."

"Ireland," my grand aunt Sybil said. More mysteries.

Reverend McCaulay began his return voyage to his four children and his ship sank in a hurricane on the way. His dead wife's sister, Edith – and why was she in Jamaica? – adopted the children and they grew up in Black River. One photograph of the four McCaulay children survives; they are dressed in frills and crinolines, even, apparently, the only boy, in front of a house that still stands in Black River. They wear black armbands for their dead mother; they did not yet know their father was soon to die as well.

When I was older, I realized there were few McCaulays in

Jamaica who spelled their name as we did. Then I heard another account of the Reverend John. It seemed he came to Jamaica with a brother, and they spelled their names with the more common "ey" at the end. But the brother ran off with his maid – unheard of in those days, my Aunt Sybil confided, and I could tell she was in sympathy with the old rules; Reverend John changed the spelling of his name in protest.

"So we might have cousins then?" I asked Aunt Sybil.

"I certainly hope not!" she said. She lived until she was 102 and her life spanned a period that encompassed kerosene lamps, buggy rides to Kingston, air travel, cell phones and computers. She did talk about the Reverend John, her father, but as he'd mostly been away and died when she was nine, her memories were conflicted and sketchy.

Anyway, at least on my father's side, it seemed we had not been slave owners. This was a relief. As I grew up, I claimed my Jamaican-born status, even as my light skin occasioned adverse comment in the streets and hostility in shops.

Then, much later, I heard another narrative about my father's family. Perhaps the Reverend John had not journeyed to Jamaica at all. His name could not be found on any ship's manifest. He appeared in the records, fully formed, in Jamaica, preaching in Cave Valley in St. Ann. It is said, my father explained, changing his story, we are descended from a famous abolitionist, one Zachary Macaulay. He could be found on a plaque in Westminster Abbey, my father said, along with Wilberforce and Clarkson. He came to Jamaica in the eighteenth century and left "without issue," according to the history books. But the story is he had a son while here and…

This was a narrative I could rally behind. I was the descendant of an abolitionist, a missionary and… well, a businessman, I suppose. My paternal grandfather, Gerald, started a public transportation company and red McCaulay's buses were a feature of Jamaican country roads. Even today, I meet older people who informed me they told time by the blaring horns of McCaulay's buses. I googled Zachary Macaulay, learned the basics of his life, and told myself a story of a young man sent away from home, to make his fortune in the Indies, a self-taught, bookish young man

(James Thomson's *The Seasons* was one of his favourites – but he also read Virgil and Horace in Latin) who liked statistics, and who somehow turned against slavery, a young man who went on to stand against the economic forces of his time, to travel on a slave ship, to become the governor of Sierra Leone, to die in England in the very year of emancipation. I imagined the circumstances that might have led him to – what? Have a child out of wedlock? Leave the child in Jamaica? That seemed at odds with his character, so I told myself a different story, of a child born in slavery, the progeny of a plantation owner and a slave, an orphan, like my own ancestors, a child the future abolitionist took back to England with him, a boy, who grew up hearing stories of an island in the Caribbean sea, and in his turn, passed those stories on. Then his grandson, my great grandfather John, would journey to the island of my birth, despite the lack of evidence in any ship's manifest. I felt that these people carried with them the seeds that formed the character of a modern day Jamaican. Eventually, I wrote this story down.

Huracan is based in part on the lives of real people, using some of the known facts, but much is a product of my imagination. I was never able to establish a link between Zachary Macaulay and my own family, and while both Zachary's father and one of his sons were named John, they were not Baptists. Some records show Zachary Macaulay's time in Jamaica to be spent near Colbeck Castle in modern day Clarendon, but I set the plantation on the outskirts of the dramatic landscape of Cockpit Country in western Jamaica. The description of the gravestone in Fortress on page 250 contains the actual words on my great grandparents' grave stone, but this is found in Santa Cruz in St. Elizabeth. To the best of my knowledge, there was no plantation called Bonnie Valley or Edinburgh, no town of Fortress or Blessing, and although there are several places called Paradise in Jamaica, the one in *Huracan* does not refer to any of them. All the modern day McCaulays are fictional characters and bear no resemblance to my own family. I wanted the three McCaulay protagonists in *Huracan* to travel to Jamaica, and although some McCaulays of my generation have left, no one has returned.

The description of the slavery exhibition on pages 270-275 is based on a 2008 exhibition called "Materializing Slavery" mounted by the Institute of Jamaica.

A word about the title: in researching the various periods, I noticed how often storms and hurricanes devastated the island. Huracan is the Taino word for storm, or possibly a god of storms, and is the origin of our word "hurricane". Although this book is very much about the various people who came to Jamaica for their different reasons, the Tainos are absent from its pages. It seemed only fair to let the title pay tribute to the Jamaica's earliest inhabitants.

My gratitude to all who helped with this book: to Jeremy Poynting at Peepal Tree Press, to Andrew Lindsay who improved my attempts at rendering Scottish speech patterns, to Ainsley and Marjorie Henriques for lending me many books, to Sheree Rhoden at the Gleaner Company who sat with me while I browsed the newspapers of the past, to Peter Espeut who talked to me about the Baptists and my own genealogy, to Esther Figueroa who listened to me talk about my characters as if they were my family, which, of course they were, and who read many versions of this story. She made it a better book in every respect. And to my other gentle readers – Celia, Jonathan, Freddy – my abiding love and appreciation.

I have written about the beloved island of my birth at different times in her tragic history; I hope I have created an authenticity, a realism. Any mistakes are mine alone.

Diana McCaulay
Kingston, Jamaica
April 2011

ABOUT THE AUTHOR

Diana McCaulay is a Jamaican writer, newspaper columnist and environmental activist. She has lived her entire life in Jamaica and engaged in a range of occupations – secretary, insurance executive, racetrack steward, mid-life student, social commentator, environmental advocate. She is the Chief Executive of the Jamaican Environment Trust and the recipient of the 2005 Euan P. McFarlane Award for Outstanding Environmental Leadership. Her first novel, *Dog-Heart* won first prize in the 2008 Jamaican National Literature awards.

ALSO BY DIANA McCAULAY

Dog-Heart
ISBN: 9781845231231; pp. 244; pub. March 2010; price: £9.99

Dog-Heart is a novel about the well-meaning attempt of a middle-class single mother to transform the life of a boy from the ghetto who she meets on the street. Set in present-day, urban Jamaica, *Dog-Heart* tells the story from two alternating points of view – those of the woman and the boy. They speak in the two languages of Jamaica that sometimes overlap, sometimes display their different origins and world views. Whilst engaging the reader in a tense and absorbing narrative, the novel deals seriously with issues of race and class, the complexity of relationships between people of very different backgrounds, and the difficulties faced by individuals seeking to bring about social change by their own actions.